O9-CFT-494

THE

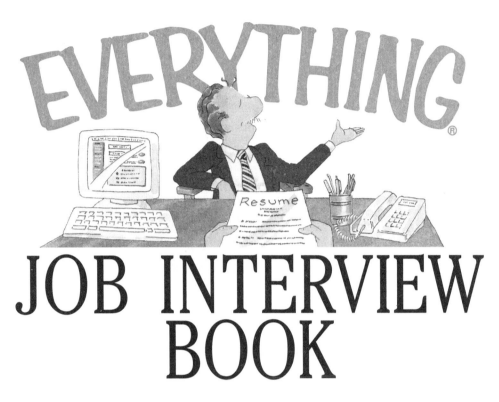

EVERYTHING

JOB INTERVIEW
BOOK

Answer the toughest
job interview questions
with confidence

Bob Adams

Adams Media Corporation
Avon, Massachusetts

Copyright ©2001, Adams Media Corporation.
All rights reserved. This book, or parts thereof, may not be reproduced
in any form without permission from the publisher; exceptions
are made for brief excerpts used in published reviews.

An Everything® Series Book.
Everything® is a registered trademark of Adams Media Corporation.

Published by Adams Media Corporation
57 Littlefield Street, Avon, MA 02322. U.S.A.
www.adamsmedia.com

ISBN: 1-58062-493-6
Printed in the United States of America.

J I H G F E D C B

Library of Congress Cataloging-in-Publication Data
Adams, Bob.
The everything job interview / by Bob Adams.
p. cm.
Includes index.
ISBN 1-58062-493-6
1. Employment interviewing. 2. Job hunting. I. Title.
HF5549.5.I6 A28 2001
650.14–dc21 2001022044

This publication is designed to provide accurate and authoritative information with regard to the subject matter covered. It is sold with the understanding that the publisher is not engaged in rendering legal, accounting, or other professional advice. If legal advice or other expert assistance is required, the services of a competent professional person should be sought.
—From a *Declaration of Principles* jointly adopted by a Committee of the American Bar Association and a Committee of Publishers and Associations

Illustrations by Barry Littmann.

*This book is available at quantity discounts for bulk purchases.
For information, call 1-800-872-5627.*

Visit the entire Everything® series at everything.com

CONTENTS

PART ONE
THE FIRST STEPS TO INTERVIEW SUCCESS

PART TWO
INTERVIEW INSIGHT

CONTENTS

PART THREE
INTERVIEW QUESTIONS YOU MAY BE ASKED

Introduction

For all the concentration and work that your resume, your cover letter, and every other aspect of the job game deserve, there is no disputing the fact that the job interview is the most important step in winning a job. Sure, a great resume will get you noticed, but it is your behavior during an interview that will get you the job!

You can never be too prepared for a job interview; from researching the company to rehearsing your answers, the job interview is one case in which practice *definitely* makes perfect. Whether you're out there looking for your very first job or are a seasoned professional, job interviews can be a nerve-wracking experience. That said, it is during the job interview that many otherwise qualified people lose their chance at employment.

It is important to know the rules of the job interview regarding what to wear, how to prepare what to say, and what to do when it's over. The goal of this book is to answer each and every question you may have when it comes to interviewing for a new job. By applying the ideas and tactics listed within these pages, you can help to ensure that your next job interview—and every one after that—will be *successful*.

The First Steps
to Interview Success

CHAPTER ONE

Discovering the
Need for Strategy

When it comes to finding a new job, it is important to remember that finding happy employment is a lot like playing a game: There are certain rules you must abide by and various strategies you can apply. In the end, however, there is usually only one winner.

The best way to win the employment game is to learn the rules ahead of time. Then apply the strategy that works best for you.

Defining Your Goals

The most difficult part of finding employment is figuring out what it is you actually want to do. Earning a degree in a particular field or working many years in a specific industry should not limit your options. In the course of one's lifetime, it is not at all uncommon for one person to have five or more careers. As cliché as it sounds, you learn something new every day about your strengths and weaknesses, your likes and dislikes. When you apply these learning experiences to choices you make as far as your career is concerned, they can be priceless bits of information.

When choosing or changing careers, there are two very important questions to consider. First, while a particular industry or job title may *seem* glamorous or enticing, are you really prepared to take on the day-to-day duties that such a position would entail? Ask yourself whether you are actually ready and willing to meet the demands of this job or whether it is just a job title you think you could impress your friends with.

Second, are you prepared to live the lifestyle that this job demands? For example, while the idea of becoming a talent agent or the assistant to some really famous person sounds like a real dream job, are you willing to be at somebody's beck and call 24 hours a day? Are you ready to deal with belittling comments and the occasional "difficult" personality? Many high profile and/or high-paying jobs

often come with a strict "very-little-free-time" price tag. If you are not sure of the customary duties and tasks of a position, try to speak with someone in the field or to a career counselor so that you can learn more about them. Read the job description carefully and make sure that you are ready, willing, and able to provide the many services that will be asked of you. Most importantly, make sure you research the job, its duties, and the company *before* accepting a position. You never know. That dream job could turn out to be a real nightmare.

Okay, so you've determined that being a rock star just doesn't coincide with your plans (all that travel just isn't worth it). Now what? One of the easiest ways to begin figuring out what kind of career you would excel in is to sit down with a pen and a piece of paper and make a list. Yes, it sounds elementary (and it is), but it works!

Divide the paper into two columns and mark one column "Likes" and the other "Dislikes." Now it's time to draw on every work, personal, and out-of-body experience you've ever had. Think about the tasks that you liked performing as well as those that you detested, and assign each activity to the appropriate column. An effective list should take at least a half hour to compile. You won't use this piece of paper to determine your ultimate career goal *right now*; rather, this piece of paper is going to serve as a reference guide throughout the rest of your job search journey. Whenever you stumble across a job that sounds interesting or whenever you are being considered for a particular position, you can take out this list and make sure that the job's duties coincide with your own objectives (as outlined in your list).

Oftentimes, your mind can get clouded with the prospect of a new job. The fact that someone is telling you that you'd be "perfect" for a position shouldn't influence what you really want. Just like the company itself, you have a bottom line, and this is not something you should compromise for the sake of a paycheck.

Remember, just because you've always thought you'd be great at a particular occupation doesn't necessarily make it so. For example, you wouldn't necessarily make the world's best

Job Search Odds and Ends

Agencies for Special Groups

- Minorities: National Association for the Advancement of Colored People (NAACP), *www.naacp.org*

- People who are visually impaired: Job Opportunities for the Blind Program, 410/659-9314

- People who are disabled: President's Committee on Employment of People with Disabilities, 202/376-6200

psychiatrist just because you like to talk and people often come to you with their problems.

Career planning is really a science of its own; in fact, there are plenty of people who dedicate their lives to mastering this science. Don't be afraid to seek out the help of career planning professionals when you are trying to figure out your next step. If you are a college student, chances are there are plenty of these professionals in the school's career planning office. If you have been in the work force for quite a while, there should be plenty of career planning centers in your own community. Pick up the phone book and schedule an appointment to meet with someone.

Career Tests

Some people balk at the idea of career tests. Well why shouldn't they? It is not always the case that a computer or some premanufactured form or even a career counselor knows more than you do. Therefore, you should not always rely *solely* on what these tests or counselors tell you. You should be open minded though. If you take a career test and the results suggest that you would make, say, a fantastic poultry engineer, why not take the time to figure out what such a person actually does. Most industries and occupations probably have an organization that operates near you, if not on the World Wide Web. Chances are they also publish some sort of trade magazine or other publication that will give you more insight into a particular line of work. It might benefit you to take a few minutes and investigate an unknown career a bit further. You never know what you might find out.

If you can't find time during the day to meet with a career professional, there are plenty of places online where you can learn more about the kinds of careers that just may be right for you. The following Web sites offer career planning information and will even allow you to take computerized versions of some popular career planning tests:

CareerExperience • *www.careerexperience.com*

Career Perfect • *www.careerperfect.com*

Experience Network • *www.experience.com*

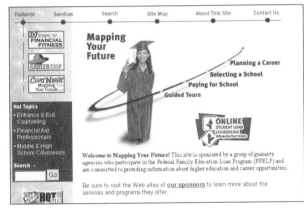

Mapping Your Future • *mapping-your-future.org*

My Future • *www.myfuture.com*

Princeton Review Online • *www.review.com*

Quintessential Careers • *www.quintcareers.com*

CHAPTER TWO

Developing
a Strategy

Insider Tips

Staying Organized

It's easy to get caught up in all the excitement of searching for a new job! One of the biggest mistakes people make when sending out a batch of resumes is forgetting to make a note of where they are going. One of the smartest things you can do, as a job seeker, is to keep a running list of all the places to which you've sent your resume. Start a notebook and keep track of the following:

- Company name and address
- Individual or department name you addressed it to
- Date you sent your resume
- Position you applied for and the duties of that job
- Reasons why you would like to work here

You may want to write a brief description of what the company does so that during an unexpected phone screening, you can speak with confidence about a company and ask relevant questions, even if it's been several months since you sent your resume.

Though the ultimate goal—to get a job—is always the same, the way in which people go about accomplishing that can be different. There are still many questions that remain as far as your strategy is concerned. For example, will you use the World Wide Web to search out currently available job postings, or will you browse the local newspaper? Will you call upon all the people you know in a field for help in finding some possible leads, or will you fend for yourself?

Job Seeking Techniques

There are several different job seeking techniques that you may employ. The most common techniques include the following:

- Answering a help wanted advertisement
- Employing the help of a recruiter or employment service firm
- Calling on personal contacts (networking)
- Sending unsolicited resumes directly to the employer (a.k.a. the Direct Contact method)

Answering Help Wanted Advertisements

When you hear the words *help wanted,* you probably think of the classifieds in your local paper. While a newspaper is certainly one place to find a help wanted ad, there are several other avenues you should consider. Advancing technology has paved the way for literally thousands of job hunting Web sites. The job listings on these sites may not fit your typical idea of a help wanted ad. In fact, on the Internet, today's job seekers can quickly access millions of job openings around the world with just a few clicks of the mouse. Magazines are another place you might choose to look for help wanted ads; they too can be accessed online.

Employment Service Firms

For people on the go (those that don't have time to pore over classifieds or print up two million cover letters and resumes, etc.), employment services are the way to go. Whether you are looking

for a temporary or permanent job, entry-level or executive, there are enough employment service agencies out there to service the particulars of any job seeker's search for employment.

But what, exactly, does an employment service do? In fact, they do as little or as much as you would like them to. Employment services can be very specialized in function, or they can be very general. They can offer only one specific service to a small group of job seekers, or they can provide a variety of services that would satisfy a large population. There are employment service firms out there that will only work with, say, experienced restaurant managers, and there are those that will help anyone, from a temporary receptionist to a *Fortune* 500 CEO. In addition to running the gamut in services, employment service firms can be run by one person or part of a worldwide corporation. They can be private or state-run agencies. And the services can be costly or free of charge.

If electing to let an employment agency do some of the work for you, it is important that you do not choose an agency blindly. While it is definitely not true of the entire industry, in the past, the employment field has seen its fair share of less-than-ethical employment service firms. Specifically, when it comes to lower-end placements, some firms are notorious for running various help wanted advertisements for jobs that don't exist. It works on both ends though; many of these same agencies are also famous for pitching fictional candidates to interested employers.

These words of caution are not to scare you away from using employment services; there are thousands of candidates out there who swear by them. It is just a warning to make sure that you research the employment agency you decide on as carefully as you would an employer, so as to not waste any of your precious time. Keep in mind that all employment service firms must be licensed within the state that they are operating; find out if there have been any business complaints regarding a particular agency.

Here are some other smart steps to take before deciding on any one employment service agency:

- Learn a bit about the history of the company, especially when it was founded. If a company has been around for a

Insider Tips

Which Method to Choose

While responding to help wanted advertisements is probably the most popular way to search for a job—both online and off—the Direct Contact method actually boasts twice the success rate of the other aforementioned options. This is not to say that you shouldn't respond to help wanted ads or that you should only employ the Direct Contact method; however, you should try and mix it up a bit. Try out both of these options and see which one works best for you.

while, chances are they are a reputable agency. Because the bad seeds in this industry seem to be exposed in a short period of time, a company that has been around for at least two years is probably a safe bet.

- Choose an industry that specializes in your profession. Because they claim to have expertise, these types of agencies tend to be more reliable. Also, because they are working within a particular industry, it is likely that news of any negative experiences on the part of job seekers would travel fast. If you are just starting out in a particular field, you may have a bit more difficulty securing employment through a specialized employment agency. Still, since many industries (e.g., advertising, banking and finance, health care, and publishing) rely on these types of services to find suitable employees, it would be worth your while to get in touch with one or more of these agencies and see what kind of jobs are available.

- Ask whether the agency belongs to any national or regional professional organization. The most notable national organization is the National Association of Personnel Consultants (NAPC). Thousands of agencies across the nation belong to this organization. In order to become a member, they are required to follow a prescribed set of business practices known as the Standards of Ethical Practice and the NAPC Code of Ethics.

Calling On Personal Contacts

Ask a number of professionals how they got their current position, and chances are at least one of them will tell you "through a friend," "through a family member," or "through a business contact." Yes folks, the Six Degrees of Separation theory is at work in the job search as well. No matter what profession you're interested in, chances are good that you know someone in that field, or know someone who knows someone, or know someone who knows someone who knows someone else. You get the picture. The point is, you should be able to find

someone in your desired field to talk to who can help you out in some way. Even if this person cannot give you a job, he or she may be able to refer you to someone who can. Making connections to other people is an easy way to break into a new field and a smart way to advance in your current industry.

If you have not found a soul who can help you, even after calling every single person in your little black book, there are other ways to make some personal contacts. Find out about any local organizations that specialize in your business and plan to attend their local meetings. If you are a college graduate, get in touch with your alumni association and find out if there is a way you can track down other graduates who work in your particular field. Another great way to meet business contacts is to go online; you could find a news group or professional forum that specializes in your business and engage in an online discussion. While job offers may not be handed to you within the first hour or so of contact, don't be surprised if you hear from these new "friends" later on, when an opportunity arises.

Sending Unsolicited Resumes

One of the biggest frustrations job seekers can experience is to contact a company, call their recorded job line, or browse through their available opportunities only to find that there are no jobs available to suit their skills. So what should you do if the company of your dreams is not actively recruiting people in your field or your geographical area right now? The answer is simple: *Send a resume anyway!*

Just as looking through the help wanted ads can be a last resort for you, *placing* a help wanted advertisement can be the last resort for an employer. Generally, employers like to promote from within their own workplace before hiring an outside candidate. If that doesn't work, they next try to find out if any current employees (employees they trust and respect, of course) know of any worthwhile candidates that might fit the bill (this is where calling on personal contacts fits in). If none of these attempts pans out, the employer will usually go through the resumes currently on

Job Search Odds and Ends

NAPC-Approved Agencies

If you are new to the whole employment agency thing, you may want to think about contacting the National Association of Personnel Consultants yourself to obtain a list of member agencies. They can be contacted as follows:

National Association of Personnel Consultants
3133 Mount Vernon Avenue
Alexandria, VA 22305
Phone: 703/684-0180
Fax: 703/684-0071
World Wide Web:
www.napsweb.org

Insider Tips

Character Flaws

While certain characteristics (e.g., loyalty, honesty, industriousness) are always highly regarded in any career, these are not the key words that a hiring manager would necessarily seek out. Instead of wasting half the page explaining what a wonderful and creative person you are, make sure to put more emphasis on your achievements. If you know the industry and the position well enough, you should be able to throw in some pertinent skills and buzz words that would interest an employer. Just keep in mind that a potential employer is much more likely to search out nouns than anything else. At the initial screening phase, educational and professional achievements are much more important than personal attributes, so skip the "boisterous" and go with the "bachelors degree."

file in their human resources or personnel office and try to select possible candidates from that pool (this is where the Direct Contact method comes into play).

If you have already sent in your resume *and* you are qualified for the position, it is very likely that the employer will call you in for an interview before he or she places a help wanted advertisement. This will save the company both time and money in the process and eliminate the amount of competition that you will be facing for the job.

Creating Your Resume

Okay, so you've figured out what you want to do with your life and how you're going to go about achieving that goal. Now what? Well now it's time to develop one of the most crucial elements to a successful job search: that is, THE RESUME! True, this book is about job interviews, but the first step to actually getting a job interview is to create an attention-getting resume.

Your resume is the piece of information that lets a potential employer know what your skills are and whether or not—on the most rudimentary, skill-based level—you would be a good fit for the available position and/or the company. For this reason, your resume must be as detailed and informative as possible, without reaching too far beyond a one-page limit. A second function of the resume is to be as attractive as possible. This is not meant in a purely aesthetic way; it simply means that you must create a resume that will draw as much attention as possible. Remember, getting noticed is the only way to get a job.

Traditional Resume

A traditional resume is the document chock full of pretty fonts and formatting that you most likely think of when you hear the word *resume*. In the past, it was just this sort of resume that you would send along to a potential employer. While this type of resume is becoming less common, it is important that you keep an updated version of a traditional resume on hand; you should bring it with you to every job interview.

Danny Rose
150 West Allen Street
Cambridge, MA 02138
(617) 555-5555
dannyrose@myemail.com

SUMMARY
Accounting manager with eight years' experience in general ledger, accounts payable, and financial reporting. MBA in Management. Proficient in Windows, Lotus 1-2-3, and Excel.

EXPERIENCE
Malcolm Corporation
Newton, MA
Accounting Manager 1996–present
- Manage a staff of six in general ledger and accounts payable.
- Established guidelines for month-end closing procedures, speeding up closing by five business days.
- Implemented team-oriented cross-training program within accounting group, increasing productivity of key accounting staff.

Dakota & Sophia Company
Wellesley, MA
Senior Accountant 1993–1996
- Managed accounts payable, general ledger, transaction processing, and financial reporting.
- Developed management reporting package, including variance reports and cash flow reporting.

Staff Accountant 1992–1993
- Managed accounts payable including vouchering, cash disbursements, and bank reconciliation.
- Wrote and issued policies.
- Maintained supporting schedules used during year-end audits.
- Trained new employees.

EDUCATION
Northeastern University, 1992–1994
Boston, MA
MBA in Management

Boston College, 1988–1992
Boston, MA
BS in Accounting

ASSOCIATIONS
National Association of Accountants

Insider Tips

Should You Include a Cover Letter with Your Resume?

Yes. While your cover letter won't help in the initial selection process, it can distinguish you from the competition in the final rounds. If you've taken the time to craft a letter that summarizes your strongest qualifications, you'll have the edge over other contenders who skip this important step.

If you're responding to a classified ad, try to use some of the same key words the ad mentions. And if you're sending your resume to a new networking contact, be sure to mention who referred you. Even in this anonymous electronic age, the old adage "It's not what you know but who you know" still holds true.

Scannable Resume

A scannable resume is a basic resume—stripped of any funky fonts or formatting—that will be fed into a scanner and spit out in the form of an electronic database listing. When employers are hiring for a specific position, they will type in a set of key words to search for, and the computer will respond with a list of possible candidates. The key to a great scannable resume is to create as many key words as possible. Think about the skills, buzz words, and characteristics that an employer might seek out when researching potential employees, and make sure you include these words in your resume. Remember, the more key words, the more likely your name will turn up in a search.

Electronic Resume

An electronic resume is a scannable resume that is sent via e-mail. Because everyone's e-mail program is different, you'll want to make sure that there is absolutely NO FORMATTING on this resume. Even boldfaced and italicized words can ruin the overall look of your resume in this case, so it is best to employ capital letters to separate sections. Unless otherwise specified, it is best to send electronic resumes in the body of an e-mail rather than as an attachment. This is done for at least two reasons. First, with the number of computer viruses that are always circulating, people are often reluctant to open e-mail attachments from unknown senders. And second, regardless of the word processing program the receiver may use, including your resume in the body of the message can help ensure that it remains readable.

Writing an Effective Cover Letter

In the job search, many people tend to shrug off the idea of a cover letter as a mere nuisance. *They're wrong!* Ask any recruiter or hiring manager, and they're likely to tell you "no cover letter, no interview." Even if you are sending your resume via e-mail, take the time to compose a compelling cover letter that really sells your skills.

Taking the time to put together such a letter shows the employer that you are interested in the position that *they* have to offer, not just any position that will bring home a paycheck. The cover letter also offers you the chance to fill in any holes in your resume. For example, if you've been out of the work force for several years, a cover letter offers you the opportunity to explain why: "Having spent the past 6 years at home with my daughter, I now feel it is time to re-enter the work force, and I look forward to doing so with much vigor." Another advantage to a cover letter is that it lets you offer up a bit of your personality. This is not to say the cover letter is a showcase for your personality; you may be the class cut-up, but a cover letter is neither the time nor the place to try out your latest comedy routine. Keep the tone polite and professional.

Strange but True

Cover Letters

Certain formats and phrases signal an employer that you're using a form letter. Some job candidates turn this blunder into an art. In one real-life example, a candidate created a form letter with blank spaces where he penned in the employer's name and position applied for. Another applicant who was indecisive about her field of interest created a list of possible positions in her letter. She then circled the most appropriate job description, depending on the company.

Danny Rose
150 West Allen Street
Cambridge, MA 02138
(617) 555-5555
dannyrose@myemail.com

SUMMARY
Accounting manager with eight years' experience in general ledger, accounts payable, and financial reporting. MBA in Management. Proficient in Windows, Lotus 1-2-3, and Excel.

EXPERIENCE
MALCOLM CORPORATION, Newton, MA
Accounting Manager, 1996–present
Manage a staff of six in general ledger and accounts payable.

Established guidelines for month-end closing procedures, speeding up closing by five business days.

Implemented team-oriented cross-training program within accounting group, increasing productivity of key accounting staff.

DAKOTA & SOPHIA COMPANY, Wellesley, MA
Senior Accountant, 1993–1996
Managed accounts payable, general ledger, transaction processing, and financial reporting.

Developed management reporting package, including variance reports and cash flow reporting.

Staff Accountant, 1992–1993
Managed accounts payable including vouchering, cash disbursements, and bank reconciliation. Wrote and issued policies.

Maintained supporting schedules used during year-end audits.

Trained new employees.

EDUCATION
MBA in Management, Northeastern University, Boston, MA, 1994
BS in Accounting, Boston College, Boston, MA, 1992

ASSOCIATIONS
National Association of Accountants

Danny Rose
150 West Allen Street
Cambridge, MA 02138
(617) 555-5555
dannyrose@myemail.com

SUMMARY
Accounting manager with eight years' experience in general ledger, accounts payable, and financial reporting. MBA in Management. Proficient in Windows, Lotus 1-2-3, and Excel.

EXPERIENCE
MALCOLM CORPORATION, Newton, MA
Accounting Manager, 1996—present
Manage a staff of six in general ledger and accounts payable.

Established guidelines for month-end closing procedures, speeding up closing by five business days.

Implemented team-oriented cross-training program within accounting group, increasing productivity of key accounting staff.

DAKOTA & SOPHIA COMPANY, Wellesley, MA
Senior Accountant, 1993—1996
Managed accounts payable, general ledger, transaction processing, and financial reporting.

Developed management reporting package, including variance reports and cash flow reporting.

Staff Accountant, 1992—1993
Managed accounts payable including vouchering, cash disbursements, and bank reconciliation. Wrote and issued policies.

Maintained supporting schedules used during year-end audits. Trained new employees.

EDUCATION
MBA in Management, Northeastern University, Boston, MA, 1994
BS in Accounting, Boston College, Boston, MA, 1992

ASSOCIATIONS
National Association of Accountants

178 Green Street
Cambridge, MA 02142
(617) 555-5555

May 18, 2001

Pat Cummings
Director
Any Agency
1140 Main Street
Boston, MA 02118

Dear Ms. Cummings:

I read about your agency in the May edition of *Save Our Earth* and was impressed by your Stop and Think! campaign to educate Boston in choosing environmentally safe alternatives for everyday living. I wonder if you might have an opening for an environmental advocate?

I have both a passion for environmental concerns and practical experience. For the past 4 years, I have been operating my own business, Recycling Renegades, in Cambridge. I successfully acquired the first recycling permit in Cambridge for ferrous and nonferrous metal, aluminum, high-grade paper, and plastic. As owner and manager, I conduct research, process materials, and distribute proceeds to community associations.

I now feel it is time to shift to a wider focus. I would like to apply my skills to developing innovative programs to promote all environmental concerns. Would it be possible to meet for an interview? I have several ideas I'd like to share with you.

Sincerely,

Chris Smith

Chris Smith

CHAPTER THREE

Applying Your Strategy

Job Search
Odds and Ends

Advantages of Online Networking

Discussion group participants often include human resources representatives and hiring managers, who lend their expertise by discussing the qualities they look for in employees. Many recruiters report visiting field-specific discussion groups to look for potential job candidates.

Participating in online discussion groups brings far greater exposure than, for instance, going to a meeting of a local industry group. A discussion group's audience is most often nationwide and may even include participants from around the world.

Monitoring discussion groups makes it easy to determine what skills and experiences employers are looking for. It's also a good way to find out which companies are hiring and what the hot topics are in the field.

You've got your resume and cover letter together. Now it's time to start sending it out. Since you've already developed your strategy, you should be all set to let the game begin. Of all the steps, this is certainly the easiest one. If you have created an electronic resume and are using the Internet to search out available positions, it is possible for you to send out tens and even hundreds of resumes at a time (depending on the speed of your fingers). Working online will also help you to employ each of the strategies listed previously. For example, while you may not have anyone to contact regarding your future in a particular field right now, Internet news groups and networking make it easy to find people who may be willing to talk with you further. If you're not using the World Wide Web in your job search, this step will take a bit longer but will be easy nonetheless.

Be Prepared for the Call

Waiting to hear from interested employers can seem to take forever and, thus, become very frustrating. In fact, finding a new job can take up to several months. And being called in for an interview does not mean that the job is yours. So try to be patient and always be prepared. Many employers like to call a person and screen them over the phone before calling them in for a personal interview. You need to be ready to wow them with your answers and experience at any time of day. If you are registered with an employment service or have posted your resume online, you should expect calls at all times. Because it is the recruiter's job to fill a position as much as it is yours to find one, recruiters will often jump at the chance to contact a potential job match. This is not to say that a recruiting firm could or *should* call you at midnight (that's completely unacceptable, regardless of how badly you want the job); but because these people often work long hours and even occasional weekends, it's not unheard of to get a call on a Saturday afternoon or later in the evening.

Make sure that you don't become stagnant after one day of hard job searching. Finding a job is a difficult game to win. You should continue sending out resumes and contacting potential employers for as long as you are seeking employment.

Getting the Interview

Getting a call to come in and interview with a company can be one of the most exciting as well as nerve-wracking parts of the job search experience. So many questions arise about what to say (and what not to say), what to wear, what time to arrive, and so on. Relax! Since nobody interviews on a very regular basis, it is natural to have lots of questions.

One main point of the interview to keep in mind though is that you have already impressed this person with your resume. Now all you need to do is show him or her that you can do the job! Sounds easy enough, right? Okay, so maybe it's not that simple. Still, like an author's pile of rejection letters, every failed interview (or any interview in which you *didn't* get the job) can serve as a learning lesson. If you can pinpoint exactly what you think you did wrong, you can avoid making the same mistake the next time around. Often it is the case that you did very well in your interview but that you still weren't offered the job.

Remember, just because you didn't get *this* job doesn't mean that you will not get *a* job.

Job Search Odds and Ends

Taking It Personally

It's not often that becoming happily employed stems from an immediately perfect equation. Throughout the process, you're likely to find plenty of jobs that you think you are perfect for while the employer doesn't see it quite the same way. Likewise, many companies may find you a perfect match for their position while you have very little interest in them. Even when an interview goes smoothly, there could be another candidate with more experience and more know-how than you, resulting in that person getting the offer rather than you.

Though you should not take it personally, the bottom line, any way you slice it, is that rejection hurts. However, if you follow the simple rules of job search etiquette, when a position opens up they'll likely think of you.

CHAPTER FOUR

Pre-Interview Priming

You are now ready to get out into the real world and see what the job market has to offer. You've got a spiffy new resume, chock full of experience; a perfectly written cover letter that is sure to wow any recruiter who reads it; and a list of industry contacts more than a mile long. Having the right experience and a great set of skills are certainly important in finding a great job. But in order to get that job, there's one more thing you need to learn: that is, how to impress an interviewer enough to (1) hire you or (2) invite you back for another interview.

In most steps of the job hunt you can rely on outside forces to help you; you could, for example, hire someone to write your resume or use your personal contacts to find out about possible opportunities. However, the interview is the one place where the fate of this activity relies entirely on you.

The Importance of the Job Interview

Many people will argue about which part of the job search process is the most crucial. While a fantastic cover letter and resume are certainly what will get you called in to interview for a job, it is the interview itself that will determine whether or not you are the right person for the job.

Think of it this way: A great resume is what gets your foot in the door of a new company; a successful interview is what lands you your own desk and a prime parking space! You could be the most qualified person on the planet, but if you can't present yourself in a professional and confident manner, a recruiter is likely to choose someone else for the job.

Remember, there is a whole science to the task of hiring new employees. Recruiters are looking for employees who not only have the skills and experience to do a job well and do it correctly but also can easily fit into the already-established company culture. They are checking to see how well your personality and ideas will complement those you will be working alongside. That said, there are plenty of ways in which you can convince an interviewer that, in fact, you are that person.

Interview Research

Preparing for an interview requires a lot of time and patience. It is not something that can be crammed into the 10 minutes you have before leaving to meet with the recruiter. Luckily, it is also something that becomes easier with time. You begin to know which questions to expect and can decide which answers work best and which fall short of perfect. The more interviews you participate in, the closer you are to winning that perfect job.

One of the most time-consuming parts of the entire job interview process is researching a prospective employer. However, it is also the most important part of the process. The easiest way to set yourself apart from the rest of the candidates is to leave the interviewer with a positive impression. And the easiest way to do *that* is to know the company inside and out. Remember, this is not something you should do early in the job search game. Company research should be reserved for the time after you have been offered the opportunity to interview.

What Kind of Information Should I Be Looking For?

Look for everything! Pretend that a professor or a supervisor has asked you to make a 10-minute presentation on the company and then learn as many facts as you can that would allow you to speak (intelligently) about the company for that amount of time. You need to know the types of products and/or services the company offers, the types of customers they most often deal with, the name and business of the parent company, and the names and businesses of any subsidiaries. You should try to learn about the company's rank in industry, sales and profit trends, type of ownership, size, and anything else you deem important. You should make yourself familiar with the company's biggest competitors and the direction in which the industry, as a whole, is headed. If you don't know much of the industry jargon already, learn it. If you know the name of the person who is interviewing you, you can even go so far as to get a little background information on him or her (not to the degree that you invade his or her privacy, but enough info to keep you talking). Pick up a trade paper, join online discussion groups, visit industry organization meetings and Web sites. Believe me, research time is time well spent.

Job Search Odds and Ends

Anxiety Types

Anxiety can strike at any time, and it can come in many different forms:

Pre-Interview Anxiety: When you lack self-confidence and, thus, are easily distracted, stress can result. This will invariably affect your performance in the interview, especially through lack of preparation due to senseless worrying.

Mid-Interview Anxiety: Suppose that after a difficult question you stumbled over, you lose your confidence and begin to falter on other points. This can snowball into a disaster if not kept in check. If you find yourself slipping, take a sip of water or do something else that will allow you a second or two to collect and recompose yourself.

Post-Interview Anxiety: There's only one thing to remember after an interview ends: Once it's over, it's over. Send a follow-up letter (provided you are still interested), and then continue to chug along in your job seeking process.

Discover every resource that you can that relates to the specific company you are applying to and their business in general. If the company has a Web site, read through each of their Web pages. Familiarize yourself with their catalog. Look into additional job openings they have posted to get an even better idea of the types of employees they are seeking. Make use of Internet search engines and read any article that comes up with that company name in it. Some people who have done this have uncovered information about a company that they did not like—information such as lawsuits or customer complaints. The more time you spend researching, the better off you will be in the interview.

Even if you get a call one day and are asked to interview the following day, don't think you can sneak through the interviewer's door—and do well—without having taken at least an hour or so to acquaint yourself with the company and its business. Though it may seem like a good idea to try and get a lot of this research work out of the way early on in the game, intensive company research should not be performed until you have secured a date and time for an interview. Otherwise, you may waste countless hours of your time researching companies that may never call you.

Internet Research

If you have Internet access, there are plenty of places online where you can get much of the needed research done quickly and effectively. The best place to start is with a company's Web site. In addition to basic company and competitor information, you can often obtain annual reports, lists of company executives, and some company history. You can learn about pending mergers and the latest and greatest happenings within a company. If there is a section for press releases, read the latest few releases. This is a great way to show the interviewer that you know the most current happenings in the company. There are also plenty of sites that will help you learn a bit more about an industry and/or a specific occupation that you are interested in. A few of these sites are profiled here:

CareerCity.com

www.careercity.com

Launched in 1985 by Adams Media Corporation, CareerCity.com serves job seekers and recruiters alike. The site is specifically designed for those technical and professional people who seek demanding and challenging positions in their chosen fields. Candidates can visit CareerCity.com to find top opportunities nationwide. If you are interviewing with an employment agency rather than an actual employer, CareerCity.com will provide you with the links to more than 7,000 American employment agencies.

www.careercity.com

CompaniesOnline

www.companiesonline.com

Run by the Lycos Network, CompaniesOnline offers Webgoers information on more than 900,000 public and private companies. When you execute a search, the link will display such basic information as phone number, address, employee size, and annual sales. By clicking on the link, you will be allowed more in-depth information including the big cheese's name and title, company DUNS number, SIC codes, and all the company's Web addresses (this is a good way to find out about the company's parent or any subsidiaries that might exist).

www.companiesonline.com

www.hoovers.com

www.jobfind.com

www.myjobsearch.com

Hoover's Online: The Business Network
www.hoovers.com

Geared toward the businessperson, Hoover's Online makes company information (general summary, key players, recent news headlines) available to you, the job seeker, as well. The site is well organized and provides a variety of links, including links to current opportunities that exist at each company. While you are probably not interested in the positions they have available (you have, after all, been called in for an interview), you may be interested in reading the listings to get a better sense of the type of employee they are seeking.

Jobfind.com
www.jobfind.com

In addition to providing tons of job postings, Jobfind.com offers job seekers the chance to research these companies further. They offer several hundred company profiles with links to current openings. While the company profiles are limited to the companies that are currently posting jobs, there are enough big and recognizable companies listed to make it worth your while to run a quick search.

My Job Search
www.myjobsearch.com

Here's another all-in-one site that can help you find a job, prepare for the interview, research a company, and negotiate a fair salary . . . all with one visit! This site is an invaluable source for job search information, no matter what stage of the game you are at. As much of the information is in the form of links to other sites, My Job Search can offer you access to a lot more information than the typical job site that tries to do it all on its own.

Wall Street Research Net

www.wsrn.com

If you are planning on playing with the big boys and girls of Wall Street—or at least the companies whose stock is traded there—this is one site that can provide you with a lot of information. Type in the stock exchange symbol, and this site will provide you with an abundance of information, including a link to the company's Web site, if there is one.

www.wsrn.com

WetFeet.com

www.wetfeet.com

This completely comprehensive site will give you the lowdown on a particular career, industry, or company, all with the click of a mouse. The site will also allow you to type in your industry, zip code, and state and learn about what the average person in your position (or desired position) earns nowadays. The site offers specific advice for those who are just starting out, those who are changing careers, and students and MBAs. While the companies they offer research on are some of the bigger name companies within each industry, this can help you if you are researching the competition for a small start-up. Whether you're just getting your feet wet or diving right in, WetFeet.com can answer just about any question you ask.

www.wetfeet.com

CD-ROM Job Search

Even if you don't have Internet access, there are various software programs out there that can help you in researching potential employers. Basically, they take the same sort of information that is available online or in the printed directories and package it in the form of a CD-ROM database. Some of the better versions are listed below:

Dun & Bradstreet Million Dollar Disc Plus
3 Sylvan Way
Parsippany, NJ 07054
800/526-0651
www.dnb.com

This CD-ROM provides information on over 400,000 companies in virtually every industry. About 90 percent of the companies listed are privately held, and all have at least $3 million in annual sales or at least 50 employees. Each company's listing includes the number of employees, sales volume, name of the parent company, and corporate headquarters or branch locations. The *Million Dollar Disc Plus* also provides the names and titles of top executives, as well as biographical information on those executives, including education and career background. Searches can be done by location, industry, SIC code, executive names, or key words in the executive biographies. This directory is updated quarterly.

Encyclopedia of Associations: National Organizations of the U.S.
835 Penobscot Building
645 Griswald Street
Detroit, MI 48226
800/877-GALE
www.galegroup.com

This CD-ROM contains descriptions and contact information for nearly 23,000 national organizations. You can search by association name, geographic location, and key words. It is available in both single- and multi-user formats.

Harris InfoSource National

2057 East Aurora Road
Twinsburg, OH 44087
800/888-5900
www.harrisinfo.com

This directory of manufacturers profiles more than 375,000 companies. All of the companies listed are located in the United States. The listings include the number of employees, plant size, and sales revenue, as well as the names and titles of top executives. This CD-ROM is updated twice a year and can be purchased in smaller regional or state editions.

Print Directories

In addition to the various electronic databases out there, there are plenty of print publications—usually in the form of larger reference books you would probably only find at a library—that list information on thousands of major employers the world over. In addition, there are various print directories available that will outline the typical tasks involved in acquiring particular job titles and allow you to map out your own career path. Below are just a few of these directories:

The Complete Guide for Occupational Exploration

JIST Publishing
8902 Otis Avenue
Indianapolis, IN 46216-1033
800/648-5478
www.jist.com

Reading *The Complete Guide for Occupational Exploration* is a great first step for those who are unsure of whether or not a particular career or job is right for them. The book gives the lowdown on more than 12,700 job titles that companies across the country often hire for. For each job title listed, the book explores the typical tasks required, skills involved, and work culture. The book is easy to use and will help job seekers at every level of employment decide on the first or next step of their career.

Insider Tips

Get the Most Out of Your Job Hunt

No job hunting experience is a bad one if you learn from it. Even if you have a horrible interview, at least you can analyze what went wrong to improve your chances in the next one. Consider each job hunting activity as an additional step in enriching your job hunting abilities and take criticisms as opportunities to improve yourself.

National JobBank
Adams Media Corporation
260 Center Street
Holbrook, MA 02343
800/USA-JOBS
www.adamsmedia.com

This annual reference publication, which lists more than 21,000 of the nation's top employers, has long been known as one of the most comprehensive publications of its kind. Covering every industry and every state, *The National JobBank* tells you all about the companies that are hiring and much more. Learn about the typical positions these companies hire for, the educational backgrounds that are often sought after, and the benefits you can expect to receive.

Occupational Outlook Handbook
Bureau of Labor Statistics
Publications Sales Center
P.O. Box 2145
Chicago, IL 60690
312/353-1880
http://stats.bls.gov/emppub2.htm

This book, which is updated every other year, provides an exhaustive amount of information on the nation's major industries and occupations. In addition to typical salary information, the *Occupational Outlook Handbook* offers information on the skills needed for each of these jobs, necessary training, and the educational backgrounds that are often required. If you are exploring various occupations or industries, this is one source that you can use to help you learn more about what each job entails.

Practice Makes Perfect

By now you've certainly heard the saying "Practice makes perfect," but did you realize how much this adage applies to job interviewing? It's true. The more you interview (or at least practice for an interview), the more likely you are to master the art of it. Refer

to the later chapters in this book to learn some of the most commonly asked interview questions (and some of the strangest), and practice your answers to them. Figure out the kinds of answers that an interviewer would be looking for, and think of a way to answer these questions as they relate to you and your own experience. If you think about the answers carefully enough and practice through a mock interview with a friend or family member, you are more likely to answer the interviewer in a confident manner.

If it's your first time out in the real world or if it's been a while since your last job interview, don't be surprised if your first interview turns out to be somewhat disastrous. Though it doesn't have to be the case that your first interview is a failure, because you are likely out of practice you should try to schedule your first interview with a company that you don't have all that much interest in. Interviewing with your dream company for that ideal job the first time out may not be a wise idea. If you don't know what to expect from an interviewer, you could blow your chances of employment.

If the first interview is less than perfect, don't despair, as interviews are the most difficult meetings to get through. That said, try and get one or two interviews under your belt before you decide to meet with the hiring manager of the company of your dreams. If that's not possible, make sure you practice until you've got it nearly perfect, as you've only got one shot at making a good impression.

If you can, get a friend or family member to sit down with you and go over your answers to some of the questions you think you may be asked. Let him or her hear the response you've prepared and ask for feedback. Do you sound confident? Do you sound capable? Do you sound desperate? These are all the questions you'll want to consider (and the problems you'll want to fix) before going to an interview.

If there's no one available to help you test out your interviewing chops, enlist the help of a tape recorder, video camera, or even a mirror. Make sure to keep an eye on your body language, as it can tell the interviewer a lot about you. Do you slouch in your chair, or do you sit up straight and attentively? Are you able to maintain eye contact without staring? When you answer a question, do you look straight ahead in a confident manner?

Insider Tips

Tie on a Dark One

For men, the tie has become one of the few creative outlets when it comes to dressing professionally. A bad choice in the neckwear department can spell certain doom for unsuspecting job seekers. The days of the "power" tie (e.g., bright colors) are as passé as acid-washed jeans. A solid dark color with tiny geometric patterns is the safest bet. Also remember: A cheap tie is one of the easiest things in the world to spot. Don't become a fashion victim.

Insider Tips

Fashion Don'ts for Men

Shiny shirts are a major no-no. These types of fabrics should be reserved for the nightclub scene. Socks should blend in well with the shoes and pants. Avoid any sort of cutesy pattern, and stick with a color that won't stand out.

• • •

Fashion Don'ts for Women

Avoid pastel colors like pink and powder blue. They may work well at an Easter parade, but they won't help you assert your profession-alism. Don't wear anything that dangles. That goes for earrings, bracelets, and neck-laces. And avoid clothes that are too tight, you'll be less comfortable and you won't be taken as seriously.

You should even go so far as to practice your handshake. Recruiters often mention that one of the most telling parts of an interview is the way the job seeker shakes hands. Too weak and limp a shake tells the recruiter either that this candidate is a bit on the shy side or that he or she is really not interested in being here. Too firm or long a handshake is a sign of des-peration or overzealousness. A firm (but not crushing) one to two shakes of the hand is the recommended way to go.

Dress for Success

You've got the handshake down. Now here's another piece of the puzzle that must be there in order for the interview to work out: proper dress! As superficial as it sounds, employers will judge you on the way you are dressed. This does not mean that if you wear anything less than Prada, the job will go to someone else. It simply means that the interviewer looks at your exterior as a repre-sentation of your interior. If it is obvious that you took the time to choose the right clothes for this interview, it is likely that you will put the same amount of thought into your work. Arriving for an interview in jeans and a sweatshirt tells the interviewer that you don't care enough about the job or the company to put your best self forward. The rules of dress for both men and women are very specific and should be strictly followed.

For Men

Though the lines between what men and women can and do wear to work on a regular basis are becoming more and more blurred—khakis and a button-down shirt can work well on either of the sexes—there are two definite sets of rules during the job inter-view process. If you are a man interviewing for a professional posi-tion, you should always wear a suit! There is no exception to this rule. A shirt and tie might make you the best dressed guy at your current job, but it won't cut it in an interview. More conservative

colors—colors like black, navy blue, or charcoal gray—are the best colors to choose. Bright and flashy colors will only serve to distract the interviewer from what you are saying. Plus, in addition to looking more professional, you can change the look of a conservative colored suit dramatically by changing the tie, the shirt, or both. If you only have one suit, these changes can help you out tremendously when you're interviewing with companies that require two or more meetings on separate occasions.

For Women

The rules of proper workplace attire for women have been changing throughout the past several decades. The "power suit" that once ruled the scene has been replaced with the traditional pantsuit that doesn't differ much from the men's version. Still, the rules of job interview dress have not caught up with workplace appropriateness. Professionalism still dictates that women wear a skirt to an interview. The length of the skirt, obviously, should be tasteful and professional. Knee length is always appropriate. Again, regardless of the company's particular dress code, women too are expected to wear a suit to the interview. Colors should be conservative. A black or navy blue skirt and jacket is the best choice.

Grooming

Personal grooming is another matter each candidate must attend to before heading out the door to an interview. Careful grooming indicates both a sense of thoroughness and self-confidence. Women should not wear excessive makeup or jewelry. If you have painted nails, make sure they are of a conservative color (Urban Decay's Roach may look great on the dance floor of your favorite nightclub, but it certainly will not score you any points underneath the track lighting of the office of your future boss).

All candidates should wear very little—if any—perfume or cologne. While you do want to smell nice for the interview, you don't want to smell like the Estee Lauder counter at your local department store. Plus, a mere spritz of the sweet smelling stuff could be enough to lead an allergic interviewer to a serious sneezing fit.

Insider Tips

Every Detail Counts

No one detail, such as the color of your tie, is going to count for much when it comes to a hiring decision. In fact, even if you cover every detail of your appearance and interviewing behavior, you still aren't guaranteed a job. However, it can take only one minor detail to seriously impair your chances at any one particular interview. Is it fair? No. But it's something you should consider.

Job Search
Odds and Ends

Map It Out Online

One of the easiest ways to figure out where you are going is to map it out. To get an exact idea of how to get to a company, try one of the following sites:

- *www.expedia.com*
- *www.mapquest.com*
- *www.trip.com*

• • •

Job Interview Checklist

❑ Resume
❑ Cover letter
❑ Writing implement
❑ Spare tie;
 Spare set of pantyhose
❑ List of professional references
❑ Driver's license and Social Security card

Men should be sure to check that any facial hair is neat and trim. If you have a beard or a mustache, make sure it is well groomed. Otherwise, men should make sure that they are clean shaven when they arrive for an interview. Even if your interview is later in the day or in the evening, schedule an extra few minutes so that you can run home quickly and shave.

Know Where You're Going

Chances are good that the person who invites you in for an interview will also offer to give you directions to the building. Take these directions! Even if you have a good idea of the location of the company, you'll want to know *exactly* where you are going!

If you are unfamiliar with the area, it might be a good idea to drive to the company before you actually have to meet for the interview. Map out the directions and time how long it takes for you to get there. Add a few extra minutes for traffic or any other unforeseen holdup. Plan on arriving for the interview at least 10 to 15 minutes early.

Know Who You're Seeing

When scheduling your interview, be sure that you know the name of the person you will be meeting with. The person who calls to screen you over the phone is not always the same person you'll be interviewing with. Find out the person's name, title, and phone number. That way, if a problem arises, you can contact this person directly.

10 Ways to Win an Interview

In addition to perfectly answering every question an interviewer asks, there are other ways in which you can make a conscious effort to impress an interviewer, and make sure that he or she remembers you, even after you've shaken hands good-bye.

1. Be Prepared

Being prepared for a job interview entails more than just knowing what questions you are likely to be asked. It means mapping out the route to your destination before the interview—maybe even driving there—and arriving to the location about 15 minutes early. Preparedness calls for bringing along an extra copy of your resume in case the original one you sent has been misplaced, and carrying some reading materials in the event that you have to wait a little while before meeting with someone.

2. Dress Appropriately

The one thing you don't want to be known as in the eyes of an interviewer is "the girl in the jeans" or "the guy in the T-shirt." Interviewers notice these things and are not likely to hire anyone who arrives on the scene in less than conservative business attire. Unless you're donning a tux or your old prom dress, you can never be too overdressed for a job interview.

3. Be Confident

Getting a call to come in and interview for a company is like a nod of approval from an interviewer. Even if *you* think you may be completely underqualified for a position, the interviewer sees something different. Always remember that the company who calls you believes you are capable of performing the job at hand; it's important for you to believe the same thing. Projecting an air of confidence—without sounding cocky or conceited—is one of the easiest ways to get an interviewer to remember you. Talk about your skills and experience with pride and—above all—let the interviewer know that *you* think you could do a good job.

4. Make Eye Contact

One of the easiest ways to project confidence is to be attentive and maintain direct eye contact with an interviewer throughout your meeting. Always look this person directly in the eye to assure him or her that you are both on the same page. If you are interviewing with more than one person (this can often be the case in bigger corporations, though usually not until a second interview or

Job Search Odds and Ends

Scheduling Multiple Interviews

There are a few advantages to scheduling a few interviews for a single day. For one, you'll already be decked out in your interviewing gear, and your briefcase or bag will be stocked with the essential spare resume, work samples, and reference sheets. Also, some people find once they've gone through an interview, they end up in a mental "zone" that can be used for a better performance in additional interviews that day. Of course, if you are currently employed, scheduling multiple interviews will also lighten up the number of days you need to take off. Still—for the sake of time and your own sanity—try and limit the number of interviews on any given day to no more than three or four.

Insider Tips

Interview Don'ts

- Don't look at your watch.

- Don't mimic the body language or mannerisms of the interviewer (this can happen when you get nervous).

- Don't be negative.

- Don't talk too much.

- Don't ask about money, perks, or things that are unrelated to the job or company at hand.

- Don't interrogate the interviewer.

beyond), make eye contact with the person asking you the question. When answering a question in front of two or more people, move from person to person, but make sure to establish eye contact with each person long enough so that you don't seem shifty.

5. Show Your Enthusiasm

Even more frustrating to an interviewer than a candidate who lacks confidence is a candidate who lacks enthusiasm. When the interviewer discusses the different aspects of the job you'd be taking on, show how willing and excited you are to take on these new tasks. Even if the interviewer discusses your having to perform a skill that you are not familiar with, show him or her how eager you are to learn. Like when showing confidence, there is a line you have to walk when showing enthusiasm. Be sure to seem excited but not obsequious or insincere.

6. Know the Position

Whatever the position you're applying for, you should know *something* about it. Reread the job description a few times to get an idea of the type of person the company is looking for. Research similar opportunities and learn more about the kind of person that makes a perfect match for this type of job. Talk to friends or people you know in the same job—or in the industry—to learn about the tasks involved. Know what you are getting yourself into before you go into the job interview; prepare answers to the questions you are likely to be asked as they relate to this job. Don't go to an interview until you can rattle off a few of the tasks you think you'll be asked to perform.

7. Know the Industry

You should also know about the industry to which you're applying, as well as whether the position can be found in many industries. For example, human resources professionals can jump from industry to industry throughout their career, as they are a needed department in almost every organization. Find out as much as you can about the industry and show the interviewer that you are well equipped to deal with the day-to-day duties of the job at hand and that you have a strong knowledge of the industry as a whole.

8. Know the Company

More important than knowing the industry, and just as important (if not more so) as knowing the job, is knowing a little something about the company to which you are applying. If the interviewer does not come out directly with a statement such as "Tell me everything you know about this company," he or she is likely to ask a few questions that will test your knowledge of the company. They may hint around at company issues to see whether you pick up on these allusions. More impressive than a candidate who has the skills to do the job well is a candidate who has the skills to do the job well *and* has a strong knowledge of the company.

9. Practice

The only way to gauge your readiness for an interview is to practice. Whether you sit in front of a mirror or role-play with a friend, practicing your answers to questions that are likely to be asked is the key to projecting a calm and confident exterior during the interview.

10. Follow Up

You've shown an interest in the company before, so why stop once the interview ends? After the interview, be sure to follow up with a quick note or a short but friendly phone call to the person with whom you spoke. A follow-up will help keep your name at the forefront of the interviewer's mind.

10 Ways *Not* to Win an Interview

Many of the following job interview blunders are simply the opposite of the aforementioned winning tactics. They're mistakes that many job seekers often make, and they should always be avoided.

1. Arrive Late

Even worse than arriving late to an interview is blaming your tardiness on the company. Explaining that you received incorrect directions or that you were told the appointment "was at 2 P.M.,

Job Search
Odds and Ends

Web
Research Tools

You can find a company's Web site at *www.dotcomdirectory.com.* You can find a company's address and phone number or a list of companies in a specific industry and location at *www.bigyellow.com* or *www.switchboard.com.*

Insider Tips

Interview Do's

- Maintain eye contact.

- Be positive.

- Show strong interest and enthusiasm.

- Ask questions.

- Act professional and confident.

• • •

Be Realistic

Most important, make sure your career plans are realistic. You have to start somewhere. Accept that most entry-level positions are usually lower paying and less than glamorous. It will probably take you a number of years to achieve your career goals and advance to your ideal job. Therefore, consider an entry-level job the first step toward attaining your long-term goals.

not 1 P.M." is a surefire way not to be hired. Always get to the interview at least 10 minutes early (though 15 is preferable).

2. Appear Bored

Slouching in your seat, looking around the room rather than at the interviewer, and yawning are all signs that you'd rather be somewhere else—such as at home in front of the television—than at this interview.

3. Forget to Do Your Research

Though an interviewer is likely to tell you about the position, the company, and maybe even the industry, he or she is also operating under the assumption that this kind of information is not news to you. "Forgetting" to research the job, the company, and the industry is one quick way to eliminate yourself from the running. While it is certainly okay to ask specific questions about the company or the position, more general questions such as "What kind of company is this?" are certainly not going to score you any points.

4. Speak in a Long-winded Manner

When an interviewer asks a question, he or she wants an answer. What they don't want, however, is to be in for a 30-minute account of your life. Be sure to answer the question with a little bit of explanation, but limit your speech to no more than a minute or two.

5. Speak in Too Brief a Manner

On the other end of the spectrum is the all too brief "yes" or "no" answers. While the interviewer certainly does not want to spend three hours in a room with you completing an interview that should have taken no more than an hour, he or she also does not want to spend just 10 minutes in there. Your answers should be brief, but a simple negative or affirmative is never sufficient. Always explain to the interviewer why you answered how you did.

6. Speak in a Negative Manner

Though you wouldn't be at this interview unless you were unsatisfied with your current employer, this does not give you a

license to badmouth your current (or former) work situation. The last thing an interviewer wants to see is a candidate with a negative attitude. Always be sure to stay positive. Even when the interviewer specifically asks you about a negative experience, speak of this as being a "learning experience." Always end your answers on a positive note.

7. Talk about Money

One mistake job seekers often make—particularly younger ones—is to emphasize the idea of money. Both you and the interviewer know that if you are offered the position, the subject of salary will definitely come up, but you should not be the one to broach it. Even when asked questions such as "What do you hope to achieve in life?" don't talk about financial security. Always having your mind on the paycheck discredits your passion for a position and will not be held in high esteem by the interviewer.

8. Appear Conceited

This is where it is important to draw a distinction between confidence and cockiness. One thing that is sure to annoy or irritate an interviewer is a candidate who has done it all, seen it all, and knows everything! While you certainly should not be afraid to talk about your accomplishments, you should be sure to emphasize the steps you took to reach these successes, and not the praise that was bestowed upon you because of them.

9. Share Unrealistic Goals

This common mistake goes back to failure to research the company, position, and industry. Unrealistic goals often assert themselves when candidates are asked questions such as "Where do you see yourself in five years?" or "What kind of salary are you looking for?" Failure to know the typical career path someone in your position would take—and how long it would take to reach certain turning points—is one common complaint from recruiters. Entry-level employees who see themselves as executive material within the next five years are not living in reality. Similarly, job seekers who don't take the time to research average salaries for the job type, industry,

Job Search
Odds and Ends

Not Sure What You're Worth?

Check out some of these Web sites to find out what you should or could be making:

- *www.salary.com*
- *http://careers.yahoo.com*
- *www.nesnet.com/salary.asp*
- *www.careershop.com*

Insider Tips

Accept All Interviews

Chances are, when sending out your resume, you have one particular company and "dream job" in mind. Still, the job market being the competitive place it is, you can't rest your hopes on one opportunity. One great way to really sharpen your job interview skills is to accept all the interviews that come your way. In addition to getting the practice that could help you if and when you get to interview for that dream job, you never know what kinds of opportunities you'll find at companies you never thought too much about. Above all, remember to always treat each employer with the same amount of respect and enthusiasm.

and area in which they would like to live often make the mistake of demanding far too much (or far too little) money for the job they are being asked to perform. To an interviewer, this lack of knowledge implies one of two things: either that the job seeker is desperate or that the job seeker is uninformed, neither of which will help get you in the door.

10. Appear Unkempt

An unkempt appearance—in job interview terms—could include dirty or unpressed clothing, as well as clothing that is too casual. Even if the company's dress code is casual, job interview attire should be strictly professional. Hair that has not been brushed, facial hair that is not neat, and an overall untidy appearance are things that are certain to get your foot in the door, and right back out again!

With these do's and don'ts in mind, it's time to learn the best and most effective ways in which you can and should prepare for a job interview. Think of your role in the job interview as that of a salesperson. What you're trying to sell is yourself to the interviewer.

Just like a salesperson would, you should take the time to get to know the company and think about why you and your skills would fit in well here. You should make a list of your most marketable skills and develop a sort of pitch for yourself. Why should this company decide to "buy" your skills? What can you offer them?

Ready, Set, Go!

With these interview preparation skills under your belt, you're all set to get out there and make a great impression. So get your suit pressed, put on your greatest smile, offer your firmest handshake, and go on out there and win that interview!

PART TWO

Interview Insight

CHAPTER FIVE

Interview Types

L ike everything else in the world of job interviewing, there are various forms a job interview can take. From an initial telephone screening to a lunch meeting with a potential employer, there are various encounters that can count as a job interview. To help you get a better idea of the types of job interviews you may encounter while seeking new employment—and what to expect from each of them—the following sections encompass the many interview types.

Interview Formats

The first way in which job interviews can be differentiated is by the format that they use. In most cases, interviews will fall into one of two format categories: structured or unstructured.

Structured Interviews

When you envision sitting in a room and actually interviewing for a position, you are most likely thinking of a structured interview. This is where the interviewer asks a prescribed set of questions and you retort with brief answers.

Unstructured Interviews

In an unstructured interview, the questions are more open ended. The interviewer asks you questions that are specifically designed to get you to reveal more about yourself than you would if just asked the same old standard questions. He or she is trying to find out more about you, your character, your skills, your background, and your aspirations.

Interviewers do not necessarily limit themselves to one style. In fact, it is common practice for a recruiter or hiring professional to start out with some basic objective questions and finish the interview with the more open-ended inquires. If you want to be on the safe side, anticipate both.

Informational Interviews

While the informational interview does fall into the category of "job interviews," it is different in that the end result does not necessarily result in being considered for an employment opportunity. Rather, informational interviews are more of a networking tool. They are a chance for you to learn about an industry without having the added pressure of having your skills and past work experiences (or lack thereof) put on display.

If you are a student about to enter the workplace for the first time, or a person changing careers after several years in the work force, an informational interview can be an invaluable resource. If you think you may be interested in a particular field but would like to learn more about what it entails, an informational interview allows you the opportunity to speak with an industry insider candidly about whether or not you might be a good match for the profession. Informational interviews allow you—the job seeker—to sit down with someone who has worked in the profession for quite some time and voice your concerns. The best part about this type of interview is that you are the one in control of all the questions. The downside? Informational interviews, inherently, exist only so that you may gain more information about a particular job, career, or industry in general. They are not meant as part of the hiring process.

The easiest way to arrange an informational interview is to enlist the help of any professional contacts you may have. Chances are good that you know someone—or know someone who knows someone—in the field you are thinking about entering. The next and final step is to call this person and try to arrange a time when the two of you could sit down and talk about what it is that he or she does.

Even without a whole slew of industry contacts, it is likely that you could find someone willing to sit down and talk with you about his or her industry just by picking up the phone and calling around to local companies that are engaged in the business in which your interest lies. Speaking with someone in human resources might be your best bet. E-mail is another great resource when it comes to scheduling an informational interview. You can send out a brief

Overcoming Anxiety, Part I

Being anxious about a pending job interview is normal, but there are ways in which you can lessen the stress. To overcome anxiety, you must first understand it. Ask yourself these basic questions:

- Am I qualified for this job? (If the answer is no, ask yourself why you applied.)
- Is there anything else in my life causing stress? (If so, try to eliminate all outside worries and focus on the task at hand.)
- What's the worst that can happen? (Unless you are applying to be a professional alligator wrestler, your job interview will not result in anything worse than simple, common rejection.)

message introducing yourself and asking whether anyone would be interested in speaking with you a bit further about what it takes to become an industry professional. If you do choose to take the e-mail route, remember to use both caution and restraint. Sending out the same e-mail to, say, three hundred employees of one company might be overkill. Find out the qualifications and current activities of each of these individuals and decide which ones are most in line with what it is you hope to do.

As in any type of interview, it is necessary that you heed the rules of proper job interview etiquette. Be sure to extend the exact same courtesies—if not more—to the person who is unselfishly volunteering his or her time to indulge your questions as you would to someone interviewing you for a job. Arrive on time, dress professionally, and send a thank-you note or follow-up letter. After all, even though the end result of *this* interview is not a job, you never know what could happen. Your sheer desire and willingness to take the time to learn about the industry could impress him or her enough to consider you for future employment.

Screening Interviews

In most companies, before a candidate can be seriously considered for employment with a company, he or she must be carefully screened by one or more members of the company. Screening interviews can take place on the phone, in person, or both.

The screening interview is the most basic interview type you can imagine. The goal of this type of interview is to decide whether or not you would be a good fit for this company, according to your skills *and* your personality. It is for this reason that making a great and lasting impression during a screening interview is a necessary first step to getting hired.

Telephone Interviews

As impersonal as the medium itself, the telephone interview is meant simply as a way for recruiters and human resources professionals to weed out those candidates who are not suited to the job

or the company. A telephone interview can happen at any time, and since it's very important that you make a great impression here, you should always be prepared to engage in one after sending out a resume. By their very nature, telephone interviews are more like "surprise interviews." They are meant to catch interested job seekers in the middle of the day to see whether they are as interested in a position as they claim to be in their resume and cover letter. While there is no way to prepare for the timing of these interviews, you can be well prepared to field the questions that are likely to be asked. After all, the goal of the phone interview is to sound interested and intelligent enough to be invited in for a face-to-face interview.

The following dialogue shows the most common parts of the phone interview dialogue, what the interviewer is trying to get at, and the best way in which you should respond to his or her statements and inquiries.

Interviewer: Hello, Mr. Smith. My name is Sally Smalls; I am the Human Resources Director at Fill-in-the-Blank Corporation.

Translation: With just this simple introduction, the interviewer is hoping to hear some recognition in your voice. He or she wants to make sure that you remember where you sent your resume.

Best Answer: The best way to respond to this introduction is to acknowledge the person and his or her company. If you know something about the company offhand, you could throw it out there. A great response to this introduction would be something along the lines of "Hello. How are you? I just read that Fill-in-the-Blank is hoping to acquire Blankety Blank. Things must be pretty crazy around the office." Keep the conversation polite and friendly and always be professional.

Interviewer: Hello, Mr. Smith. We received your resume the other day, and I was wondering whether you had a few minutes to speak with me so that I can get a better idea of what it is you're expecting from this position.

Translation: Your resume caught our attention. Before we bring you in for a face-to-face interview, we would like to get a feel

Insider Tips

Name Dropping

Be sure to drop names; it's one of the most important ways to get ahead in the business world (e.g., "Ally Kendreck suggested I call you"). As you continue networking, you'll probably find yourself dropping names of people you've met only by phone. Don't be uncomfortable with this; this is the way it's done. You need to do everything you can to increase your chances of finding a job.

Job Search Odds and Ends

Overcoming Anxiety, Part II

Tried all the previous suggestions and still can't keep your anxiety at bay? Relax!

- Take deep breaths (not where people can see or hear you). A short walk to collect your thoughts can also help.
- Think about your past achievements. Even small things such as scoring the winning basket in a high school basketball game can bolster your confidence tremendously.
- Imagine what your life would be like if you were to get the job. The more enthusiasm and confidence you portray, the better you will be seen.

for the kind of person you are. Can I take a few minutes of your time to screen you before inviting you into the office?

Best Answer: "Absolutely." Part of the test here is to see whether you are ready to talk about your qualifications and desire to work with this company at a moment's notice. From the time you start sending out your resume, always be prepared to hear from a recruiter over the phone. Above all, take it as a compliment that you received a phone call; some people don't even make it this far. If you are really taken by surprise by such a phone call and don't think you would be at your best to speak with the interviewer (i.e., you were in the midst of a mid-afternoon nap or were catching up on the latest *Real World* marathon), don't be afraid to ask to reschedule the interview. You should, however, try to reschedule it for as soon as possible and say something along the lines of "Right now is not a very good time, but I would be able to speak with you in another hour or so, if that would be okay?"

Interviewer: I see here that you are currently working as a sales representative for Addison Company. Why do you want to leave?

Translation: Why do you want to leave your current position?

Best Answer: Talk about your desire to branch out or grow and the lack of opportunity you have to do that with your current employer. Even if you are asked this question during a phone interview, be prepared to answer it again during a face-to-face interview. Be sure to prepare a strong answer to this question. Remember, whatever you say, do not slander your current employer. Tip: The best reasons to give for leaving a job include lack of growth opportunity or an unchallenging environment.

Interviewer: What led you to apply for this position?

Translation: Why do you think you would be a good match to this position, company, and industry?

Best Answer: Be honest. What are the reasons that influenced you to send your resume out to this particular company? How do you think a job with this company would benefit you? What do you want to accomplish?

Interviewer: What would your ideal job be five years from now?

Translation: Are you looking for a *job* or a *career*? If we were to hire you, would we be making an investment in the future of the company? Is there any chance that you would even be around in five years, or are you hoping to make a quick buck and get out of here?

Best Answer: With the typical career path of someone in your position in mind, describe the types of things you see your-self doing in five years. What are some of the everyday tasks you envision as being part of your job? Without giving specific job titles, give the interviewer an idea of the types of profes-sional activities you would like to be involved in within the next several years.

Interviewer: The final part of the conversation—which should last no more than five to 10 minutes—will usually consist of the interviewer telling you a bit more about the position. He or she will let you know the hours, what would be expected of you, the qualifications they are seeking, and all the other perti-nent information.

Translation: Are you the right person for this job?

Best Answer: Assure the interviewer that you meet if not exceed the criteria mentioned. Talk a little bit about your skills, and state your interest in the position, especially now that you've learned more about it. Remember to always be *extra* brief when on the phone. There will be plenty of time to talk about your myriad talents and skills when you meet with this person face-to-face, which is your goal in this final answer!

Interviewer: We will begin interviewing candidates on site next week. Would you be interested in coming in and speaking with us a little further?

Translation: You've passed the phone screening. Now it's on to the next test!

Best Answer: Absolutely. What day and time would work best for you?

Remember, it is very likely that you will be asked the exact same questions during a face-to-face interview that you were asked over the phone. While you should be careful when answering these questions a second time, you should also be aware that you will be given more time to prepare the best answers possible in the time between this interview and a real one—if there is one. Just like in a face-to-face interview, remember to always stay positive and *never* mention salary or anything about monetary compensation!

Face to Face Screening

Though the telephone interview can certainly count as a screening interview, a screening interview can also happen face-to-face. As the telephone can be a rather informal means of communication (we all know that one person who is so pleasant on the telephone and so miserable in real life, or vice versa), the company may want to screen you in person so that they can get a look at you and see how you interact with other people.

Screening interviews, for the most part, take place with a company recruiter or human resources professional. These are people who deal with hiring and firing people for a living. While this person may not know about the particular job for which you are applying, it is he or she who will be the initial driving force behind deciding whether or not your candidacy gets pushed forward.

Screening interviews will most likely be your first face-to-face encounter with an employee of a prospective company. That said, this is probably the most important of all the interviews. Passing this interview is the only way in which you can be considered for employment later on. Also, in passing this interview, you will have succeeded in triumphing over much of the competition.

As the point of the screening interview is to establish yourself as a strong candidate, it is very important that you use this time to provide evidence of your skills and really use your experience to your advantage. You want the interviewer to walk away from the interview thinking there are very few more qualified candidates than you. From the screening interview, you will move on to one or more of the interview types described in the following pages.

One-on-One Interviews

Though hiring processes are different between companies, you can usually count on engaging in at least one one-on-one interview. This is where, rather than being faced with a fusillade of questions from a crowd of people, the candidate sits down, one-on-one, with a human resources or other hiring professional.

Individual Interview

An individual interview is the type of interview that probably comes to mind when you think of a traditional job interview. This is the situation in which you are invited to meet with one person—whether that person is a human resources professional, your potential boss, or a coworker—to speak, in depth, about your qualifications and how you might benefit the company. In order to reach this step of the interviewing process, you will have already passed the company's screening process (a phone interview or a face-to-face screening). You will have already assured the company that you have the skills and experience to do the job well. But there will be others who have shown them the same thing. You will now have to show them that—above all other candidates—you are the one the company should pick.

An individual interview is one of the interviews in which you should try your hardest to build a strong rapport with the interviewer. The interviewer's job, in the case of the individual, one-on-one interview, is to find a reason *not* to hire you. Their objective is to further decrease the size of the applicant pool; thus, with each of these individual interviews, the job of the interviewer is to decide who will stay and who will go.

In addition to restating your various skills and qualifications, you must make this interviewer like you as a person. He or she is trying to decide whether or not you will fit in with the rest of the company, or whether there might be a possible conflict of personalities. Getting along well with the interviewer will show that your personality is in fact compatible with those of the other employees.

Insider Tips

Waiting by the Phone

While you should be prepared to field phone calls from recruiters after sending out your resume, you should definitely not spend all your days waiting for the phone to ring. In preparation for these telephone screenings, however, there should be one item by the phone: a notebook. The best way to prepare for a telephone interview is to keep a running list of all the companies you have sent your resume to, the positions that they are hiring for, and a little bit of background on the company. When an interviewer calls and mentions the name of his or her company, you can—quietly—flip to the appropriate page in your notebook to see why you sent your resume to this person in the first place. If you are conducting a large job search, this is a particularly good idea, as it can be easy to confuse companies.

Group Interviews

One way in which companies can save time as far as the hiring process goes is to conduct one or more group interviews with a candidate. In a group interview, employers place you in a room with several people at a time, rather than have you meet company members individually, one-on-one. The tricky part to the group interview is that those "other people" can be either current company employees or other potential candidates.

Committee Interview

Though it sounds a bit intimidating, committee interviews are becoming more and more common in the workplace, as they can save the company time. This is when a potential employee is asked to sit in a room with several senior-level employees and answer a whole slew of questions. Questions can come from any one at any time, and you will be evaluated by each of the committee members.

Though the idea of being scrutinized by five or so people at a time can seem a bit daunting, think of it this way: You've got the power of a democracy on your side. Rather than have only one chance to charm one person, you are being given the opportunity to enchant various company members all at once.

If you are asked into a committee interview, be sure that you always address the person asking the question. If, for example, the woman or man on the right asks you a question, answer her or him directly; maintain strong eye contact, and pretend as if you were the only two in the room. The key to succeeding in a committee interview is to remain focused. Don't let the number of people squeezed into the room frighten you. Treat each member of the committee with respect and kindness, and they will be sure to see what a great match you are for the job.

Joint Interview

A joint interview takes the idea of the committee interview one step further. Rather than bring together a group of employees who have the ability to "yea" or "nay" your candidacy, the joint interview brings together the entire candidate pool and interviews them at one time. Though this certainly saves time for the interviewing committee, a joint interview can be a bit intimidating for a job seeker. In addition to being made fully aware that there are other candidates in the running, you are forced to socialize with them!

A joint interview consists of two or more potential candidates sitting in a room together and engaging in a discussion. The interviewer (there can be one or more) thinks about a topic and then introduces it to the candidates. He or she will begin a discussion and expect the candidates to join in. If you can remember what it was like to take an oral test back in your school days (or the times when you were graded on your class participation), the joint interview is a very similar experience. In addition to listening to your insights into a particular topic and gaining a bit more knowledge as to your experience, the joint interview allows the interviewer to see how well—or poorly—you are able to engage in discussion with your peers, and whether or not you have trouble interacting with them.

Above all, a joint interview allows the interviewer to put your leadership skills to the test. The interviewer wants to see whether you have valid points, and the ease with which you are able to persuade others of these convictions. Observing your behavior within this group of competitors is a great way for an interviewer to assess whether you might be a good candidate for a management position someday and whether you have the ability to act in a professional and pleasant manner—even with all this competition breathing down your neck. The best way to prepare for this type of interview is to spend as much time as you can sharpening your interpersonal skills.

Insider Tips

Who's Interviewing You, Anyway?

Once you step into your prospective employer's environment, put your best face on. Everyone you meet, from the front desk clerk, to the recruiting department's secretary, may be asked for input on what they thought of you. You may also be introduced to a few people, in which case it's a sure bet that their first impression will be heard by the recruiter. Remember to smile and show confidence.

Departmental Interview

Another way to conduct a group interview with an applicant is to place him or her in a room full of department or company coworkers. By gathering together several key members of a department or company and letting them interact with a candidate, hiring managers can observe how this person's personality and manner fits in with that of the department as a whole.

A departmental interview is not just about socializing, however. The candidate's peers will be asking questions and discussing certain situations that are likely to arise to ascertain how the person would react. Members of the department may throw out some hypothetical situations ("What would you do if an irate customer called you and . . ."), or they could offer a little more information on the job itself. What is great about this type of interview is that—again—you are in the position to persuade several people, rather than just one, that you are the perfect person for the job. At the same time, you can ascertain the real truth about this job, both its rewards and its pitfalls. Unlike a human resources professional, whose job it is to hire and fire people, these people can tell you, for sure, what a typical day is like. They can answer questions about how stressful the work becomes, the worst day they've ever had, and the best day they've ever had.

If you reach the stage at which you have been asked in for a departmental interview, you have probably already persuaded the personnel staff as well as the department manager of your skills and abilities. That said, you should then try to build rapport with the other members of the department during this interview, as their say could be the final one.

Interactive Interviews

One of the great things about interviewing—for the candidate—is that it can be easy to figure out which questions you are likely to be asked by an employer; thus, you can come up with some great answers to these questions ahead of time. Still, after hearing hundreds of candidates rattle off the same, premanufactured interview

question answers, recruiters sometimes look for a bit more from a candidate. This is where the interactive interview comes into play.

Rather than ask candidates the same questions again and again (and have to listen attentively through the same answers), employers try and elicit physical proof of a candidate's abilities. The interactive interview allows an employer to adopt a "show me" attitude to the interviewing process, and the results can be quite telling.

Professional Portfolio Interview

In a nutshell, the professional portfolio interview is the chance for the candidate to illustrate his or her craft—on the spot—at the request of the employer. For more creative types (e.g., photographers, graphic artists), this would merely consist of the applicant showing his or her scrapbook of past work. For, if you will, noncreative types—sales and marketing professionals, for example—a professional portfolio means something quite different.

For many professional positions, job candidates will be asked to do more than just talk about their strengths, weaknesses, and experiences; they'll be asked to prove them as well. In an interview for a sales position, for example, the interviewer may hand the candidate an everyday item like a pen or pencil and tell the candidate to "Sell This!" Someone looking for a marketing position may be asked to devise an ad campaign—on the spot—for something as simple as a cardboard box. A professional editor may be asked to read a brief manuscript and make recommendations.

The point is that these interviews can happen at any time, and you should always be prepared to showcase your skills to an interviewer. Also keep in mind that you must be very careful not to boast or exaggerate your skills to an employer. If you claim that you can type 150 words per minute, you better be prepared to prove it!

Shadow Interview

Another way in which an interviewer can put your skills and experience to the test is to put you on the job (before actually hiring you). While this is different from the portfolio interview in

Strange but True

Interview Scenarios

- An interviewer walks into his or her interview only to be told that he or she is to face the wall—not the interviewers—when answering questions.

- An interviewer walks into his or her interview only to be told that he or she is to face the window—not the interviewers—when answering questions.

that you do not have to show any direct proof of your skills or work, be assured that every question you ask or suggestion you make is certainly being evaluated.

In a shadow interview, you will be asked to come into the office for an agreed upon amount of time (anywhere from an hour to an entire day). Once there, you will sit with a selected member of the team and follow this person around. When he or she gets a phone call, you'll listen. When he or she has a meeting, you'll attend. When he or she eats lunch, you'll eat too. You get the picture.

While you are certainly the one being evaluated in this case, you should also look at shadowing as a chance to get a day in on the job before deciding whether or not you would like to work with a particular company. Far too often, employers and candidates alike are on their best behavior when it comes to the interviewing process. Both parties are wearing their finest clothing and putting on their best act. A shadow interview offers you the opportunity to see what happens when a company can't predict what is going to happen.

Case Interview

One type of interview that is certainly specific to one group but does require its own designation is what is known as a case interview. For the most part, case interviews are reserved for people looking for employment as a consultant, engineer, or some other profession that requires an extensive amount of logical thinking and strong problem-solving abilities. Rather than ask a candidate "How would you react if . . ." the interviewer gives the candidate a situation or problem and asks him or her to solve it. The point of the exercise is to see how this person's brain works. Is the candidate able to develop a logical plan to solve the problem? Does he or she show an impressive display of reasoning, or does it seem like the candidate is questioning his or her own answer?

The case interview sounds intimidating, and it is. But that just goes to show how necessary it is to have different types of interviewing styles. To succeed at this type of interview, a candidate needs to be intelligent and quick thinking. Victory over a case interview

requires a keen problem-solving ability and great insight. Candidates must have knowledge of business and the world in general, as it is simple facts that the candidate will need to use to solve the problems he or she is faced with. Coming up with new and feasible solutions is something that recruiters will look upon very favorably.

Multimedia Interviews

As computers and the Internet become more and more important to the daily functioning of any business, they are slowly making their way into all aspects of the company's day-to-day duties, including the hiring process.

Computerized Interview

Computerized interviews are becoming more common in big and small companies alike. For the most part, computers are used to take the place of a screening interviewer. A candidate comes in and rather than occupy the time of a human resources professional, he or she will answer to a computer for the next hour or so.

Because these types of interviews can be very intricate (and because it's likely you'll encounter one in your upcoming job search), the entire next chapter has been devoted to computerized interviews.

Videoconferencing Interview

Videoconferencing interviews meld the personal interaction of a face-to-face interview with the cost-effectiveness of a computer. Candidates sit in front of a camera and interact—in real time—with an interviewer who asks all the same questions he or she would if the two were sitting next to one another in an office somewhere.

It is now estimated that approximately half of the largest companies in the United States use some form of videoconferencing in their hiring process. The main reason? Since larger companies often pay the travel costs of those they recruit (most often those in more senior-level positions), videoconferencing saves the company huge sums of money throughout the year.

**Job Search
Odds and Ends**

**Don't Be Afraid
to Be Bold**

If your interview is going well and you feel like you are sure this is a job you want, don't be afraid to say so. Ask if they are interested in you, but be ready for what could be a serious blow to your ego. Wrap up your interview by giving some of the reasons you like the company before asking about your prospects. Make it clear that you think this job was made for you, and vice versa.

Strange but True

Interview Behavior

Upon arriving at the interview, the job seeker seemed gracious and enthusiastic. While engaging in small talk, she informed the interviewer that this was her third meeting of the day. That said, as soon as they sat down, she pulled out a slice of pizza and a can of soda and proceeded to eat her lunch. Apparently, amidst all the job interviews, she hadn't found the time to eat.

If and when you are asked to take part in a video interview, you should prepare in much the same way you would for a face-to-face interview. Arriving in front of the camera with your pajamas on (or even a suit jacket with pajama pants) will certainly not win you any points. Think of how you would appear on camera, and dress in something that will present itself well (black or another dark color is always a wise choice).

Alternative Interview Types

Depending on the company, each meeting you have could introduce an entirely new way of interviewing for a job. Many companies may have found the aforementioned interview types to be effective in some ways and ineffective in others. In response, they may have created their own interview composite. Still, the themes covered in this book are the ones you're likely to experience. And the commonly asked questions that are listed in the following chapters are the ones you're likely to be asked. Still, to be on the safe side, here are a few other interview types to be aware of—and prepared for.

Lunch Interview

The lunch interview is a fairly common type of interview, and it comes in many forms. On the one hand, you could sit face to face with the hiring manager, enjoy a bite to eat, and at the same time try to convince him or her of your skills and compatibility to the company. On the other hand, you could sit amongst two or more human resources professionals, possible coworkers, and maybe a potential boss or two.

Though the rules of proper interviewing etiquette certainly apply here—that is, the rules of dress and how to answer a question—the lunch interview introduces the added concern of eating. That's right. Even the act of consuming food has a few rules attached to it when it takes place during an interview. The most important rule to remember is this: Do not repulse your lunch companion(s) with bad table manners. For example, if you like to eat with your hands,

reserve such barbaric behavior for private moments at your own dining room table.

Be sure to order food that is easy to eat and easy to keep under control. Avoid foods that are likely to end up between your teeth. Can you imagine discussing your most recent role in a major corporate merger, only to find out later that you delivered this discourse with a piece of spinach lodged between your two front teeth?

Don't be fussy about your food, and don't complain about it. The surest way to do well in this type of test is to follow the lead of the interviewer or one of your dining companions. Above all, don't exert more concentration on trying to stuff your fajita than on the interviewer's questions. Finally, don't order the most expensive thing on the menu. Just because you're not paying doesn't mean that you should treat yourself to the lobster.

Remember that this is a lunch *interview*, not a lunch date! Keep the conversation focused on your skills and experience. Regardless of what the table topic turns to, never stray too far from the reason that you are here: that is, to get a job!

Stress Interview

There are several different versions of the stress interview. On the one hand, you can be asked to come into a company only to realize that for the next hour or so, you will be bombarded with a variety of questions that seem near impossible to answer. In other cases, a typical face to face interview can quickly turn into a stress interview—and then back into an easygoing one. The point of the stress interview is to gauge just that: your level of stress. How easily do you become anxiety-ridden?

Stress interviews can be done on a one-on-one basis or in groups. You could be answering the stress questions of just one interviewer or five. Likewise, you could be sitting alone or with several other applicants for the position. Though many people claim that the stress interview is not a reliable way of measuring one's competence, they are nonetheless employed quite often.

The Lunch Meeting:
Etiquette Counts!

In recent years, the idea of a lunch meeting has become a staple in the business world. If invited to lunch with a potential employer, there are several things to keep in mind, as proper manners are part of what you are being tested on here:

- Don't be indecisive when it comes to ordering your food. Your mind should be focused on the interview ahead, not the meal.
- Think about what you want to order ahead of time, and make sure it is something you can easily cut into bite-sized pieces. Avoid anything that is messy or will require lots of attention.
- So that you don't drink your future supervisor's water, remember to eat to the left, drink to the right.
- Your napkin goes on your lap—don't leave it on the table, tuck it into your collar, or turn it into a cute little hat.
- After you take a bite, put your knife and fork on your plate until you are ready for another bite.
- Maintain eye contact while speaking but be wary of staring while the interviewer is trying to ingest his or her food.
- Avoid alcohol! Even if the interviewer is imbibing an alcoholic drink or two, your best bet is to err—and drink—on the safe side.
- Don't complain about the restaurant, the food, or the service. Even if your meal is barely just this side of edible, swallow it down with a smile. You've faked liking a meal before; now is the time to revisit those acting skills!
- Don't argue about who pays the bill here. In any business setting, the person who arranged the lunch (in this case, the interviewer) pays for the lunch.

Remember, the point of the stress interview is to disorient you. You will be asked rather forthright questions (in a rather forthright manner). Questions will not be spaced out properly, and they may overlap others. The key to succeeding in this type of environment is to really take control of the situation.

When you first enter the room, you will probably be introduced to each of the interviewers. Before the firing of questions begins, take a moment to get to know each of these people. Find out who does what for the company, and decide who the key people in the room are. Who are the people you should try the hardest to impress? Once you've figured this out, you can begin to prioritize the questions that are thrown at you. If your future boss and coworker both ask questions at the same time, you'll know which person it is more important to answer first.

Remember that the key to winning this type of interview is to remain calm under all the pressure. Make a conscious effort to maintain your composure. Always speak in an even, calm voice. Don't let your body language give away the uneasiness you are feeling. Answer each question carefully and to the best of your ability. The best way to think of the stress interview is this way: The interviewers are the ones acting unprofessionally and out of control; by remaining calm and unaffected by what's happening in the room around you, you are proving to be the only one in control.

Strange but True

Interview Scenarios

An unsuspecting job seeker walks into his or her interview, only to find that he or she has been invited in for a marathon interview. This is when you have an hour interview with the hiring manager, as well as an interview with a different member of the company every hour until lunch time (and yes, there's usually a lunch interview scheduled as well—kind of a reward for all your hard work).

CHAPTER SIX

Computer-Assisted Job Interviews

As stated in the previous chapter, the role of the computer and other technology is becoming increasingly important in the workplace. This reliance extends to the job interviewing process as well. Though computerized interviews have been used in the past by companies that tend toward large volumes of workers (banks, hospitals, restaurants, hotels, and retail stores are just a few examples), the benefits of the computerized job interview are quickly introducing themselves to all sorts of companies. While, in most companies, it is typical to have designated "screeners," screening interviews can take just as long as a selection interview. The interviewer still needs to make the time to talk with the applicant and assess his or her qualifications for a particular job. Though screening candidates has been made easier with the use of a telephone, this can still be a timely and costly task.

In an attempt to save both time and money, technology-savvy companies are now scheduling candidate meetings with a PC rather than an actual human being. While computerized interviews are still a relatively new technique, you shouldn't be surprised to find many more companies (including smaller companies that can't spare the time to interview hundreds of people for one position) employing some sort of computer-assisted interview format.

Preparing for Your Virtual Interaction

First interviews with a computer have the same goal in mind as first interviews with a human resources representative: that is, they are meant as a way of screening a candidate to determine whether or not he or she would be a good fit for the position at hand. The only difference here is that the computer does the asking and your fingers do the answering. You should prepare for a computerized interview in the exact same way that you would a face-to-face interview. You should always wear appropriate business attire and be prepared to answer any question that might arise.

If you are taking a computerized interview, be aware that although *most* programs pose questions in the form of a true/false or multiple choice format, there are programs

out there that will ask for a full response. In these latter cases, there is usually a preset time limit attached to each of the questions, so you should be prepared to answer each question quickly. Topics most often covered include your professional and educational backgrounds, as well as your relevant skills and qualifications. Once completed, the computer compiles a summary of your answers, which the recruiter will then use to determine whether or not you will advance to the next round of interviewing. Depending on the program used, the computer might either recommend a possible next step or provide the interviewer with a list of follow-up questions that would be important to ask.

The Structure of a Computer

While you can never know which questions to count on—or even anticipate—when you're interviewing with a computer, the one thing you can count on is a little structure. Though the computer programs differ between manufacturer and company, computerized job interviews are always based on the principle of the structured job interview. As discussed before, a structured interview is an interview in which each candidate is asked the same set of questions. The reason computerized interviews are all structured interviews is so that all applicants can be fairly screened. Since each interviewee answers the exact same set of questions, the computer's recommendation to bring the candidate back for an interview—or not—is determined fairly. Supporters of the computerized interview like the idea of the structured format because by asking each candidate the same question, companies essentially are able to compare apples with apples (to use a cliché—which you should *never* do in the job search process).

Advantages of Using a Computer

In addition to a sense of uniformity that is brought to the interviewing process with the employ of the computerized job interview, there are various other advantages to using this method. In keeping

Insider Tips

Dress for Success

If an employer calls to tell you that you have been invited in for a computerized first interview, don't take this as an invitation for informality. Even if the typical handshake is being replaced by a mouse click, you always want to be properly attired in a business suit. As you will be interacting with live humans at some point (who will be noting your appearance, etc.), always dress for success.

with the idea of uniformity, one could also argue that the computerized interview succeeds in doing away with any prejudices that might be placed upon a candidate by a biased interviewer. For example, if an interviewer were—illegally—hoping to fill the position with someone of a particular sex or race, use of the computerized interview would help to alleviate such unfair practices. This is not to say that these same biases could not creep their way back into the hiring process at a later point, but it does assure the candidate and the employer that all hiring is being done impartially.

Another advantage of using a computerized interview—and one that benefits the company—is that employers can be given the opportunity to word each question carefully, ensuring that nothing they are asking is illegal (the topic of illegal questions is covered later in the book). It is important to stress that although illegal questions do occur, this is usually because the interviewer does not realize that what he or she is asking is illegal. For example, in companies in which all employees must be over the age of 18 years, an employer is likely to bring up the topic of age during the interview. Depending on the way in which the question is asked, the interviewer may be asking an illegal question. For example, to ask the employee "Are you over the age of 18?" would be okay. To ask the job seeker "How old are you?" is, on the other hand, illegal. Using a computerized job interview to screen applicants is a great way to alleviate the company's fears that interviewers might ask anything that is inappropriate or illegal.

A further benefit of using a computer rather than a person is that essentially the computer does a better job of screening candidates. When an interviewer steps into a screening interview, he or she wants to find out several different things: Does this candidate have the skills necessary to perform the job at hand? Does this candidate have the education necessary to perform the job at hand? Does this candidate have the right personality to fit in with the job at hand? And the final question, Can I be sure that this candidate is being straight with me as far as his or her skills and resume go?

This final, all-important question is the one question that the computer is much better equipped to answer. As is the nature of a computer, one of the ways in which it makes an evaluation is by

comparing all of the candidate's responses. Computerized job interview programs are built to flag any inconsistencies in a candidate's answers and to make these discrepancies known to the recruiter.

Yet another benefit of using a computer rather than a person is one that should certainly soothe all those candidates who become anxiety-ridden at the mere mention of a job interview. Candidates report being much less nervous over the impending meeting when they know they are meeting with a computer rather than a human interviewer.

Still another benefit is one that companies report after using computer-assisted interviews. These companies say they experience an increase in productivity. They also claim that because of the accuracy with which a computer can pinpoint a strong company "match," they have experienced stronger customer service, lower employee turnover, less employee absenteeism, and less theft in the workplace.

A final and significantly important advantage to the computerized interview is that overall it is more efficient. While two humans interacting in a room might be tempted to let a conversation run off on a tangent, a computer is programmed to ask the exact same questions, in the exact same way, in the exact same amount of time *every time it interviews a candidate!* That said, a computer is able to gather more information in a shorter period of time and therefore is more efficient.

Disadvantages of Using a Computer

Amidst all the praise of the efficiency and effectiveness that computer-assisted interviews bring to the workplace, there has been some nay-saying. For the most part, these issues center around the fact that a computer is just that—*a computer*! Those against the use of computers in the job interviewing process contend that the absence of humanity itself is at the core of this problem. While this is a legitimate point, and one that is well taken, it should also be noted that—for the most part—computerized job interviews are simply used as a screening device for busy recruiters. However, the software manufacturers are taking these negative claims into account.

Insider Tips

Avoid Absolutes

Try to avoid using absolutes such as "always" and "never." A large number of "always" and "never" answers might make it look as if you're lying—or worse, be a signal of extreme behavior. Employers look for moderation and tend to stay away from extremists.

They are making it so that after answering the questions, candidates can type in any comments they would like to have considered.

One of the main problems that people report with the computerized job interview programs is that the questions are biased against certain groups, especially when it comes to minorities and women. Another complaint is that a computer lacks the ability to take special circumstances into account, like a history of unemployment due to disability. If the candidate is asked a question such as "Are you currently employed?," the only recourse the person has is to say "Yes" or "No."

A final argument against whether or not computer interviews are a fair means of screening is one that can work both ways. The central complaint is that a computer is not a person and that therefore it cannot measure a candidate's eagerness to enter the workplace, enthusiasm for a particular field, or willingness to work hard. Yet, on the other hand, one could argue that the computer lacks the ability to gauge a candidate's negativity or pessimism.

What to Expect from the Computer

Computer-assisted interviews go something like this (note that they begin in the exact same manner as a more traditional, face-to-face interview): A company representative—usually a recruiter or other human resources professional—gives you a call and works with you to schedule a mutually convenient time when you can come into the office and meet. At the interview, you initially meet with a real live human being but then are led into a room where you meet your actual "interviewer"—the computer. The company representative shows you how to use the computer and probably sticks around for a few minutes just to make sure you have no problems or questions. After that, it's just you and Mr. IBM!

If you have even the smallest bit of familiarity with computers, you should have no problem navigating the computer interview program. Because these programs are designed to screen applicants at all levels, they are constructed in a universally friendly manner. The

basic format of the computerized interview is this: You are given a specific time period in which you are to complete the interview, typically this time limit is 30 minutes (about the same time as a face-to-face interview should take to complete). When you've finished, the computer then provides the hiring manager with a summary of your qualifications and a recommended next step, should they want to take one.

Computer-assisted interviews generally consist of about a hundred questions that relate to your educational and work background. Following are some examples of questions that may be asked during a computer-assisted interview. The questions are taken from the ApView computer-assisted interview from SHL Aspen Tree Software:

Q: Are you currently employed?
 A. Yes
 B. No

Q: Why did you leave your last job, or why do you want to leave your present job?
 A. I was dismissed
 B. I was laid off
 C. To take a better job
 D. Relocation
 E. To go to school
 F. I am not leaving my present job
 G. Other reason

Q: How often do/did you experience conflict with your coworkers?
 A. Often
 B. Sometimes
 C. Rarely
 D. Never
 E. Cannot say

Q: What kind of recommendation do you think your most recent supervisor would give you?

A. Outstanding

B. Above average

C. Average

D. Below average

E. I don't know

Q: On previous jobs, how often were you able to develop new or better ways of doing the work assigned to you?

A. Most of the time

B. Usually

C. Sometimes

D. Seldom

E. Never

When they were first introduced, computer-assisted interviews consisted entirely of multiple choice or true/false questions. Since that time, computer-assisted interview programs have been quickly advancing. As more and more companies become dependent on computers to screen possible job candidates, the software manufacturers have looked to human resources professionals for input on what kinds of techniques would be most beneficial. Based on the input received, many companies are now creating job interview programs that allow the candidate to type out an extended written answer instead of a multiple choice question. ApView, for example, allows its customers the option of asking open-ended questions instead of or in addition to multiple choice questions. All written answers are later reviewed by a human resources professional—not the computer itself. That said, if you are asked an open-ended question in the course of a computerized job interview, you should be sure to answer it in the exact same way you would if it were asked by someone sitting in the chair across from you. As most computer programs are tailored to a specific company or position, it is important that you still do all the recommended research and other steps necessary to properly prepare for an interview.

Accuracy Matters

The key to succeeding in the case of a computer-assisted interview is to remember that accuracy counts. Be sure to answer each question that you are asked just as you would in a face-to-face interview. Don't exaggerate your skills and accomplishments and think that the computer will not know you are lying. Though a computer cannot read body language—as a recruiter can—as mentioned previously, it *can* do something much more powerful: A computer is able to quickly pick up on any inconsistencies given in your answers. A computer also has the power to report these discrepancies back to the recruiter. Remember, a computer-assisted interview is just the first step. Your goal during the computer-assisted interview is to answer the questions honestly enough that you are invited back for a face-to-face interview. If the computer thinks that you are not being truthful with the answers in your screening test, it is not likely that you will be invited back again.

Be Honest . . . but Not *Too* Honest

As in every other task involved in succeeding at your job interview, there are certain boundaries and lines that apply to the computerized interview. A few moments ago, we went over the importance of being completely accurate and honest in the answers that you give during a computerized interview. Now we're going to modify that advice just a little bit. While it is true that you certainly don't want to lie to a computer or exaggerate your skills, you don't want to be too honest either! You don't want to confess all your sins and flaws on the spot—to a computer—and not be able to explain yourself.

Recent studies have shown that job candidates who sit down and interview with a computer rather than another human being have a tendency to become far too honest. The reasoning is that because the candidate is staring into the glare of a computer screen rather than the eyes of a recruiter, he or she is likely to be much more honest. People are likely to disclose more personal information about themselves to a computer than they would ever dare dream to say to a recruiter. Is it therapeutic? Who knows! The only thing we

Job Search Odds and Ends

Time Flies . . . When You're Lying?

Recent studies have proven that on average it takes longer for a human being to tell a lie than it does for him or her to tell the truth. The reason for this is unclear. Perhaps it has something to do with the split-second moral dilemma that takes place in your brain. In any case, software manufacturers who create job interview programs have taken this fact into account. One of the things a computerized interview program does is measure the time it takes for you to respond to a question. When a computer summarizes your answers for a recruiter, it also highlights delayed responses or, in other words, answers that are perhaps dishonest.

can be sure of is that—above all—it is detrimental to your getting the job. So, before you start unveiling all the skeletons in your professional (or other) closet, remember that your answers will be read by an actual person as soon as you step foot out the door. Though the computer is the one facilitating the interview, it is a human being who, in the end, will be judging you. That said, a good rule to follow is to *never* tell a computer anything about yourself that you wouldn't tell a human resources professional face to face.

What the Computer Will Say

After you complete the interview, it is up to the computer to determine the next step. The computer analyzes your responses and presents a summary of your qualifications to the recruiter. In less advanced programs, the computer may just regurgitate your answers; in more advanced programs, the summary will include contradictions in your responses, a list of possible follow-up questions that should be asked, and a recommendation as to whether or not you would make a good candidate. The most advanced computer programs now even allow employers to create a standardized "employee profile" for their company. Based on the successful hires they've made in the past, a recruiter can tell a computer the type of employee that works best in their company setting—according to the amount and type of experience they've had and so forth. When a candidate comes to interview for the job, the computer can then compare this person's answers to that of the "ideal employee" created by the recruiter. The computer analyzes the candidate's answers with this model employee as a guide and decides whether or not you the candidate would make a good fit. By comparing your answers with those of successful hires, the computer can predict—usually with measurable success—whether or not you'll be a successful employee.

The recruiter reads the report and makes a decision as to whether or not you should be brought back for a second interview. Though it should really go without saying, if a recruiter has reason to believe that you may have fibbed a bit during your interview, it is not

likely that he or she will want to meet with you for a second time. How can you avoid this? If you are always candid and completely truthful in your answers, such contradictions should never arise.

Types of Computer-Assisted Interviews

The computerized job interview can occur via the Internet. And it can come in various forms, including the scenario-based interview.

Internet Job Interview

Use of the Internet as a platform to administer screening interviews is a method that is quickly gaining popularity. And why not? For long-distance job screening in particular, the Internet can be both fast and cost-effective (for both employer and potential employee alike). If, for example, you live in Boston and are applying for a job in Seattle, getting through the initial screening via the Internet can save you the time and money of having to fly across the country. Faultfinders claim that a telephone screening is a better way, but companies who employ the Internet method don't seem to be listening—the number of computerized interviews conducted via the Internet is rising each day.

Again, the process of an Internet-based interview starts out the same as any other: You are contacted for an initial screening interview and, instead of a telephone or face-to-face interview, are provided with a password that gives you access to the company's in-house computer system. Some companies may arrange a time for you to log on and take the test; others may give you a deadline. After agreeing on the time or the deadline, you log on to the company's job interviewing site and become engaged in what is essentially a computer-assisted interview. Like other screening interviews, you are asked basic questions about your skills, experience, and education. Once completed, the computer analyzes your answers and creates a report for the recruiter to read. If, at that point, the recruiter decides you are an employee worth pursuing, he or she calls to arrange a face-to-face meeting. Only *then* should you start worrying about paying the costs of travel!

Scenario-Based Interview

As the name implies, a scenario-based interview involves more of the "show me" attitude that you would find in the portfolio interview. In these computerized interviews, the candidate is faced with a virtual customer or situation and asked to react. Scenario-based interviews are used to see how candidates behave in simulated work situations.

Learning Systems Sciences, a leader in this type of computerized interview, reports that their clientele consists primarily of banks and retail establishments, including many large department store chains. These interviews—like the structured variety—are most often used for screening purposes. These tests are typically only used for positions in which there is an extremely high turnover rate. After passing these simulations, candidates are next brought in for a face to face interview.

Retail establishments and other companies who devote much of their time to hiring new employees each year find this type of interviewing to be far superior to more traditional methods. Rather than ask the candidate "How would you feel if an irate customer approached you and demanded their money back?" and getting the typical canned answer, an interviewer can see for himself or herself how this person would react and thus determine early on whether the candidate would be able to handle difficult situations in a professional manner. The computer screen might show, for example, an irate customer yelling about a product he bought that he believes is faulty to see how the candidate would deal with such a customer.

How is the candidate rated? Since an actual interviewer isn't likely to be in the room, the computer—somehow—needs to record the candidate's reaction to this test. Rather than key in a set of answers as to what he or she would say to this virtual complainer, the computer will record the candidate's voice. Once the test has been completed, the recruiter can then review this recording and determine whether or not to bring the candidate back in. The recruiter can tell a lot about a candidate just by *listening* to how he or she reacted to this test. Did the candidate remain calm and polite, or did he or she sound harried and rude? Candidates are usually graded on a predetermined scale.

For instance, apologizing to the customer for the problem might score the candidate a point or two, but not sounding sincere could take some of those points away!

Assessment Tests

Assessment tests are nothing new to the world of job hunting. For years, applicants have been asked to take them to evaluate their suitability to a particular job or company. The reasoning behind these tests is simple: Hiring new employees is a time-consuming and expensive process. By carefully screening applicants with both structured, computer-assisted interviews *and* the addition of a computerized assessment test, recruiters can greatly reduce the chances that a new hire will leave after only a few months. These tests only serve to further enforce the fact that a good candidate is likely to make a great employee. The three main types of assessment tests that you are likely to find as part of the job interviewing process are skills, integrity, and personality tests.

Most positions require some type of skills test—for example, a math test for accountants, a proofreading test for editors, and a typing test for administrative assistants. There is really no field that is exempt from some sort of testing, even those applying for a job as a computer programmer are often asked to write a short program as part of their pre-employment testing. If you're applying for a position in which you'll be dealing with goods or money, you'll probably be required to take an integrity test. Personality or psychological tests can be used in virtually any situation but are especially common if you're interviewing for a management position or one in which work with sensitive material is required.

Skills tests can often be part of the initial screening process, but personality and integrity tests are usually one of the last steps of the interviewing process. Depending on the nature of the test, you may answer multiple choice or true/false questions or transcribe written information into a computer program. Like the screening interview itself, computerized integrity and personality tests typically contain upwards of a hundred questions. For the

Job Search Odds and Ends

Why the Scenario-Based Interview Works

Scenario-based interviews are applauded for many reasons, including:

- Such interviews give candidates a very realistic idea of what to expect from a job. For example, they can experience what it might be like to deal with an incensed customer.

- Companies that employ scenario-based interviews report a lower turnover rate along with improved overall quality in their employees. As a result, customer service seemingly has improved, as well as the overall attitude of the company.

most part, these questions are of the multiple choice, yes/no, true/false, always/sometimes/rarely/never variety. You are given a time limit. Once your time is up, the computer will score your work and, if applicable, compare your answers to a specified profile. It then generates a report that tells the recruiter how a candidate rates in relation to other candidates.

Computer-Assisted Skills Tests

Skills tests are the most straightforward type of computerized assessment tests. They are used to measure your aptitude for performing a specific task or duty that would be required of the job for which you are applying. If you have ever done any work as a temporary employee—or worked with an employment service firm—you are likely to be familiar with this type of testing. This is where, as a condition of your employment, you are tested on your computer skills, typing speed, accuracy, or some other skill that is important to the job. Skills tests tend to determine your proficiency in word processing, spreadsheet, and database programs.

To complete the test, you are asked to do some basic exercises using the various applications. With some tests, especially those that are testing you on various word processing programs, you are given a certain amount of time in which you must format and write a document, for example. The computer's assessment of your skills is based on several factors. The accuracy with which you completed the task is obviously of the utmost importance. In addition, the computer records how much work you managed to accomplish in the specified time period. In some cases, if you finish the entire task before the time period ends, you are judged on the time it took you to finish as well. Similarly, a spreadsheet test might judge you on how quickly and accurately you can enter data and perform different functions. A typical use of a skills test would be, for example, to test the mathematical or logical reasoning skills of an accountant or engineer.

Typically, computerized skills assessment tests are measured by your raw score. This score is then compared to a mean—or average score—of everyone who has taken the test. A score of 75, with a

mean of 68, for example, shows the employer that you have above average skills in the areas in which you were tested.

Unfortunately, there's no way to prepare for a skills test, except, of course, to practice the skill. For example, if you know that you will be asked to take a typing test, practice your typing so that you may increase your score, or if you know that you will be asked to take a short math test, be sure to brush up on your basic arithmetic skills.

Computer-Assisted Integrity Tests

Integrity tests are used by companies to measure your honesty, morals, and ethics. In addition to being important in cases where an employee will be dealing with sensitive information, an integrity test is used to determine an applicant's overall level of honesty or moral standing. In addition to determining larger issues such as whether someone is likely to embezzle company funds or steal from the cash register, such tests can also determine whether someone is likely to be tardy or leave work early, socialize excessively during the workday, take long lunches, "borrow" office equipment, and so forth.

In addition to overall honesty, integrity tests allow employers to measure a candidate's reliability, work ethic, and trustworthiness—each of which is important in determining an employee's performance. Questions are most often posed in the form of always/sometimes/rarely/never.

When taking an integrity test, the best strategy is to be honest. Try to avoid absolutes, like "always" or "never." Though a recruiter may *want* to believe that you have "never" lied, it is not likely that he or she will. Then again, to say that you "always" lie probably will not get you a second interview either. Simply be honest, but don't reveal more than you have to.

Computer-Assisted Personality Tests

Personality tests are definitely the most complex of all computerized assessment tests. In general, they are used to determine whether a candidate's personality is suited to the job at hand.

Pinkerton's Adult Personality Survey, for example, measures traits such as work motivation, adaptability, and trustworthiness. The results of such a personality test are then compared against a standard—or norm—that is determined by those who have previously taken the test or those that have been successful in filling a similar position. For instance, if you are applying for a position as an insurance underwriter, your score will be measured against a standard group of successful insurance underwriters.

Again, this is one test in which honesty is always the best policy. Avoid using absolutes, unless they accurately reflect your personality. You never know how the group you are being measured against answered these questions, and straying too far from the desired scores—whether above or below—is likely to take you out of the running.

Employers like personality tests because they allow an accurate measurement of how well you will fit in with the rest of the company. While whether or not you are invited out for drinks after work may be unimportant to you, it is important to a company to know that you fit in well with the rest of the company. In the end, such a factor benefits both you and the employer. If you don't fit in well with the company, you are not likely to be a happy employee. If you're not a happy employee, it's quite possible that you'll begin to seek employment elsewhere. If you do, in fact, find employment elsewhere, it affects the company tremendously. Not only do they have the added task of hiring someone to fill your position, but they have wasted both time and money to train you in the first place.

The Stanton Profile, which is another Pinkerton test, is a hybrid personality/skills test that measures work preferences to determine general employability. After completing the test, your score is measured against the minimum requirements of a particular job. For instance, the test will ask you a question regarding, say, your adaptability. Adaptability is a good trait for an administrative assistant but less important for someone working in a stockroom, who will likely be doing the same tasks day after day. Depending on your answer, the test will assess—taking both your skills *and* personality into consideration—whether or not you would make a good employee.

If you thought that preparing for a skills or integrity test was difficult, you'll find that preparing for a personality test is near impossible. First, many people aren't sure whether they should let their "true" selves answer the questions or whether they should base their answers on the "personality" they assume the company is looking for. Experts differ on the subject. While some suggest that you should use your work personality to answer these questions (your work personality is usually somewhat different from your at-home personality), others say you should just be yourself. Still other experts claim that the best way to succeed at a personality test is to come up with a "professional character" based on successful friends and colleagues. When answering questions, think of how this "character" might respond.

While it can be useful to look at the traits that have made others successful, you should first look at the characteristics that have gotten you where you are. If you've spent any time in the work force, you know that your work personality differs from your personality outside work. Therefore, use what you've learned in the workplace—what is and isn't acceptable workplace behavior—to answer the questions.

As with the other types of tests, try to avoid using absolutes like "always" and "never," as an abundance of absolutes can signify to the employer either that you are lying or that you engage in extreme behavior. As stated previously, employers seek moderation in their new recruits; they tend to stay away from extremists.

CHAPTER SEVEN

The First
Defining Moments

T he first minute or two of any interview are the most crucial. As the saying goes, you only get one chance to make a great first impression, and this is when you want to do just that. By applying the skills discussed previously (proper attire, firm hand-shake, direct eye contact, etc.), you should have no problem wowing the interviewer and getting an offer of employment.

What Time Should I Arrive?

Like many issues in the job interviewing process, figuring out the best time to arrive at an interview can be tricky. The one rule you always want to remember is that being late to an interview—even if it's just "casually late"—is never acceptable. In fact, arriving late to an interview is one of the reasons recruiters often cite for not hiring someone. Unless there are some extenuating circumstances (and you've called ahead to let the interviewer know that you will not be arriving until a little bit later), you should always plan on arriving early.

The best time to arrive for an interview is approximately 10 to 15 minutes early. Anything less may seem like you're cutting it close; anything more may seem like you are too anxious (there are lots of thin lines like this in the job search process). Remember too that you are taking time out of someone else's workday. It could be the case that even if you do arrive on time, the interviewer may not be ready to speak with you. If, when you arrive, you are told that it will be a few minutes, take a seat and wait patiently.

Waiting for the Interviewer

You've probably heard the stories—which have now reached urban legend proportions—about the sadistic recruiters who force their interviewees to sit and wait for them for sometimes as much as two hours or more. While it is probably true that somewhere in the annals of job interviewing, a candidate has been forced to wait for

someone for an extended period of time, you can also be sure that this was probably not intentional.

Still, having an interviewee wait an extra five to 10 minutes is the route that many interviewers like to go. This is not done to watch them squirm in their seats a little longer, it's simply a way for the interviewer to see how the candidate reacts when something doesn't go according to plan. Does the interviewee sit patiently and look calm and relaxed, approach the receptionist and demand that the interviewer see him or her immediately, or storm out after only 5 minutes of being ignored? How you react to a situation like this before you are hired can determine how you will react to similar adversities after you are hired.

Since it's likely that you will have a few minutes to spare before the interviewer can see you—especially if you've arrived the suggested 10 to 15 minutes early—you should bring along a magazine or a book (one that you wouldn't be embarrassed by if someone else saw you reading it) and use it to occupy your time while waiting.

Above all, do not show any annoyance. If the receptionist informs you that it will still be a few minutes, simply respond in a gracious and unaffected manner and sit quietly with a magazine or book until the interviewer appears.

Introducing Yourself

When the interviewer finally does arrive, remember that it's show time. Be sure to show him or her, right from the start, that you are the *only* candidate who should be considered for the position. If you appear shy or intimidated, an interviewer may not want to dig too deep and embarrass you; that said, he or she will not ask you the really difficult questions—the questions that get you the job. It's human nature to judge a person by the first impression, so in the case of the job interview especially, you want to make sure it's a good one.

Strange but True

Interview Stories

When pressed for the most disastrous interview ever, one recruiter recounts "the time there was no interview. When the receptionist informed my interviewee that I had been held up in a meeting and would be a few minutes late, the woman responded 'Tell him it's his loss!' and stormed out the door."

Making a strong first impression is easy, as long as you know what it is the interviewer is looking for. Lucky for you, the secrets to making a great first impression lie within this book. The four main pieces to the puzzle are these:

- Maintain eye contact.
- Offer up a firm handshake.
- Engage in a bit of small talk.
- Set a tone.

Maintain Eye Contact

When the time for your interview finally arrives and you get the chance to meet the person who will be grilling you for the next hour or so, be sure to stand up and greet this person with a warm smile, and be sure to maintain constant eye contact during your articulate introduction. Establishing eye contact is probably one of the most important parts of your introduction. You want to make sure that you look the interviewer directly in the eye as you are being introduced and/or are shaking hands. At the same time, you don't want to make this person uncomfortable, so be sure not to stare at this person.

Offer Up a Firm Handshake

Similar limitations are placed on the handshake; while you don't want your handshake to be so light that the interviewer is forced to check for a pulse, you also don't want to be so enthusiastic that this person winds up in the emergency room with a fracture. A firm grip with a quick shake or two of the hand is appropriate; don't hold on for dear life.

Engage in a Bit of Small Talk

Before getting down to the important stuff—like why you would do well with this company—it is likely that the interviewer will engage you in a bit of small talk to get the conversation flowing. Prepare for these questions as well. Don't mistake, for example, "How was your ride in?" or "Did you have any problem finding us?" as anything other than small talk. He or she is really not interested in whether or not you hit any traffic or encountered any accidents on your way to the office. If you anticipate simple questions like these, you can be better prepared to answer them.

All too often, job seekers make the mistake of launching into a huge dialogue about how long it took them to get to the office, how they found a great short cut, and so on. The last thing an interviewer wants—or needs—in response to these initial questions is anything longer than "Great," "Fine," or "No Problem!" Don't be verbose; it can cause the interviewer to question your suitability to the company immediately. Also, regardless of how nervous you may be, don't let small-talk questions like these dumbfound you. After all, if you have trouble answering "What's the weather like out there?" how are you going to help this company come up with a winning marketing strategy?

Upon arriving at the office or area of your destination, wait until the interviewer tells you to be seated before sitting down (sit, don't plunk) on a chair or sofa. And remember the following words that your parents, teachers, and others used to tell you: "Be on your best behavior"—the traditional rules of etiquette should be observed at all times during a job interview.

Set a Tone

The tone of the meeting depends on the personality of the interviewer. He or she may ask a straight line of professional questions and answers, or be more lighthearted and laid back. Regardless of the manner of the interviewer, you should always prepare your answers in a very professional way.

Job Search Odds and Ends

Be Confident— You've Earned It!

On average, at least 80 percent of all applicants do not even make it as far as the interview stage for any job. For prime positions, that figure can be as high as 99 percent. So, when you're invited to an interview, you should be proud of yourself for that achievement alone.

Strange but True

Job Interview Answers

When asked "Why should we hire you?" an interviewee responded, "Because I wouldn't steal anything."

While it is most likely your resume that got you a call for this interview, it is the personality you show during the interview that will dictate whether or not you go any further in a company. One mistake that candidates often make is to prepare for each question by brainstorming the "perfect" answer. They think about the kind of answer the "perfect candidate" would give and use that. In most of these instances, the job seeker is wasting the company's time. Trying to project the perfect image can only result in disaster, because often the interviewer sees right through it. On the other hand, if the interviewer buys into the candidate's "prefect persona," he or she may be surprised when—once hired—the candidate does not perform as "perfectly" as expected.

Though you shouldn't necessarily reveal your true nature to the employer right from the start—warts and all—you should also not pretend to be someone or something you are not. Many career experts think that the best way to set and maintain a professional tone throughout an interview is to create a sort of "job interview persona." Think about the many aspects of a person a job interviewer would be interested in, and be sure to project these characteristics. Which traits that you possess would make you a strong candidate and set you apart from the rest of the candidates? Think about the many successful people you know or have heard about and the personality traits that make them good leaders. How can you convey to the interviewer that these qualifications are part of your own professional nature? When preparing answers to the questions you think you will be asked, be sure to keep these traits in mind and answer the questions accordingly.

Think of yourself as a calm, cool, and collected individual; be relaxed enough to allow a bit of your true personality to seep out. Remember that in the end you have no control over the outcome of an interview; you do not decide whether or not you get the job. In many cases, you could conduct yourself perfectly throughout the interview and still not get the job. On the other

hand, you could feel like you've botched the entire interview and still receive an offer.

The only thing you *do* have control over during the interview is what you do and say while you're there. That said, always keep the following key qualities an interviewer is looking for in the back of your mind and be sure to convey your aptitude in each of them:

- Adaptability
- Competence
- Confidence
- Creativity
- Dedication
- Dependability
- Easygoingness
- Enthusiasm
- Leadership Ability
- Motivation
- Problem-Solving Ability
- Resourcefulness

Think of these qualities in every answer you give and every thing you say, and you should have no problem projecting the image of a confident and competent candidate.

CHAPTER EIGHT

Getting Down to Business

So you've managed to get through the first few moments of the interview without any scratches, and now you are on to the main event. It's time to get down to business and talk about the skills you possess and how they relate to the job and company at hand.

Making an Impression

Do you know how many candidates the typical recruiter or hiring manager of a specific department has interviewed in his or her lifetime? Depending on the number of years they've been in the business, it could be hundreds, maybe even thousands. In fact, they see so many different candidates come and go that it can become very difficult to differentiate between them. It is likely that even just a week or so after your meeting, the interviewer has forgotten all about you. That is why—above all else—your main job in an interview is to make a lasting impression or, more specifically, to make a lasting *positive* impression. But what can you do to make sure that your name, face, and resume stand out from the hordes of others? Following are some suggestions.

When an employer begins to describe the activities of the company and the typical duties that your desired job will entail, listen carefully. Think of ways in which you have demonstrated aptitude at these sort of duties and draw parallels between the company's needs and your own experiences. Describe your experiences in the same way you would on a resume. Emphasize your achievements and don't be modest. On the other hand, don't exaggerate to the point of disbelief.

If you are interviewing for a competitive position or with a large company, the first interview is the most difficult. Though an initial phone screening is used to weed candidates out, the first interview is where the competition becomes even more fierce. Those who do not pass the first interview are the ones who get the obligatory "Thank You For Your Time" letter, and the

rest of the candidate pack move on to the second round. It is for this reason that making a great impression, especially during the first screening interview, is so important. Focus on a few of your greatest strengths—ones that you know would be looked upon favorably by the company—and emphasize them throughout the interview.

Let the rules of the first few moments of the interview follow you into the interviewer's office as well. Always maintain strong eye contact with the interviewer. Be attentive and listen carefully to all that he or she is saying. Answer questions with brief but complete answers, and provide evidence for the answers you give. If you claim to be a loyal employee, talk about a situation in which you've proven this. Be sure to highlight some of your greatest achievements, both personal and professional. Telling stories about past experiences is one of the best ways to leave an impression; an interviewer is more likely to remember a story that you told than an answer you gave, so be sure to cite evidence where and when you can.

Showcasing Your Knowledge

Ask any interviewer and he or she is likely to tell you that a knowledgeable employee is a desirable employee. If you've done your homework and researched the company, position, and industry, you should have no problem demonstrating your knowledge to a potential employer.

At some point in the interview, it is likely that the interviewer will begin to tell you a bit more about the position and the company in general. If you have done your research, you should already know a lot of this information. Without sounding like a know-it-all, you may want to indicate your familiarity with this information. If he or she mentions a current happening in the company—perhaps a new product they are about to launch, or an impending merger—you may want to try and engage in an intelligent conversation about this topic. This is a great way to build rapport with the interviewer (and leave an impression).

Strange but True

Interview Questions

One job seeker found herself caught completely off guard when the interviewer asked, "So why do you hate your boss so much?"

Strange but True

Interview Questions

"What would you say if I told you that this job will require you to work harder than you ever have before but that you will receive no credit for your work?"

Again, if you have done your research, it is likely that you will be able to discuss something that the interviewer mentions. Without interrupting (or correcting this person), try your best to tactfully mention your familiarity with the topic and hope it grows into a conversation between equals.

Emphasizing the Positive

There's no disputing the fact that a positive person is a likable person. Show the interviewer your optimism and ability to handle difficult situations with ease by remaining positive throughout the interview. Even when asked about the worst job you've ever had, or the most difficult project you've ever worked on, be sure to emphasize the positive points of these experiences. Think of all your experiences—bad and good—as learning experiences. Think about what you have learned from them, and use that information to further impress the interviewer. For example, instead of saying "I hated my position as a telemarketer because I was forced to bother people night and day," think of that job as a learning experience. You could say, "I realized that cold calling wasn't my strong suit. Though I really enjoyed being able to interact with people, I decided that my talents could be better utilized in a face-to-face situation." Even the most horrible job taught you some sort of lesson; figure out what it was and talk about it.

Downplaying the Negative

In keeping with the previous sentiments, it is always important to downplay your past negative experiences in the course of a job interview. Do be forewarned, however, that your resolve will be tested. Recruiters often ask candidates specifically about negative situations and difficult tasks they were asked to perform simply to see their reaction. Though it may be true that you hate your current boss, job, and company, you should never—under any circumstances—let the interviewer hear or see your bitterness. Again, all

experiences—even bad ones—have taught you a lesson. The best way to downplay a negative topic is to introduce the situation only briefly and focus the rest of your answer on the positive experiences that emerged from it. Keep the slanderous remarks or disparaging comments to yourself. The only thing such comments will convey to the interviewer is the possibility of a future attitude problem, which probably will not place you too high on the "Must Hire Now" candidate list.

Answering Questions

When answering an interviewer's questions—no matter how simple or difficult—there are certain rules you must follow. First and foremost, you must be clear in what you are saying. Don't skirt the issue at hand; be sure to answer the question that you are being asked. Candidates that ramble and seem to go off on their own tangent are not candidates that are likely to be hired.

Where you can, be sure to cite evidence or tell the interviewer some sort of story that supports what you are saying. If you claim to be, for example, a strong leader, discuss a time when you demonstrated strong leadership skills.

Try to ascertain the heart of each question, and be sure your answer clearly articulates your capabilities. If you are unsure of what the interviewer is asking, or what he or she is trying to get at with a question, don't be afraid to ask. Asking for clarification during any part of the interview will not be looked down upon, unless you start asking for clarification on every question.

The most important thing to remember when answering any question is to always project an air of confidence. Even if the interviewer is questioning your abilities or skills in a particular area, answer with confidence and conviction.

Insider Tips

Eliminate Your Weaknesses

Do not ignore your weaknesses, because the interviewer is certainly going to try and find them. Once you know exactly what your biggest weaknesses are, spend time alleviating them. Once you've taken some steps toward overcoming obstacles, you will be able to talk about it with your interviewer with a certain level of pride.

Insider Tips

Talking Money

During an interview, one of the worst questions you can ask is, How much will I be paid? Even more tactful variations of this question (e.g., What type of salary would accompany this wonderful position?) are inappropriate. While some employers will tell you the salary up front (and whether or not it is negotiable), others will wait until the final stages of the game. If the interviewer asks you what type of salary you are looking for, make sure you give them a range instead of an actual figure. For example, "$25,000 to $30,000" is much easier to negotiate than "$29,000."

Answering *Difficult* Questions

Having an impossible question (one which you don't have an answer to) thrown at you is probably one of the worst things that could happen during an interview. Yet, this is something that happens quite often—as a result of the recruiter's deliberate attempt to stump you. Many interviewers admit to asking candidates questions they know they can't answer, simply to see how they react. This is one test you want to make sure you pass!

In interviews for high-pressure jobs especially, you should be prepared for questions that are both utterly complex and absolutely zany. When asked such a question, do you stumble and stutter nervously? Do you try and make something up? Do you admit that you do not know? Often, there is no right or wrong answer to these questions, but there are right and wrong reactions.

If you have an impossible question thrown at you, the best way to handle the situation is to think about the question for a few seconds. If you come up with an intelligible answer, great! If you can't, a simple "I don't know" or "I cannot answer that question" will do just fine. Avoid making apologies! Don't be sorry just because you don't know the answer; simply say you don't know and move on with the interview. Regardless of what you say, always remain confident in your response—even when you don't have an answer at all.

Preparing Your Own Questions

In a typical interview format, one of the last (if not *the* last) questions an interviewer will ask you is, Do you have any questions of your own? Even if you feel you have heard everything there is to know about this company and this position, be sure to ask something! If you don't have any real questions, choose from a list of insightful questions that you have prepared ahead of time. Make sure you prepare more than one question so that if the interviewer answers your questions throughout the course of the conversation, you have a few backups. Responding something along the lines of "Nope! I think you answered 'em all!" is not likely to make a lasting impression.

Worse than having *no* questions to ask an interviewer at this juncture in the interview is asking a question that has already been answered. For example, asking about the hours you will be asked to work when the interviewer has already gone over this in detail will only serve to lower your status in the eyes of the recruiter. In addition to thinking that you are inattentive, he or she may believe that you are incapable of absorbing large amounts of information in a short period of time.

Are there other questions to avoid at this point in the interview? Avoid asking anything about salary—unless it has been discussed before (though, even then, this could be an iffy subject)—as well as questions about other benefits or issues that could be considered "selfish," such as tuition reimbursement. Also avoid reading directly from the list of questions you have prepared.

Are there ways to really shine at this point in the interview? If you have done your research, this is another point where you can subtly demonstrate your knowledge. By asking questions that pertain to this particular company, you are showing the interviewer that you know what you are talking about. Be sure that your questions don't turn into an interrogation. Avoid asking questions the interviewer may find difficult or awkward to answer. And steer clear of questions that don't pertain directly to the job. For example, while it may interest you to know whether or not all the company's catalogs are printed on recycled paper, now is not the time to ask. Ask intelligent questions that will underscore your interest in the position as well as a long-term career with this particular company.

Some Questions to Ask

Are you still unsure of what kinds of questions would be appropriate at the end of an interview? Below are some successful questions that job seekers have asked interviewers in the past and the kinds of questions that an interviewer looks for:

Insider Tips

Refrain from Reading

When it comes to asking questions, you should always have some prepared for the interviewer ahead of time. And while you may want to write these down for your own reference *before* the interview, never read directly from this list during the interview.

- Could you talk a little bit about what a typical work week would be like for a public relations executive at Fill-in-the-Blank Corporation?
- If I were hired and able to prove my worth, what would be the typical career path of someone in my position?
- What are some of the strengths you believe the ideal candidate for this position should have?
- Why did the last person leave this job?
- How long do people tend to stay in this position?
- What opportunities for advancement are there in this position?
- How much interoffice interaction is there? Do departments tend to work independently of one another, or is there a fair amount of intercommunication?
- How does your company measure employee performance? How often is this done?
- In your opinion, what is the best part of this job?
- In your opinion, what is the worst part of this job?
- How long have you worked for Fill-in-the-Blank Corporation?
- What do you feel is the best aspect of working for this company?
- What do you feel is the worst aspect of working for this company?
- I know that much of the industry, in general, is looking toward the Internet as the wave of the future. How is your company responding to this new technology?
- If I were hired, how many others would there be in my department?
- What is the overall size of the company?
- How would you describe the management philosophy at Fill-in-the-Blank Corporation?
- How many others are interviewing for this position?
- When do you think you will be making a hiring decision?

Illegal Questions

One thing that you should certainly be aware of—when asking and answering questions alike—is the types of questions that are considered illegal. There are plenty of questions that an interviewer is not allowed to ask, by law, and you should be aware of these in case one comes up during an interview.

Federal law prohibits employers from discriminating against a candidate on the basis of sex, age, race, nationality, or religion. If you are asked a question that seems to probe one of these private matters, it is most likely an illegal question. For instance, an interviewer may not ask you about your age or your date of birth. However, he or she may ask you if you are over the age of 18, as that may apply to the job. If you are asked an illegal question during an interview, don't jump up and try to make a citizen's arrest. And don't be so bold as to demand that the interviewer retract the question immediately. The truth is, many employers simply don't know what is legal and what is illegal to ask an applicant. That said, if asked a question that you believe to be illegal, be tactful about *not* answering it directly.

One strategy you can employ is to address the purpose of the question. For example, an interviewer who asks you about your plans to have children could be concerned that you will not be able to fulfill the travel requirements of the job. Address the heart of the matter by saying, "I'm not quite sure I understand." If you can determine the interviewer's concerns, you can allay them with a reply such as "I'm very interested in developing my career. Travel is definitely not a problem for me. In fact, it is one of the aspects I enjoy most about this job."

Other ways to deal with illegal questions include just to answer the question anyway, or to tactfully point out that the question is illegal and decline to answer it. Though the situation is one that will probably lead to defensiveness on the part of the interviewer, avoid reacting in a hostile fashion. Remember, in many cases, the question was asked out of simple carelessness, or to help the interviewer make small talk.

Insider Tips

Make Yourself Part of the Question

Rather than asking "What kind of departmental structure does your company have?" try "What kind of departmental structure will I be working in with your company?" This will not only make you seem more confident but also give the sense that you want to work for this particular employer.

Job Search
Odds and Ends

Most Common Interview Complaints

- The candidate did not research the company.

- The candidate lacked enthusiasm.

- The candidate did not ask questions or did not ask the right questions.

- The candidate was too fidgety.

- The candidate did not make enough eye contact.

- The candidate's attire was too casual.

- The candidate spoke too quickly.

- The candidate spoke too much.

The responses below outline some of the many ways in which you could go about answering what is, essentially, an illegal question.

Q: What religion do you practice?

1. I make it a point not to mix my personal beliefs with my work, if that's what you mean. I assure you that I value my career too much for that.
2. I'm not quite sure what you are getting at. Could you please explain how this issue relates to the position?
3. That question makes me a bit uncomfortable. I'd really rather not answer it.

Q: How old are you?

1. I'm in my fifties and have over thirty years of experience in this industry. My area of expertise is in . . .
2. I'm not quite sure what you are getting at. Could you please explain how this issue relates to the position?
3. That question makes me a bit uncomfortable. I'd really rather not answer it.

Q: Are you married?

1. No.
2. Yes, I am. But I keep my family life separate from my work so that I can put all my effort into my job. I'm flexible when it comes to travel and late hours, as my references can confirm.
3. I'm not quite sure I understand. Could you please explain how this issue relates to the position?
4. That question makes me a bit uncomfortable. I'd really rather not answer it.

Q: Do you have children?

1. No.
2. Yes, I do. But I keep my family life separate from my work life so that I can put all my effort into my job. I'm flexible when it comes to travel and late hours, as my references can confirm.

3. I'm not quite sure what you are getting at. Could you please explain how this issue relates to the position?
4. That question makes me a bit uncomfortable. I'd really rather not answer it.

Ending the Interview

The end of the interview should not come as a surprise to you. The interviewer will most likely ask whether you have any further questions and tell you that he or she has none left for you. He or she may then offer up the next stage of the process by saying something like "We're interviewing candidates for the next two weeks and hope to make a decision by the end of the month." If the interviewer does not tell what comes next, don't be afraid to ask. Find out whether the company will contact you directly or whether it will be up to you to call someone back and check the status of your application. Ask how long it will be before they make a decision.

It is a good idea to write this information down, so that you can be sure of the agreed upon next step. If the interviewer doesn't offer you his or her business card, ask for one. Even if he or she doesn't have a card handy, write down his or her name (be sure to ask for the correct spelling), title, and phone number (if you don't have it already). Keep this information alongside the names and titles of anyone else you may have met with in the company, as these are the people you will want to thank.

While you might like to think that the only thing left to do now is sit around and wait for the phone to ring, it's not. In addition to having plenty of "after the interview" tasks to take care of (see the next chapter), you should never stop working on finding a new job until you have received an official offer. Even if you think the interview went great, there's no guarantee that you got the job until the company tells you so. Continue sending out resumes and scheduling more interviews. While it's okay to hope for employment at one company, it is not wise to stake the future of your employment on one interview. Finding a new job is a full-time job in itself; you must be prepared to work hard to make the job offers come rolling in.

Insider Tips

Closing Words

You may feel as though you have little control over how long your interview lasts. However, a typical first interview will take about 30 minutes. Do not look at your watch or make an obvious glance at a clock. When the interview approaches the 30-minute mark, be aware of any signs that the interviewer might be wrapping things up. Try to finish off strong, but do not try and hold your interviewer captive. A longer interview is not necessarily a better one, especially if your interviewer has somewhere to go. When the interview is over, do not show signs of relief or dejection. With confidence, express your appreciation of the interviewer's time and remain positive. Even if you think things went poorly, the interviewer may have had a different view.

CHAPTER NINE

After
the Interview

While you may be tempted to put your feet up and sit by the phone after a successful interview, don't pat yourself on the back yet. Interviewers see plenty of promising candidates all the time, and though they may wish they could hire all of them, they usually have to make decisions. Even if the interview went well, it does not mean you got the job. Even if the interviewer asked you questions about your salary requirements or asked something along the lines of "If we were to hire you, when could you start?" it doesn't mean they've made their decision. After you've shaken hands and said good-bye to the interviewer, there are still plenty of tasks left to be done.

Saying "Thank You"

Though many people think of the thank-you as superfluous—sometimes even toadyish—it is quickly becoming a mandatory part of the job search process. Many recruiters even claim that the thank-you letter, which is essentially the same as a follow-up letter, is sort of a last test of a candidate's suitability. If they receive the letter within the next few days, the candidate scores some definite points with the interviewer. If they do not receive a letter, the job may go to another candidate who had the courtesy to thank the interviewer for his or her time.

Aside from being a recruiter test, sending a thank-you letter to the person or people with whom you met during your interview can be a way for you to underscore your continued interest in the position and the company. If you've ever been in the situation where you've come up with the perfect response to a question—three hours after the

fact—the follow-up letter is the forum in which you can express such a response. Though it should be short and sweet, you should feel free to (tactfully) mention any details you may have forgotten in the course of the interview. If the interview didn't go as well as you had hoped it to, the thank-you letter is also the time to win back some lost points.

Be polite and make sure to express your continued interest in the position, as well as your ability to perform the duties the job requires. Make sure to proofread the letter carefully and, if you're unsure of how to spell the person's name, call the company and ask the receptionist or someone else who might know. While a handwritten letter on a piece of nice stationery is the best way to do it (provided your writing is legible), sending a quick e-mail is okay too. If the interviewer's e-mail address is listed on his or her card, use it. If not, don't ask for it. Make sure to write and send this thank-you letter immediately following the interview so that your meeting is still fresh in the interviewer's mind. It will help to put a face to the letter and, it is hoped, a face to the position they're hiring for.

Anatomy of a Letter

For a rough idea of how to write a thank-you letter to an interviewer, see the anatomy of a great follow-up letter below. Remember, you should send a note to each person you spoke with during your visit to the office. If sending multiple letters, make sure that each one of them reads a little bit differently; you certainly don't want all these people to get together, compare notes, and question your creativity.

Insider Tips

You Snooze, You Lose

Never wait for the employer to make the next move. By doing so, you not only put the ball in his or her court but also hand the job off to another applicant, most likely the one who called a few days earlier.

Your Street Address
Your City, State, and Zip Code

Today's Date

Interviewer's Name
Interviewer's Title
Company Name
Company Street Address
Company City, State, and Zip Code

Dear Mr./Ms. Interviewer's Last Name:

The first paragraph doesn't need to be much longer than two to three sentences. Its purpose is to say thank you to the interviewer for his or her time, and to mention something about the interview that might jog this person's memory as to who you are.

Use the second paragraph to restate your interest in the company and the position, and make mention (again) of your most relevant skills. If there is something you forgot to mention during the course of the interview, this is the place to say it—just be sure that it's done tactfully.

The final paragraph will allow you to say a final thank-you and let the interviewer know how much you are looking forward to hearing from him or her. If you have made definite plans to follow up—that is, if you are supposed to call the interviewer the next week—be sure to remind him or her that you plan to do so.

Sincerely,

Your Name
Your Name

When closing the letter, be sure to use "Sincerely." Contrary to popular opinion, "Love" will not score you any points. Also, be sure that you both type *and* sign your name to the letter. Proofread the letter carefully and make sure there are no errors. If you find mistakes or typos, rewrite the letter completely. Pen scratches and correction fluid are completely inappropriate

Following Up

Besides sending a thank-you letter, there are other ways in which you can follow up with the person who interviewed you and work to keep your name in the forefront of his or her mind, though the key to doing this successfully is not to seem too pushy or anxious. Allow enough time for the interviewer to receive and read your thank-you letter. If, after ten days, you still have not heard anything about the job, you should feel free to get in touch with the interviewer again (unless, of course, the person told you ahead of time that no decision would be made for at least another month or so).

The best way to express your continued interest in a company and a position is with a brief telephone call. Figure out what you plan to say ahead of time so that you don't waste a lot of time listening to an uncomfortable silence. Make it short; ask whether or not a decision has been made and when the applicants will be notified of a decision.

A great way to follow up with an interviewer—though there are only certain circumstances in which this could apply—is if, during the course of your interview, the interviewer provided any possibilities for a follow-up conversation. For example, if the interviewer suggested a book you might enjoy or told you to check out a recent magazine article, this allows you the perfect "excuse" to call. Call and thank the interviewer for the recommendation and mention how much you learned from the piece or how much you enjoyed it. A word of caution: If you were lucky enough to have been afforded this great way of following up, *be sure to read the book or article that the interviewer mentioned!* Calling two hours after the interview to tell the person how much you enjoyed reading *War and Peace* is not likely to win you any points.

Press On

If you still haven't received a phone call a day or two after the interview, don't panic! Depending on the number of candidates applying for a position, it can often take several weeks—or even months—before a company is ready to make a decision. At the end

Insider Tips

When *Not* to Call an Employer

In an age of e-mail, pagers, and voice mail, making personal contact with unsolicited follow-up phone calls is nearly impossible. Still, there are always good and bad times to catch an employer. Here are some of the times to avoid calling:

- Monday mornings and Friday afternoons. The body may be at work, but the mind is mired in the weekend.
- Just before 12 P.M. and just before 5 P.M. You may catch them at their desk, but most people are too preoccupied with lunch or getting home to give you their full attention.
- The few minutes before any hour can also be difficult. Meetings and appointments are often scheduled for these times, so try and call 15 minutes before or after the hour commences.

Strange but True

Interview Behavior

When an interviewer told the applicant that he wasn't sure that his skills and educational background really fit in with the job they were trying to fill, the job seeker threatened the interviewer with "If you don't hire me, you'll be sorry!"

of the interview, find out how many candidates they are interviewing and when they expect to make a decision. Just remember, it could be a while before you hear any news, so don't sit around waiting for a phone call.

Even if you know that the job you just interviewed for is the perfect job for you, don't count on getting it. Make sure you spend the time between interviewing for a position and hearing about the company's decision wisely. Send your resume out to other firms and set up other interviews. Even if you have your heart set on working for one specific company, it always helps to have a backup plan. Keep in mind that having a number of opportunities on the table will put you in a much better position to negotiate a better deal for yourself.

Taking "No" for an Answer

Though it hurts to say it, into everyone's life a little rejection must fall. Just as a cover letter and resume are a necessary part of the job search process, so is rejection. Depressing as it is, having to deal with rejection is inevitable; we will all experience it at some point.

With so many job seekers out there and only so many positions to be filled, it is unlikely that you will get every job you apply for. Though any rejection hurts, rejection in the job market is not something that should always be taken personally. Don't swear off ABC Company or organize a boycott of XYZ's products just because they chose to pursue another candidate. The best way to deal with rejection as it relates to job seeking is to turn it around.

One of the best things about rejection in the job market—as opposed to rejection elsewhere—is that you can turn it around and make it work for you. One way you can do this is by contacting each of the interviewers who rejected you and—again—thank them for their time. You also have the opportunity to tell each of these people that though you weren't selected for employment this time around, you would love to be considered for any future positions.

If you feel comfortable enough with the person who interviewed you, maybe you've spoken with him or her on a few occasions

since your initial meeting, you may even want to ask them for help. Ask the interviewer if he or she has any suggestions about how you might improve your chances of getting hired in the industry. You can even go so far as to ask the interviewers for the names of any people or companies they may know of that are hiring. Remember, this is not a technique that is appropriate for everyone. First, you must be confident enough that these questions sound professional, and not desperate. You must also have built up a strong enough rapport with an interviewer that he or she doesn't feel like your questions are bothersome.

If you do, in fact, decide to contact interviewers after they have informed you that they will not be needing your services, there are two important things to keep in mind. First and foremost, don't ever—under any circumstances—ask the interviewer why you weren't hired. In addition to being completely out of line, this is a question that will definitely make the interviewer feel a bit uncomfortable and, most likely, unwilling to help you in your search for employment. Second, if you do decide to ask for suggestions, make sure that the conversation evolves to this question; in other words, don't make it obvious that you called specifically to ask for a list of contacts. By engaging the interviewer in a friendly (but brief) conversation that eventually leads to offering suggestions, he or she likely will be much more willing to help you.

Securing a Second Interview

Depending on the company structure, it can often be the case that rather than a hiring decision, the next step after a first interview is a *second interview*. In fact, there are very few companies that simply rely on the opinion of one person to make a hiring decision. In many companies, the first interview is with a human resources or personnel professional who then makes a judgment of the candidate's suitability and passes this information on to the head of the department that is hiring. The purpose of the first interview is to narrow down the number of candidates that the company will then seriously consider. That is why your goal for the first

Insider Tips

Baby Steps

Obviously, the ultimate goal of your job search is to land the dream job you've always hoped for. Because this is such an enormous task, setting that as your one and only goal, however, can actually serve to hurt your motivation. The best way to solve this problem is to set mini-goals that can easily be achieved in a period of days rather than months. Those little pats on the back will help keep your spirits high.

Strange but True

Interview Scenarios

A job seeker walks into a room only to find an empty chair and ten interviewers sitting around it. Once the job seeker sits down, the interviewers quickly introduce themselves and begin firing questions without a moment's hesitation.

interview is to stand out and be remembered. When going back for later interviews, there is a bit of a different strategy involved.

By making it through the first interview, a candidate has proven that he or she has several strengths that could benefit the company. That said, the purpose of second interviews and beyond will be to find out about your weaknesses and other limitations. Your goal in second interviews and beyond, therefore, should be to present yourself as a well-balanced candidate.

In later interviews, try and figure out the underlying concern at hand for each of the questions you are asked. Remember that the interviewer has previous knowledge of what your weaknesses are, and he or she is trying to gauge whether or not that weakness should be cause for concern. In your answer, try and dispel any apprehensions you can make out on the part of the interviewer.

In many cases, you will interview with several people who are only in a position to reject your hiring—not push it forward (examples of these types of people include department heads of other departments). Thus, you should focus on building a strong rapport with these interviewers.

For most professional positions, you will have two separate interviews before a decision is made. For higher-level, executive positions and such, three interviews are common. There are even companies out there who are well known for conducting no less than six interviews with a candidate before making a decision. Though this could seem like a rather nerve-wracking experience, remember that with each further interview, you are proving yourself a more valuable candidate and that the competition is becoming less. That said, you should begin to feel more relaxed and comfortable as you return for further interviews.

CHAPTER TEN

The Job Offer

After sending out all the resumes and cover letters, long after you've done the company research, and once you've completed a few rounds of job interviewing, you'll most likely be led to the final stage of the job search game: that is, the job offer. While it might seem that the actual offer should be the most exciting part of the entire process (it can be), being offered a new position can also be nerve wracking. As it's likely that you will be interviewing with several companies at once, it is also possible that you will be offered more than one job at once. Deciding which offer to accept can pose a number of questions and concerns. On the one hand, if you've been looking for a job for quite some time, you're likely to find yourself screaming "YES! I'LL TAKE IT!" before the recruiter even finishes stating the offer. On the other hand, you may be worrying that something better will come along just as you accept the offer (that's just your luck, right?).

As job seekers are faced with far too many conflicting emotions at the last stage of the game, it's easy to see how so many people can make unnecessary and costly mistakes now. It is far too often the case that eligible job seekers—with a lot to offer any company—sell themselves short. They don't believe they will be hired anywhere else (and they don't feel like spending the time looking), so they accept an offer without even exploring the rest of their options. On the opposite end of the spectrum, there are those job seekers who have wildly unrealistic expectations of what they are worth as an entry-level employee. For those job seekers who go straight to where the money is, they're overlooking some very important aspects of a job that will come back to haunt them later. You can help avoid making these last-minute blunders by answering the following set of questions.

Do You *Really* Want This Job?

If you are going to seriously consider a job offer, make sure it is a job you want. Make sure that it is a job (and company) that you will enjoy going to every day. Be sure that the career path you are embarking on is the right one for you and that this job is just

another logical step along your path. Think about the following questions as well: Are you willing to live and work in the job's location? Is the work schedule and job lifestyle one you believe you will enjoy? If you are just graduating, is the job in the field you'd like to pursue?

Will This Job Help Your Career?

Though for many people the determining factor in accepting a job offer is what the pay is, there is one more important aspect that is often overlooked: that is, Will this job help your career? In some organizations, you may be given a lot of responsibility right from the start but then find that job growth ends there. Before accepting the position, make sure you know whether or not the company offers room for advancement. Find out about periodic performance reviews, including when they are conducted.

Is This Job Environment One You Will Be Comfortable In?

You wouldn't want to live in the country if you enjoyed the pace of the city, and you wouldn't want to live in Alaska if you didn't like the cold. That said, you shouldn't want to work in an environment where you wouldn't be comfortable either. In fact, an uncomfortable work environment has been known to hinder one's productivity.

One of the main goals of the entire interview process is to determine whether or not you and your personality will fit in with the work environment of the position. Consider specifics, including office or workstation setting, privacy, proximity to other staff, amount of space, noise level, and lighting. What is the level of interaction among coworkers? While some organizations strongly encourage teamwork, others promote individual accomplishment. Think about which approach works better for you. Remember: If you don't like the work environment before you accept the job, you probably will

Insider Tips

Keep a Poker Face

When discussing money, try not to reveal what you're thinking. Even if the salary offer seems barely above poverty level, it wouldn't be wise to inform the recruiter of that fact. Similarly, if the offer is much higher than you expected, doing cartwheels around the room probably wouldn't be appropriate either.

not like it as an employee. Don't accept a job only to realize this mistake a month or two later.

What about the Money?

Questions about salary and benefits are often frightening to those new to the workplace, as they're not issues that have had to be considered before. If you're a recent graduate, the closest you've ever come to negotiating a salary is getting a raise from minimum wage to a dollar more. However, talking about salary with a potential employer does not have to be as scary as it sounds. As long as you prepare for the inevitable mention of the topic, you should do just fine.

Again, before talking about salary with a company, you should be well aware of what the going rate is for someone with your background (education, experience, skills, specialization), in your position, and in your geographical area. If you find out that the median salary is $27,000, tell a recruiter (if and when asked) that you were looking for between $25,000 and $30,000. While an employer will be quick to alert you to any set salary requirements and whether or not your needs exceed it, it is best to not make yourself seem self-important (or completely clueless) by requesting $100,000 a year for a $30,000-a-year job.

Negotiating a Salary

Depending on the company you are dealing with and the position you're applying for, a company will do one of two things when asked to negotiate a salary: that is, stand firm or negotiate. You can easily determine whether or not a company is willing to negotiate on a salary simply by asking "Is that salary negotiable?" The question is a very common follow-up to the big salary disclosure, and it is not a question that should be taken the wrong way on the part of the employer.

If a company says that they are willing to negotiate a salary, your next move is to justify the increase. You want to assure them of your interest in the position but explain why the proposed salary

probably wouldn't be enough. Rather than saying you simply are worth or want more money, give solid evidence as to why more money is needed. For example, explain why their offer doesn't sufficiently cover your living expenses or moving expenses.

Remember that the art of negotiating is not a one-sided battle in which the job seeker names a price and the employer says yes or no. Negotiating entails listening to the employer and giving his or her offer consideration, even if it's not as much as you were looking for. Set realistic expectations for salary—and be able to justify this amount—and it's much more likely that an employer will be willing to match it.

How Much to Expect

Again, average salaries change with just about every aspect of the job. There are plenty of online sites where you can type in your job and geographical location and get back a list of average salaries for your position. Other ways in which you can find out a realistic salary expectation is to read the trade journals for your industry, read the newspaper help wanted ads, browse through some online job posting boards, or ask the question in an online discussion group of industry professionals. If possible, talk to current employees. The U.S. Department of Labor's *Occupational Outlook Handbook* lists salaries and other information about a variety of jobs. It can be found at your local library.

Get It in Writing

If you receive an offer and decide to take it, the most important next step is to get it in writing. After you have discussed all the aspects of the new job, including both salary and benefits, be sure to ask if you can have the offer outlined in writing. This is a normal request from job seekers, and it's not something you should be afraid to do. What you should be afraid of is an employer who is reluctant to provide you with a written outline of the job offer. An offer like that is one you may want to rethink before accepting.

Make Sure You Are Happy

Sure, a six-figure salary is certainly an enticing perk, but it's important to remember that salary isn't the only aspect of the job that will determine your happiness. Finding a job that you enjoy and can grow with is just as important. Similarly, finding a job that lets you showcase your skills and be yourself is equally important. If the starting salary of a job is fairly low but the job seems to present a great and unique opportunity, think about the benefits of taking this job. Before deciding to depart from your original career path, think about your professional future and where you want to be.

Still, if there's a great opportunity being offered but you just can't get past the low salary, you may want to take a while to think about it. Rather than start out a job with a negative attitude, it is best to shop around and wait until all the pieces come together and the perfect job opportunity makes itself available to you. Always trust your instincts. Figure out exactly what it is you are looking for in a job, and don't be afraid to wait until just such a job comes around. In the end, it is your overall happiness that matters, and that is certainly something you shouldn't negotiate.

Interview Questions You May Be Asked

CHAPTER ELEVEN

Your Ability and Compatibility

Skills and Experience

One aspect that is obviously important to an employer when interviewing potential employees is skills and experience. Think about the most important skills you possess and how they will aid you in a particular position or field. When the interviewer asks you questions about your skills, be sure to offer specific examples to illustrate your point. Avoid using clichés or being too general. Make sure you don't cross the line of confidence by sounding too pompous or arrogant. Employers will never believe that you "saved the world from mass destruction." They will, however, believe that you "increased departmental sales by 25 percent."

Q: What are your key skills?

✔ **YES:** After spending the last six years as a senior systems analyst, I've developed a number of important skills including business modeling, process re-engineering, software-package evaluation, and advanced programming capabilities in UNIX and C environments. I was very pleased to discover that these are the skills you are seeking. Would you like to hear about specific examples of my work?

✗ **NO:** I am a hardworking people person who wears many hats.

Talk about your key skills and how you'll use them in this job. Avoid using clichés or generalities. Offer specific evidence, drawing parallels from your current or previous job to the job you're interviewing for. Don't be afraid to ask a question in your answer. However, the last thing you want to do is seem garrulous, so find out if the interviewer would like to hear specific examples and, if so, oblige him or her.

Q: What sets you apart from other applicants?

✔ **YES:** Once I'm given a job or a project, I tackle it with indefatigable energy. I want to learn everything I can, and my goal is to

achieve results beyond the expectations of my supervisor. I really strive to excel in all I do.

✗ NO: I have experience in the field, and I am a college graduate.

Your answer should demonstrate confidence in your abilities without sounding conceited. A good way to illustrate your worth as an employee is to talk about what others, preferably past and present supervisors, would say about you. If you have specific skills that relate to the job, be sure to emphasize this point as well. Make sure that the reasons you give for your uniqueness are well thought out. Citing your own experience in the field—unless it is unique or a special skill in high demand—is pointless, as many of the other applicants are probably experienced as well.

Q: What are your strengths?

✔ YES: I would say that my strong interpersonal skills are one of my greatest strengths; I work easily with others and am always open to various points of view. I also have good judgment about people and an intuitive sense of their talents and their ability to contribute to a given problem. Given the type of employee you are looking for, I think that these skills directly relate to the job. I am extremely hard working. In addition to maintaining an active membership in various professional societies, I have spent the past two years taking evening classes to further my education and knowledge of this industry.

✗ NO: I am smart as a whip, and I am looking for a company just like yours so that I can hone my skills and talents even more.

Describe two or three skills you have that are most relevant to the position. Avoid using clichés ("I'm a real people person") or generalities ("I'm loyal!"). For each strength you give, be prepared to back it up. To say that you have initiative but then be at a loss for an example of this trait will not work for you. In addition to describing how your strengths have worked for you in the past, talk about the ways in which these skills could be put to use in the new position.

Insider Tips

Organize Your Skills

When it comes to talking about your skills, keep in mind that there are several different skill categories that an employer may be interested in hearing about:

Functional skills: Functional skills are the skills you have spent the entirety of your work time developing. They include such things as organizing, problem solving, writing, listening, and communicating.

Personal skills: Personal skills tell an employer how well your personality will fit in with those around you. These skills include such things as how well you work with others, how well you deal with authority, whether or not you are able to assert authority, and your time management abilities.

Technical skills: Technical skills are just that; they refer to such things as your computer knowledge and customer service skills.

Q: What are your weaknesses?

✔ YES: On some occasions, it has taken me longer to complete a project than I had originally anticipated. I consider myself a bit of a perfectionist; I refuse to turn a project in if it is not the best it could be. While this serves me well in some respects, it can also set me behind schedule sometimes. For the past month, I have been taking a time management class once a week. Already, I can see that the skills I'm learning are helping with this tendency to dwell on certain projects.

✗ NO: I really can't think of anything.

This question is really one that can make you or break you in the eyes of an interviewer. While you want to be honest, you want to make sure that you don't shoot yourself in the foot. Think about the many duties the job entails, and try not to point out a weakness that would be a major obstacle as far as your potential duties are concerned. Try and think of a weakness that (1) is not **too** big of a deal and (2) can be overcome. Another smart move is to discuss how you are working to strengthen this weakness.

Q: How does your experience relate to this job, in particular?

✔ YES: In my current job I've recently completed three re-engineering projects. I gathered all the necessary market data, developed a benchmarking program, and put together a team to do the evaluation and analysis. As a result, I'm ready to tackle the major re-engineering project that you've listed as the priority of this job during the first year. In my past job, I was the liaison between the project engineering group and the instrumentation group in the testing of a new turbo engine. This experience will also help me tackle this job, which involves a close and careful working relationship between your technical group and your field-testing group.

✗ NO: Because I just graduated from college and have spent the last several years working as a waitress, I don't think my experience serving food could really translate to your organization.

However, if given the opportunity, I would promise to work very hard.

When you read a job description, you should try and envision the many tasks that the position will entail and relate these tasks to past experiences. Draw parallels from your current or previous job to the requirements of this job. With first interviews especially, the interviewer may very well be a human resources professional—not someone associated with your job or industry. He or she may not know much about the field to which you are applying. A similarity that seems obvious to you may not be so obvious to the recruiter. By showcasing your own knowledge, you are demonstrating that you are a knowledgeable employee. Even if you are new to the professional job market, have only held a part-time job, or have never held a job, you have done things in your life that you can count as experience. In the above example, the waitress could talk about the interpersonal skills she learned at her job and the way in which she learned to deal with customers in a friendly and effective manner. Don't discount *any* experience you may have, no matter how inconsequential you think it might be.

Q: What skills do you think are most critical to this job?

✔ **YES:** As technology is ever changing, I think that it is important to keep up with the latest marketing trends. Knowing what kinds of new technologies exist and how to go about incorporating them into my own marketing plans is what will keep me ahead of the competition. Creativity is also of major importance to the marketing industry; new ideas can quickly become stale and stagnant. A successful marketing associate will always be looking ahead to the next big revolution. If, just a few years ago, I had not been aware of the important role that the Internet would play in our day-to-day duties, my current company could have been wiped out by the competition.

✗ NO: I think that to be a great salesman, you have to have a keen lying ability. As any number of my friends and family can attest to, I am a born liar!

When describing the skills you feel are most important, make sure (1) that you know how these skills relate to the position at hand, (2) that you possess these skills yourself, and (3) that you can illustrate how the cited skills have helped you in your current and/or past positions.

Q: What skills would you like to develop in this job?

✓ YES: I'd like to develop my negotiating skills. I've had considerable experience interpreting and implementing large contracts, but I've been limited in negotiating the actual conditions, costs, and standards for a major contract. I believe this job will offer me the opportunity to be a member of a negotiating team and thereby to begin acquiring the skills necessary to lead the team.

✗ NO: As an assistant manager at Hamburgers Are Us, I would hope to be able to learn the skills that will allow me to open up my own fine dining establishment within the next six months. With no prior restaurant or managerial experience, I think this position would afford me the perfect opportunity to run my own international franchise one day.

Make sure you are not inhabiting an imaginary world with your answer to this question! First, be sure that your answer coincides with skills that this job will help you develop. Second, be sure that you've already covered some of the prerequisites to developing the skills you mention. For example, you wouldn't want to apply for a job as a receptionist with the Joffrey Ballet and say that you hope to develop your ballet skills. Think about your current job and several aptitudes you have not been able to develop fully. For example, your opportunity to manage the department might have been hindered because your supervisor plans to stay in his or her job at least five more years.

Q: If you were to stay in your current job, what kinds of tasks would you spend more time on and why?

✔ **YES:** If I were to stay at my current job, I'd like to gain more experience in labor negotiating. In particular, I'd like to help negotiate labor contracts, resolve grievances at the step-4 level, and prepare grievances for arbitration. Though I have a very strong background in all areas of human resources, I believe that a strong grasp of labor relations experience will round out my skills so that I could have the opportunity to move up to a position of department head and possibly vice president.

✘ **NO:** As my attempts to further myself in my current company have been unsuccessful, I would probably try and spend more time working online to find myself another job.

In answering this question, think about the aspects of your job that interest you most. What are the areas that you would like to strengthen and advance in? What are the areas that you need work in so that you could advance? Talk about the current responsibilities that give you the most satisfaction. Another smart move (and one that will score you points in the motivation department) is to talk about the possibility of advancement. Again, make sure your goals are realistic. Talk about the career path you are heading down and how the sharpening of certain skills can help you attain your goals.

Q: How do you explain your success in the workplace?

✘ **YES:** In this age of technology, human contact is an underrated thing. I know how frustrated I get when I call a company and am met with a barrage of computer voices telling me which number to hit and whom to call. In business, I never assume that a customer is satisfied until he or she has told me so directly. That said, I take a very personal approach to following up with every customer. The feedback that I have received—both positive and negative—has provided valuable insight into the quality and characteristics of our products. What augments my

Insider Tips

Clichés in the Job Market

Just like within a particular industry itself, there are plenty of catch phrases that get thrown around in the search for a new job. Just like clichés in everyday language, these are words and phrases that an employer can certainly do without. But how can you avoid using clichés or obvious comparisons if you don't even know what they are? The following list represents the most commonly heard clichés among personnel professionals:

- I am a people person.
- I am a jack of all trades.
- I wear many hats.
- I am interested in honing my skills.
- I am a multitask-oriented kind of person.

Insider Tips

Chatterboxes Need Not Apply

One of the most difficult parts of the interview is trying to figure out how much of an answer the interviewer wants. Will a quick yes or no do, or are they expecting you to retrace all of your achievements, starting with your first birthday?

It is not at all wrong to ask the interviewer this question. If you're really unsure of how detailed an answer they are seeking, just ask!

past successes even more is how much the customer appreciates these follow-ups, especially when there's been some sort of problem and you still have the opportunity to correct it on a timely basis. And the customer feedback doesn't just benefit me; I'm always passing on customer comments to our production and design teams so that we can ensure we are making the best possible product.

✗ NO: I think that I have been lucky enough to have several managers who recognize true genius when they see it. I have contributed to much of the success of my last ten companies, and I'm sure any one of them would take me back as an employee in a matter of seconds.

Again, the key to answering such personal questions is to be honest, but not arrogant. You should not be embarrassed to toot your own horn a little. If you've accomplished something in the workplace (or anywhere else), don't be afraid to talk about it. But rather than discuss how great you are ("I'm an excellent employee; really—ask anyone who knows me"), you have to show the interviewer. Discuss the steps you've taken to ensure that you are considered a worthwhile employee, and mention that little bit extra that you do. Talk about observations other people have made about your strengths or talents. This question is similar to the question, What sets you apart from the crowd?

Q: How well do you write?

✔ YES: I would say that my writing skills are above average. I made a very conscious effort to develop these skills while I was working towards my MBA. I even took an entrepreneurial class in which the chief assignment was to develop, write, and continually rewrite a business plan. I have brought it along if you would like to see it.

✗ NO: I am a horrible speller, and I have a bit of trouble with correct grammar. But I always use spell check, and I would definitely hand my work over to someone else before sending it out.

A great way to prepare for an interview is to overprepare. If you anticipate a question such as this one, bring along a sample of your

work. For more creative positions (photographer, graphic artists, etc.), always be sure to pack your portfolio so that the interviewer can see your work and assess your talent for himself or herself. Even if the job you are applying for is not creative in nature, there may be some writing involved. A sharp set of writing skills is always a great asset.

Q: Could you tell me a little bit about your computer skills?

✔ **YES:** I would consider myself very well versed when it comes to computers. In my current position, I tend to use a PC with office software such as Microsoft Word, WordPerfect, Lotus 1-2-3, and Excel. I am also familiar with various graphic design programs including Quark, Photoshop, and Adobe Illustrator. I have some experience with Macintosh systems as well. I am a pro when it comes to navigating the Internet and have even picked up a bit of knowledge as far as HTML programming goes.

✘ **NO:** I try to avoid having to learn new technologies. If I have to write something, I take out my trusty old pen and paper or use a typewriter.

Computer literacy is a must in today's job market, no matter what the position. A working knowledge of a word processing program such as Microsoft Word is essential, and familiarity with database management or graphics programs is valuable as well. If your computer experience is rather limited, talk to a friend who has a computer or visit the local library and try to find your way around some of the most basic word processing programs. These programs are simple to learn and will allow you to avoid having to say that you have no computer skills. As the Internet is playing an increasingly important part in the day-to-day business of just about every company, familiarity with the Internet—and possibly some of its programming languages—is a much desired skill. While most companies use PC-compatible computers, many business in more creative fields such as publishing or advertising, use Macintosh computers. If you're interviewing in one of those fields, you might find it helpful to familiarize yourself with Macs.

Job Compatibility

One of the easiest ways to eliminate yourself from the running for *any* job is by not researching the position properly. Before you apply for a job (and certainly before you interview for one), you should be well aware of the job requirements. If long hours and lots of travel are not what you are looking for, perhaps that seemingly great sales position is not for you. During the job interview, the employer will be testing you to see just how compatible you are with the position you are applying for. Make sure that when asked about qualifications that relate to the job, you are answering in a way that shows you're the right person for the position.

Q: What are the most rewarding aspects of your current job?

✔ **YES:** I would have to say that the most rewarding part of my job as a career counselor is knowing that I have made a difference in somebody's life. I know that in some way I have helped that person to become happy. I try and keep in touch on at least a monthly basis with all of the people I have counseled and worked with. Hearing the stories about their successes, their promotions, and everything else positive in their life is the best reward I could get.

✘ **NO:** There's no doubt in my mind that the paycheck is the most rewarding part of my job. With the salary I receive, I have been able to buy a gorgeous house, an oceanfront summer home, and an all-leather luxury car, and all of my kids have gone to great schools.

When an interviewer asks about a "reward," he or she is interested in knowing—on the most intimate level—why you continue to do this job. Monetary compensation, discounts, and other company benefits should never factor into your answer here. You need to reveal the reason why you chose this profession and why you intend to stick with it. Talk about your passion for your job and what keeps you motivated. Make sure that these "rewards" can also be obtained in this new position. Conclude by focusing on the new experiences you are seeking in your career.

Q: What do you see as some of the limitations of your current job?

✔ **YES:** I think that the main limitations in my current job really exist in the industry overall. It's simply not in a strong growth mode. That's really the main reason I have become so skilled in defensive marketing. Retaining our current customers is the key to having an edge over the competition. By introducing various customer satisfaction programs and other such promotions, I think I have helped to counter this limitation a bit. Though the industry isn't seeing much growth as a whole, my current company is becoming stronger.

✗ **NO:** As an aspiring actor, being a marketing assistant just isn't helping my career.

Answer this question—briefly—with one or two areas in which or reasons why you think your current job is hindering you. Though it's been said before, remember that you should always remain positive. Don't bad-mouth your company or your coworkers. Most importantly, make sure that the growth you say you are looking for would be available in this position. Even if it would not be immediate, figure out whether taking this job would allow you the growth you desire or whether you'd be conducting the exact same interview in another year or so.

Q: What are you hoping to achieve in your next job?

✔ **YES:** I am looking for the opportunity to try marketing a service as opposed to a product. Since graduating from college, I have held two different jobs in marketing. In each of these positions, it was my responsibility to market the products the company manufactured. While I have enjoyed this very much, I am looking for a little more of a challenge. Marketing a service involves a whole different thought process, and it's something that I am looking forward to exploring.

✗ **NO:** I am looking forward to achieving financial independence. The company I work for now is rather small, so even their highest officers aren't paid as much as middle management in a corporation as large as yours.

In this question, the interviewer expects you to express your inside passion for a job. He or she wants to see that the goals you are setting for yourself illustrate a willingness to achieve greater things, and a passion and dedication to your job. Make sure that your answer is realistic as far as time and experience goes. If this is only your first or second job since graduating from college, you may not want to talk about your desire to run the company. Discuss the reasons that led you to apply for this position and how they relate to your idea of the perfect job. Also make sure that the goals you cite as hoping to achieve will be made available to you in this position.

Q: What would your ideal job be like?

✔ **YES:** No matter what happens, I'd like to stay in a position in which training is the main part of my job. I had always thought about being a teacher, but I knew that I was too interested in business to teach as a full-time job. By training new employees, I am being given the opportunity to use my business skills and educate others. While I would definitely strive to climb the ladder in my career, I would never want to stray too far from what I am doing right now.

✗ **NO:** I would be the world's biggest rock star!

Though many people may be tempted to talk about their fantasy job ("I would be the King of England"), this question isn't really about make-believe. The interviewer is trying to gauge a bit about your personality and the kind of job that you would be most happy in. While you don't want to be too obsequious and say something along the lines of "Exactly the job I'm applying for!" you also don't want to stray too far from your career path. If you're ideal job is not within the actual industry you are applying to, think of a way in which these two industries (or jobs) can be connected. For example, if you're starting out as a salesperson, it would be okay to talk about how you would like to one day become involved in marketing. Since

these two functions really go hand in hand (it's sometimes difficult to differentiate the two), you can draw various parallels as to how you would get there.

Again, it is always important to keep the idea of the career path in mind. Will this position get you where you want to go? How? How will you go about doing that? Remember that it is important to always keep your professional goals in mind.

> **Q: If you had unlimited time and financial resources, what would you do?**

✔ **YES:** I'd love to be able to use the time and money to go back to school or partake in various seminars. As international business has always been an interest of mine, I would like to travel the world and learn the ways that business differs from country to country. Of course, having this time to travel, I would try and see as much of the world as possible, but I think that all of my travels would be an exercise in business education.

✗ **NO:** If I had unlimited financial resources, you certainly wouldn't see me here. The first thing I would do is quit my job! My daily task of lying on the couch watching soap operas and cartoons would only be interrupted by my jaunts around town in my brand new Ferrari.

Again, this is one of those questions when the interviewee may forget that he or she are in the midst of a professional meeting, not at home playing "What if . . ." with the kids. When giving an answer, be sure to stick to work-related pursuits or to educational efforts that could be used to help you in your job. Again, think of ideal jobs or activities that are related to the job at hand. If you are applying for a teaching job, for example, you might want to talk about how you would become a volunteer for an adult literacy program. Though it is not exactly teaching, it demonstrates a passion for your field, even when the paycheck factor is taken away.

Job Search Odds and Ends

Top Five Ways to Tell That You Didn't Get the Job

1. The recruiter ends the interview by saying, "Don't call us and we won't call you."
2. The recruiter hands back your resume and says, "We won't be needing this."
3. The recruiter leaves the room during your "I am the smartest person in the world" speech.
4. The recruiter brings in a janitor as a substitute for the second part of your interview.
5. The recruiter falls asleep during the interview.

Q: After learning more about this job, which aspect interests you most?

✔ **YES:** I'm particularly interested in your recent joint ventures with two processing companies in Latin America. My father was an army officer, so we lived in Latin America for three years. I am very interested in seeing what happens with these agreements. What are your plans for the next few years?

✘ **NO:** There's really no one aspect of the job that interests me. The whole thing sounds intriguing.

In the section regarding your motivation, the interviewer asks a very similar question: What particular aspect of the company interests you most? Essentially, there is no real difference between these questions except the way that they are worded. In the aforementioned question, you are being asked to talk directly about the company in an effort to prove that you have done your research. In this instance, you should feel free to talk about the company—as that is something you'd be inheriting with the position—or about the position itself. Describe your qualifications for the job and how well the job fits your natural skills and abilities. Give evidence that you've performed well in similar work. What proof can you offer that you'll excel in this job? The best answer to this question would address both the company and the position. More specifically, it would focus on what you could do for the company in the position at hand. If you've researched the company properly, you should have no problem answering this question quickly and authoritatively.

Q: After learning more about this job, which aspect interests you least?

✔ **YES:** In my last position, I was able to find more success by spending time on my major accounts rather than scheduling one-on-one interviews with smaller accounts. Though every salesperson has his or her preference, I think that this is really where my strength lies. In my time there, I was able to increase

my key account business by 20 percent. I would like to be able to continue with this personal style within your company to obtain even better results.

✗ NO: I know that you had mentioned something about occasional overtime and some weekend work being a possibility. While this is not a real problem per se, the idea of spending my weekend in a cubicle instead of at my beach house or in front of the tube watching football is a little disheartening.

This is another one of those questions that job seekers hate to be asked. Forcing you to talk about a potentially negative aspect of the job can be a little intimidating, especially when you're trying to impress this person. One way to kind of skirt the issue is to talk about a situation in your current position that you find to be a negative aspect and find out whether this job would have a similar downside. Another way to counter this question is to ask why the last person left the job? Respond to the interviewer's answer and then go on to discuss what you see as the positive points of this job, even if you've done so before.

Q: What aspects of this job do you feel most confident about?

✔ YES: As the companies I have worked with in the past have been engaged in the manufacture of very similar products, I feel that I will be able to fully integrate myself in no time at all. With a strong knowledge of your company's products, I think that I will be able to jump right in with lots of creative and fresh ideas and translate my past success to your company.

✗ NO: I think that I have very strong people skills, and I am confident that everyone in your company will love me in no time at all. After only a week with my current employer, I began dating my supervisor!

Make sure that when answering this question, you are selling the skills that you have that relate to this job—and not just selling yourself! The interviewer probably already has a good sense of your personality and you as a person; this is a chance to plug

More Support
for Inline Text

If you're still not convinced that pasting your resume within the body of the e-mail is a good idea, consider this comment from one hiring manager: "Sending your resume as an attachment is an invitation for rejection. Aside from viruses and all the other technical problems associated with attachments, the receptionist tends to judge a candidate's suitability upon his or her cover letter. If the cover letter is not a dynamic and persuasive piece of writing, it's not likely the resume will be opened at all."

your applicable skills and how they relate to the position at hand. Talk about your skills in relation to the larger scope of things: that is, how they relate to this job, this company, and the industry.

Q: What concerns you most about performing this job?

✔ **YES:** As my past experiences relate directly to this position, I am confident that I could perform the job well. Other than that I have never been the key manager of a department, I am a little concerned as to whether or not there will be a large enough customer service network. As one of the key points of this company is a 24-hour service line, I just want to be sure that there are always enough people here to answer the phones.

✘ **NO:** Though many of my past duties have been similar to those required in this job, I have never done this job exactly. I guess my main concern right now is that I will be a failure.

Even if the job you are interviewing for will bring about many brand-new responsibilities and is not something you have much experience with, you always want to project an air of the greatest confidence. One way you can answer this question is to turn it around and say, "Nothing that you have mentioned so far concerns me. I am fairly confident that I could perform the job really well. Are there any aspects of this job that you are concerned with me performing?" If the interviewer comes back with a few questions, respond with the same confidence in your abilities. Address each one of the recruiter's concerns and make him or her sure that your interests are compatible with the position. Offer proof that will dispel any doubts the interviewer may have.

Q: Which of your skills do you think is most relevant to this job?

✔ **YES:** I think that my past experiences—as far as both my education and work history are concerned—are what make me well suited to this position. I have spent the past five years at a company that produces very similar products, and my business

degree only helps to augment the success and experiences I
have found in the workplace.

✗ **NO:** As the president of my high school's student government
association, I think that I would make a great manager in your
company. I know how to be diplomatic, and I know how to make
people like me. Also, that stint taught me a lot about politics.

Yes, the interviewer is interested in learning all about you, but
delving too far into your past shows a lack of achievement—or
confidence—in your more recent endeavors. Though you may be
tempted to recap your entire employment history, the interviewer
is likely looking for one reason why you think you would be a
good match for this job. Your answer should be similar to your
prepared response to the question, What interests you most
about this job? Use examples to back up the most relevant infor-
mation from your resume.

Q: In your last job, how did the realities you experienced differ from your initial expectations?

✔ **YES:** The hardest thing to foresee in my last job was how my
market research department would be viewed by other depart-
ments within the company. Apparently, because there had been
so many incompetent employees in the past, many of the other
departments contracted outside companies and organizations to
do market research for them. While I made several attempts to
try and help the reputation of my department, it was to no avail.
Working at a job in which it seems like no one respects the
work you do can be very frustrating. That is what led me to
apply for this position.

✗ **NO:** During my interview, the recruiter had talked about the need
for more competent managers within the company and how by
being hired I would be on the fast track to a career in manage-
ment. After nearly six months there, I had not heard a word
about a promotion or any management position opening up. I
just always assumed that the "fast track" would not take so long.

This question is specifically geared at judging whether or not your ideas about the job—and your abilities—are realistic. Do you expect too much too fast? If you were not given opportunities in your past position that you thought would be offered to you (a promotion perhaps, or even specific tasks to be performed), is this a reflection on your work? Another aim of this question is for the recruiter to ensure that any past disenchantment will not be repeated in this job or with this company.

Q: If you were hired for this position, there would be some travel involved. Would this cause a problem for you?

✔ **YES:** When given proper notice, I can arrange to travel at almost any time of year. In my current job, I usually travel about once a month. It's really one of my favorite aspects about this kind of career.

✗ **NO:** As I have a family to consider, I do prefer to let other people do the traveling. If given enough notice, I can usually manage to travel at least once a year, though.

A question like this should be obvious to you. In certain careers—a job in sales, for example—travel is one aspect you should anticipate. Your response to this question should be consistent with the demands of the job. If you travel frequently for your current job, let the interviewer know how often. If you were unaware of the travel aspect—and are not happy about doing it— let the interviewer know now. Telling the interviewer you have no problem with travel but then shirking your travel times when they come is unethical and misleading. It's possible that, by telling the interviewer you are reluctant to travel, you will lose the opportunity, but this is obviously a position you are not well suited for.

Q: Why is this a particularly good job for someone with your qualifications?

✔ **YES:** Based on what you've told me about the last person who held—and excelled in—this job, I believe we share many

similarities and, therefore, am confident that I would do a great job. We seem to have the same educational qualifications and similar work experience. I also think that I would work well with your audit team. I come from a similar kind of environment and know exactly what a client can do to make the consulting relationship more productive.

✗ NO: I think that my resume really speaks for itself.

The key to answering this question is to draw upon experiences from your current or former job and talk about the positive experiences you have had. If you know anything about the success and background of the person who formerly held this position, that's also a great way to prove that you are a great match for the job. Being too specific can be detrimental to this question, as it indicates that you may not quite understand what this position is all about.

Q: In what type of work setting do you feel you are the most productive?

✔ YES: The best way that I have found to keep on top of things is to have an hour of uninterrupted time in the morning. As much as I can, I try to get into work an hour or so early and take the time to plan out my day. As far as the rest of the office goes, I like to be in an environment where everyone listens to one another. I like to hear everybody's input and feedback and to feel a real sense of community within the office. From my past experiences, I think I feel better working tirelessly when I can see that everyone else is busy too. It lets me know that we're all working together to reach the same end.

✗ NO: I prefer to work in an environment where there isn't someone looking over my shoulder every second, questioning what I'm doing, and making suggestions.

The interviewer is trying to determine the effect your working environment has on your work. If the office is a little busy, are you going to be distracted or have trouble concentrating? Will your job performance suffer as a result of this company's work

**Job Search
Odds and Ends**

If Your Skills Aren't Appropriate . . .

If it looks as though your skills and background don't match the position the interviewer was hoping to fill, ask him or her if another division or subsidiary could perhaps profit from your talents.

environment? How well do your needs fit in with the position, the layout of the department, and the particular work group you'd be assigned to? The best way to answer this question is to emphasize your ability to work in a variety of settings; talk about how you've succeeded in various environments, including those that were less than ideal. Make sure that you are describing the environment at the company that is interviewing you. And don't give the interviewer reason to become suspicious about why you prefer a certain working environment. For example, if you say you don't like someone looking over your shoulder, the interviewer might suspect that you have a problem with authority.

> **Q: When it comes to the structure of your typical work day, do you prefer continuity or frequent change?**

✔ **YES:** I enjoy change and challenge, which is why I frequently ask for the tough assignments. For example, I asked for the last two projects we discussed. I don't allow myself to get bored.

✘ **NO:** It doesn't matter to me. Whenever I find myself bored with my job, I usually take a couple days off to recharge.

Your response to this question should be in accordance with the job description. Will you be forced to switch gears several times throughout the day? If so, talk about your ability to accept frequent change. Your answer should be consistent with the job description. Describe environments that have allowed you to remain interested and learn new things without getting bored.

Culture Compatibility

In addition to being compatible with the duties of a particular job, employers want to make sure that you will be comfortable in the job *environment*. If you comment that you don't like working for a large corporation, chances are that Microsoft will not come knocking at

your door. In addition to researching the qualifications of a particular job title, you should be sure to research the particular company to which you are applying. That way, when the interviewer asks you a question specifically to find out whether or not you'd adapt well to the company environment, you'll know how to answer.

Q: What would your friends tell me about you?

✔ **YES:** My friends would probably tell you about my energy and enthusiasm. I spend more time at work than any of them, yet I see more of my friends than any of them as well. I guess I just really believe in doing things with gusto.

✗ **NO:** My friends would probably tell you that I am a little bit on the shy side. They make a joke out of the fact that when making plans, I always just go along with the crowd.

The interviewer is trying to get a better sense of your personality. How do you act when you're not at work (or not in the midst of an interview)? He or she is interested in the parts of your personality that will naturally be revealed in time. Make sure that the personality traits you reveal are ones that would be looked upon favorably by the company.

Q: Tell me about your relationship with your current and past supervisors.

✔ **YES:** I have been fortunate enough to have had a lot of great supervisors in my past. They have all been extremely intelligent and talented people. The lessons I have learned thus far in the workplace have been mainly from these people. I think that in many respects I have become the favorite sounding board for my past supervisors. Though the obvious balance of wisdom and expertise was theirs, I believe that I was always helpful to them in their decisions about customer problems.

✗ **NO:** In both of my past two positions, my supervisor has been my reason for leaving.

The interviewer is trying to get a sense of your personality as it relates to that of your prospective supervisor. Would the two of you get along well in the workplace, or would you be at each other's throats? Talking about past bosses gives the interviewer a good idea as to how you work and makes him or her aware of any potential problems that may arise. Remember to avoid being negative. Be honest, but do not slander your previous supervisors. If you have had an occasion where you and your previous supervisor did not get along, try and put a positive spin on it. What did you learn about yourself by finding out what kind of boss you didn't work well with? What does this say about your attitude in the workplace and preferred working environment? End your response by emphasizing the type of boss you work well with, as it's always better to go out on a positive note.

Q: Tell me about your past relationships with coworkers.

✔ **YES:** I have never had a problem with any of my coworkers. As I am sure any of them would tell you, nothing ever seems to set me back too much. That trait came in really handy in cases where they were experiencing problems and needed someone to advise them. By helping to come up with a solution, quickly and calmly, I have always been willing to pitch in wherever I can. If you asked them which two words described me best, they'd probably say constant and dependable.

✘ **NO:** I have been lucky enough to establish immediate friendships with virtually every coworker in my past. If we're not meeting up for dinner or drinks after work, we're spending half the day catching everyone up on what is going on in our lives. I swear, it sometimes takes me at least a half hour to get to my desk in the morning. I have to stop and say so many hellos.

Here's another one of those questions that require careful consideration. On the one hand, you want to prove to the interviewer that you can easily mix in with different types of people. On the other hand, you don't want the employer to think that you'll spend half the day chatting away with your chums. Speak specifically of

your working relationships with your coworkers. How well have you worked together? What kinds of things have you done to create a real camaraderie in the office? What types of people do you enjoy working with? In answering this question, you are letting the interviewer know how you'll get along with not only their current employees but also their customers. The interviewer wants to be confident that any surprises about your work personality have been uncovered.

Q: Talk about a work environment that you think would be ineffective for you.

✔ **YES:** The one thing I have trouble with is when there is no room for communication or feedback. In the past, I have been in situations where I was assigned a project and told exactly how to accomplish it. While I am always open to other people's suggestions, I need to be able to infuse my work with my own personal and professional style. In any project, there needs to be the latitude to make adjustments, and that is definitely something I look for in order to be an effective worker.

✘ **NO:** I wouldn't like to be in a work environment in which everyone is always serious. I know that I definitely need a little humor throughout the day to keep me going. How about you?

Rather than go on and on about the negative situations you don't want to see yourself in, focus on the environments in which you can be effective, and explain why. Make sure that your answer reflects something of a professional nature. Focusing too much on your personal needs throughout the workday (your desire to make friends rather than work hard) only shows the interviewer that you have a difficult time separating your work life from your personal life.

Q: What situations excite and motivate you?

✔ **YES:** I really enjoy being able to work on a project all the way through. I like being involved from the initial idea conception and

Strange but True

Interview Questions

"Tell me the funniest joke you've heard recently."

brainstorming phase all the way through to the completed project. Knowing that I was able to see a project all the way through and then look at the tangible results is really an exciting thing for me.

✗ **NO:** I am a big fan of company award programs. I think that knowing there could be a bonus, a gift certificate, or some other little prize at the end of a long and tumultuous project is enough to keep me going strong.

Make sure that you answer this question in a way that reveals the kind of work that inspires you. Far too many people bring monetary or other selfish rewards into this question. Talk about what motivates you to keep going. Why do you work in this job, or even this industry? Talk about your passion for your work. Remember that the answer you give should be compatible with the type of work you'll be asked to perform.

Q: How do you think your last employer would describe your work habits and work ethic?

✔ **YES:** At my last job, I was awarded a sort of MVP award at the end of the year for all the extra efforts I put into one of our major accounts. Earlier in the year, that same company was so angry with a situation that had arisen that they threatened to pull their account entirely. Upon hearing this, I quickly stepped in and took care of the problem, even though it required me to work through a holiday weekend.

✗ **NO:** I think that they would tell you they were just about the same as those of everyone else on staff.

The interviewer wants to hear that in hiring you they're hiring a future star of the company. Knowing that you went above and beyond the call of duty in your current position, or in a past job, assures the interviewer that you will work hard here as well. It indicates a strong work ethic and dedication to your job. Be sure to give examples of your reliability, dedication, and corporate loyalty. Make sure to exude confidence without cockiness.

Q: How well do you work with your current clients or customers?

✔ **YES:** Since I started at my current employer more than three years ago, my client base has changed very little. Sales have increased tremendously, which was my main goal, and I have acquired new clients—mainly through recommendations from other clients—but I have been lucky enough to work with the same clients for several years now. And I have fantastic relationships with all of my clients; we keep in touch on a fairly regular basis, so I have really been able to get to know these clients as people more than business contacts, which is a great feeling.

✘ **NO:** I have never had any major problems with any of my clients. But because they are constantly changing, I have never forged any really strong relationships.

This question is quite revealing when it comes to your interpersonal skills. Though you may not realize it, your customers' reactions to you can have a big impact on how you are perceived professionally. Though you've never had a problem with any of your customers, why aren't they coming back for more service? Be careful to think about this question before answering. If you have maintained close working relationships with several of your clients or customers, consider listing one of them as a professional contact. It's a great way to show a new company how easy you are to work with and how concerned you are with great service.

Q: Whom did you choose as your professional references, and why?

✔ **YES:** The three references listed include my current supervisor, a coworker, and one of my key customers. I chose these three people so that you could really gain a well-rounded perspective as to who I am, professionally. By choosing these three references, you're learning how I am perceived in each arena of my professional life.

✘ **NO:** I chose to list a former coworker, one of the customers who frequented the bar I worked at in college, and an old high school buddy of mine. I figured that this would give you a great deal of insight as to who I am as a person, both at work and in my personal life.

Collecting References

Prepare a list of three to five references. Unless you are new to the work force, at least two of these should be professional references from previous employers or close business associates. Other potential reference sources include teachers, professors, volunteer committee heads, and friends who are well respected in business circles. Don't list family members as references.

Family members and friends do not make great references. However, there are plenty of people who would make great and logical choices to serve as professional references for you. Consider, for example, former or current supervisors, former or current coworkers, professors, customers or clients you have dealt with extensively. Also, remember to describe what you'd expect each of them to say about you.

Q: Is it okay that we call all of your references?

✔ **YES:** Absolutely! Though I'd prefer that you hold off on contacting my current boss until I have been made a firm offer. I certainly understand your need to verify the accuracy of my employment, but I just want to be the first to tell her if I am leaving.

✘ **NO:** Though I put my current boss on that list, I'd actually prefer that you didn't call her.

This is one question that is designed to protect you and your current work situation. If you hand over a list of references and the interviewer does not ask whether or not it is okay to contact everyone on the list, be sure to volunteer this information. One of the worst things that could happen would be for a future employer to contact an unsuspecting current boss. Interviewers understand what a touchy subject this can be and should not question you if you request that they wait to contact your current supervisor.

Q: Tell me something you learned from reading a recent book.

✔ **YES:** When it comes to choosing reading material, I really enjoy reading biographies. I especially enjoy reading the biographies of people who lived in a different era. Recently, I was able to read Martin Gilbert's biography of Winston Churchill. I was really amazed at what I learned from reading about this man. He taught me the value of strong leadership skills as well as having a good rapport with the public and those around you in times of stress and uncertainty. These are certainly lessons that I want to incorporate into my own life.

✘ **NO:** I am a big fan of biographies, and I was recently able to read Kitty Kelley's account of Frank Sinatra's life, *His Way*. If I hadn't

been in awe of this cultural icon before, I certainly am now. He's a prime example of a man who really knew how to get what he wanted in life, no matter what the cost. It's that kind of determination and courage that I admire.

Though this question is geared toward your personal life (it asks about something you've read in your free time), it can be very indicative of your work performance. Learning about your outside interests is a great way for an interviewer to decide how well you will fit in with this new environment. One of the best ways to answer this question is to use a classic piece of literature that the interviewer can relate to or a biography you have recently read.

Q: Tell me about a time when you had to drop what you were doing to help a coworker.

✔ **YES:** I think it would be safe to say that in my current position, assisting a coworker is pretty much a daily occurrence. Throughout the week, we all have various questions and projects that we need help with, and there is always someone who is willing and able to put his or her own work on hold to do it. Just this week, I assisted a coworker in preparing our latest catalog to be sent to the printer. As any sort of spelling or item number mistake could really hurt sales, it's important that you have someone else take a close second look. It's comforting to know that you are working with such a great network of people; you know that if and when you have a problem, there will be someone to lend a hand.

✘ **NO:** Though I had dinner plans of my own, I agreed to take a coworker's cousin out to dinner the other night. She was visiting from out of town, and he had already made plans, so I agreed to help him. I really like having such a strong network of people to count on at work.

Talk about your unselfish willingness to pitch in. Do you understand the importance of helping others, even if you have your own work to do? Showing that you enjoy being part of a team, even if you tend to work independently, shows the interviewer your commitment to

your job as well as a respect for those you work with. Demonstrate your ability to understand that what is good for one worker can be good for the entire workplace.

Q: Do you prefer working alone or in a group?

✔ **YES:** I think that a logical mix of both is necessary to complete a project to the best of your abilities. I definitely like to have a little private time so that I can plan my course of action, or make a schedule, but I also like to have lots of activity taking place around me. I like to engage in brainstorming sessions; I enjoy being able to share my ideas and see what everyone else is thinking. No one person has all the answers. At some point, you need to work with others to figure out the best way to accomplish a goal.

✘ **NO:** I definitely prefer working in a group. In the past, when I have been given independent projects, I have really struggled to complete them on my own. I am much more confident in my own work when I am given a direct assignment from someone in a higher position.

There are two goals in answering this question: to be honest but to seem flexible. If you prefer working alone, tell this person. If you're better working in a group, let them know that as well. The key is to let your preference be known, but also to communicate that you are a flexible person who has no problem adapting to various environments. It might be a smart idea to figure out what the typical work style is for the position you're applying for and to demonstrate your desire to work that way.

Q: Tell me about a situation in which you found it difficult to remain objective.

✔ **YES:** I was given a project in which part of the assignment involved contacting various professionals within the computer field and interviewing them about certain trends they thought would occur, and their predictions for the future. After several weeks of playing phone tag, talking to industry professionals, and composing my final report, my

boss decided to cancel the project. While I certainly understand the need to revise budgets and schedules, I just found it frustrating that I had become so excited about a project and worked so hard at it, only to have it pulled once I was satisfied.

☒ NO: The manager of my department had given his two weeks' notice, and the search to replace him became sort of a race between me and the other senior workers in the department. Though I had been with the company the least amount of time and had not been schooled as extensively, I felt that I was certainly the most qualified as far as my character went. I have never really gotten over the fact that the job went to someone else.

The best way to answer this question is to think of a time when you put a lot of thought and energy into something, only to see the project canceled at a later time. Another way to answer this question would be to think of a time when you found that a project you had worked on was less strategically sound than you'd hoped. In concluding your response, be sure to demonstrate that—although you were frustrated—you were able to readjust your thinking and understand why the project had to be canceled.

Interpersonal Skills

All the education and skills in the world will not make you a great communicator. One of the most important skills an employee can have is the ability to communicate well with coworkers, whether they be assistants under that employee or the big cheese of the company. A popular way for employers to find out about your interpersonal skills is to ask about former and current bosses. Regardless of your personal feelings toward your bosses past and present, be sure you think about their management *style* and incorporate that into your answer. Figure out what traits (e.g., good listener, willingness to help) your dream boss would possess and which characteristics (e.g., never around, not interested in new ideas) you could do without.

Insider Tips

Don't Catch Your References Off Guard

You'll most likely be asked for references when applying for a new job. After compiling a careful list of references—who you are sure will say only positive things of you—be sure to let them know that a potential employer may be calling. Give each reference a call and let him or her know the type of position you are applying for and what the skills involved would be. You might even want to send along a copy of your resume and cover letter so that the reference has a better idea of the kind of characteristics they should emphasize.

Q: Tell me about an effective manager you have known.

✔ **YES:** The best supervisor I ever had was the person who led my training group when I was first starting out in the business. We spent two weeks going through an intensive training program in which we learned various sales techniques, industry jargon, and business concepts. This person would really watch our faces as he taught us something new. When he saw that we looked a little confused, he would ask what we were having difficulty understanding. Before moving onto the next topic, he would make sure that everyone in the group fully understood the previous one. He never assumed too much when teaching us new things, and he never made us feel dumb for not grasping an idea quickly.

✘ **NO:** The best manager I ever had was at a part-time job I held during college. Since he had just graduated from college himself, he was always very understanding when we wanted to take off early or have a few days off. In fact, he made it a policy that if you wanted to leave early to get to a party or some other social function, you could do it as long as you invited him along.

Sometimes our favorite supervisors are the ones that we can really pal around with. While everyone would like it if his or her best buddy were in charge, an irresponsible manager—and your affection toward him or her—will not impress an interviewer. When you discuss a supervisor you respected, make sure that you are taking that person's business savvy into account, and his or her ability to manage people. Talk about his or her interpersonal skills, and why you respected his or her style of management. How was the person able to accomplish so much and get your support in the process?

Q: What type of management style do you think is the most effective?

✔ **YES:** I've always learned well from people who act as coaches rather than experts. When someone comes to me with a

problem, I try to act as if I'm reasoning through the problem with the person, learning as I go. I never just give an answer. I want employees to develop confidence in creating answers for themselves.

✗ NO: I like a manager who doesn't continually remind you that he or she is your superior. I respect the kind of person who leaves you alone and lets you get on with your own work.

This question is very similar to the previous one, "Tell me about an effective manager you have known." That said, it can be answered in very much the same way. Rather than give a particular example of the manager or leader you've admired most, talk about the attributes that person possessed. You can even add a personal or popular example of someone who you think is an effective leader. If you can, let the question lead to your own management style; talk about the things that you have learned from these leaders and how you try and incorporate them into your own managing persona.

Q: How would you describe your own personal management style?

✔ YES: Rather than tell someone what to do or answer a question directly, I try to encourage my employees to help find the solution. For example, if someone asks me a question about how to proceed on a project or task, I will prompt them to tell me what they think we should do. In addition to questions, I want to hear solutions. I like being able to lead my team, but I want to know that they are working to help solve problems as well. I like to think that by involving everyone in questions and problems that arise in the department, I am teaching them how to be an effective leader.

✗ NO: I'm explicit in my directions. I tell my staff what needs to get done, how to do it, and when to finish. The work is up to them.

Talk about your management style and interpersonal skills with your staff. Do you allow them to be creative, or are you a

Job Search
Odds and Ends

Top Five Interview Misdemeanors

1. Forgetting to bring extra copies of your resume and references
2. Wearing jeans to the interview
3. Not knowing the name of the person with whom you are interviewing
4. Arriving late
5. Using foul language

take-charge sort of person? Think about how your staff, or those you've managed in the past, views you. Describe a particular skill you've learned from a leader you admire, and how you try and incorporate that into your own management style. Be careful that you portray yourself as a fair leader, and not as a tyrant.

Q: What type of people do you work with most effectively?

✔ **YES:** My favorite type of coworker is someone who is not afraid to voice his or her opinion. I love to work with people who are creative, and willing to brainstorm ideas before deciding upon a particular solution. Confidence is always important as well.

✗ **NO:** I like working with people who are confident in their work and who show a lot of pride. I can't stand working with people who leave all the answers up to someone else . . . you know . . . those people who do what they are told but never volunteer any of their own opinions. I really hate working with those kinds of people.

The key here—and in every question, really—is to remain positive. Far too many people answer this question in a way that fails to highlight the positive points they like in their coworkers; instead they drone on and on about the things they hate. A negative attitude is never in a job description, and it's certainly not something you should convey—either intentionally or unintentionally—during an interview. Make sure that the characteristics you are describing are something that this company would approve of. For example, if you are a bit of a chatterbox, you might love to have a few other talkative people in your department, but this is not the type of thing you should mention in your interview. Always remember that the interviewer is interested in how well you will fit in with the company's other employees, not how well they'll fit in with you.

Q: Is there anything that your current supervisor does that you really dislike?

✔ **YES:** The one thing that really makes me uncomfortable is when my supervisor gives feedback in front of others. Whether the feedback is

positive or negative, I just think it is more appropriate for any commendation or criticism of one's work to be done in private.

✗ NO: I don't like it that my boss always has to have the final say. Even if other people muster up the courage to offer their own opinions, he always goes with the solution he came up with in the meantime.

Though this question obviously targets a negative situation, the goal is to eliminate the negative spin as quickly as possible. Briefly touch upon an issue that has bothered you in the past, but try to describe it as a positive learning experience. And as stated previously, avoid personal criticism of a current or former supervisor, as it may only serve to lessen the interviewer's opinion of you.

Q: What are the steps you take to organize and plan for a major project?

✔ YES: The first step I take in planning any project—no matter how big or small—is to brainstorm the best, worst, and most likely scenarios that could occur. Then I work backwards: I ask, What steps can I take to ensure the most desirable outcome? What can I do to avoid the worst case scenario coming true? I then compose a schedule that allows for a realistic time frame to complete the project. By figuring out all the possible scenarios in the beginning, I find that I am well prepared to deal with any problems that may arise during the project.

✗ NO: Because each project I work on is so different, I plan for each one in a different way. I feel that I work better and more effectively when I take a fresh approach to a project.

Whether or not you approach each project in the same way, it helps to have a similar plan of action that you use time and time again. It is just this sort of planning that shows you have strong time management skills and that you are a real professional. Describe to the interviewer your general approach to mastering new projects. What are the steps you take before you

begin? How do you set a timetable, determine priorities, delegate tasks, and still have enough work left over for yourself?

Q: Tell me about a time when you've had to work under intense pressure.

☑ **YES:** I was working on a strict deadline to complete an end-of-quarter report at the same time that I was on the road working. I did not have all of the files and information in front of me, so there was a lot of calling back and forth. Luckily, my staff really pulled together to help me, and the report turned out great.

☒ **NO:** My boss had gone on a vacation for two weeks, so my department decided that we could take a mini-vacation as well. As the time drew nearer to my supervisor's return, we realized that we had spent so much time talking and doing other non-work-related things, that we had fallen way behind. We had to cram two weeks' worth of working into just two days. It was difficult, but we did manage to pull together, work as a team, and get everything done.

Be sure to concentrate on your time management skills when answering this question. Also be sure that the situation you describe is one you succeeded in. You want to show the interviewer that you are a hard worker who knows how to deal with difficult situations. You also want to assure this person that when faced with these situations, you can easily emerge victorious. Be sure to give a specific example, and give enough detail to communicate both the intensity of the situation and the ease with which you handled it.

Q: How do you manage your time on a typical day?

☑ **YES:** I always reserve the beginning of my day for work with my major accounts. Because these are the accounts with a higher risk and return potential, I like to devote as much time as I need to these people. After I finish servicing all of my accounts, I engage in general correspondence. Internal correspondence is

usually the last thing that I do, unless there is a pressing issue that I think needs immediate attention.

✗ **NO:** I really prefer to let the day handle me. I tend to prioritize duties as they come my way throughout the day. What is my most pressing task one moment could be my least important 10 minutes later. That ever-changing aspect of the job is one of the things I enjoy most.

Again, the interviewer is trying to find evidence of your time management skills. Though the ability to juggle many tasks as they occur is important, the interviewer also wants to know that you attack each and every day with a certain plan in mind. He or she will also want to be sure that you don't give priority to the more exciting work and avoid dull, necessary routines that are important in the long run.

Q: Describe a time when you acted on someone's suggestion.

✔ **YES:** At one point, some of my employees commented that my office hours were inconvenient for them. They suggested that I keep open office hours earlier in the day so that they could find the time to come speak with me when there was something bothering them or something they wished to talk about. I changed the hours and have found a lot more employees dropping by to share feedback with me, which I really appreciate.

✗ **NO:** Each morning, I would arrive to the office about 10 or 15 minutes late. My boss suggested that I start waking up an extra 10 or 15 minutes early in order to get to work on time. I did, and I haven't been late since!

The interviewer wants evidence of your willingness to listen to other people's ideas, and to act on them. Show that you are willing to accept constructive criticism and suggestions and to use them, if you think they could be beneficial. In answering this question, you're also revealing how coworkers feel about you. Have they felt comfortable enough to offer you suggestions in the past? Are you an approachable person? Do coworkers believe that

Strange but True

Interview Questions

"If a movie were made about your life, what actor/actress would be cast to play your character?"

Strange but True

Interview Stories

The following is a true story: One job candidate finally got a call for a job he really, really wanted. Although he was deathly ill with the flu, he accepted a meeting for a final interview on the following day.

Shortly after the interview started, the manager's phone rang, and he excused himself for a few minutes. Our hero sat there waiting in his best suit. Suddenly, the worst happened. He realized he was going to be sick to his stomach. There was no time to get to the bathroom, and he didn't see a trash barrel.

So he got sick into his jacket, folded it up, placed it beneath his chair, and recomposed himself. A few minutes later, the manager returned. And believe it or not, he got the job.

if given a suggestion you'll listen fairly and objectively? When given a suggestion that leads to some sort of improvement, do you give credit where it is due? In answering this question, you want to reassure the interviewer that you are a reasonable and fair person and that you respect the ideas of others.

Q: Tell me about a time when you had to defend an idea to your boss or someone else in an authoritative position.

✔ **YES:** After working for my current employer for just a few months, and getting feedback from many of our West Coast clients, I realized that many of our biggest accounts were not happy with the public relations services we were providing. It seemed that our Manhattan-based PR firm was having difficulty satisfying our West Coast clientele. As West Coast companies make up nearly 80 percent of our business, I approached my boss about changing PR firms. Because we had been using the same firm for nearly 10 years, he was quite reluctant to change. When I showed him the demographic shift in our customer base and had him to speak with several of our clients who had voiced concerns to me in the past, he agreed that we might be better off switching agencies.

✘ **NO:** After talking to many of my company's employees, I found that they were in serious need of some motivation. I went to my boss and suggested that we try to make the workplace a bit more fun by doing things like "Hawaiian Shirt Day." Though my boss and all those above him laughed at these suggestions, I still pursued the idea. In the end, I was never able to convince them that such an event would work, but I was happy that I had tried nonetheless.

The most important thing here is to make sure that you describe a time or situation in which—after defending your idea—you were able to see it through successfully. By explaining such a situation, you are telling the interviewer three important things about yourself: (1) that you have good ideas, (2) that you will fight for what you

believe in, and (3) that those in higher positions respect your opinion and are willing to take a chance on your ideas.

Q: Which aspect of your own management style would you like to change?

✔ **YES:** One thing that I have been working on is not telling people what to do when they ask me a question. Rather than tell them the answer to the question, I like to talk to them and help them work out the problem. This is something I have been working on for a little while, and it's a technique in which I can already see improvement.

✘ **NO:** I would like to be able to control my temper a little bit better. Far too often I find myself yelling at employees who come to me with a small and simple question. It's just that I've usually got so much on my mind that I can't stand to take the time to answer another question. I have been working on this problem, and it's something I am making progress in.

Though this question specifically asks you to bring up a negative point of your personality, it doesn't mean you can't speak in a positive way. One of the best ways to answer this question is to talk about an aspect of your management style that you are already trying to improve. Make sure to point out a characteristic that you wouldn't be embarrassed or afraid to mention otherwise. Rather than focus on the problem at hand, explain the steps you are taking to improve this characteristic, and be sure to give evidence that you're making progress.

Q: Have you ever become defensive around your boss or peers?

✔ **YES:** For several years, the book publisher I worked for had always printed its flyers in a black-and-white, four-page layout. While I understood the need to remain economical, I suggested that we change our format to an all-color, two-page layout. The cost would be about the same, but I strongly felt that the overall

effect would be significant. My boss complained that we couldn't afford to do that, but I assured him that we would pay just about the same amount of money to do it my way. In the end, my boss agreed to try it, and the result was fantastic! Sales generated from our new flyers increased by 30 percent.

✗ NO: I feel like I am always on the defense in my current job. Though one of my main duties is to come up with new and creative ways to sell our products, it seems like my current boss has his own set way of doing things and laughs at any idea that is not his own. On several occasions in the past few months, we have gotten into heated debates about whether or not my ideas would do well. Defending my ideas is just another one of the things that I have come to accept as an everyday thing.

You should describe a situation in which you emerged victorious. Think about a time in which you were passionate about something or convinced that an idea would work and had to work your hardest to sell those around you on the idea. Discuss the ways in which you persuaded those same naysayers to okay the idea. Avoid any discussion of personality clashes, feelings of resentment, or heated exchanges. Tell what the outcome of your persistence was. Be sure to end on a positive note.

Q: Have you patterned your own management style after someone in particular?

✔ YES: If anyone has taught me about this business so far, I would have to say it was my first boss. I began working for him right out of college, and he really taught me everything there was to know about the business. He was extremely organized, articulate, and business savvy. His tremendous interpersonal skills allowed him to deal with people very easily, and I was always impressed by the way people seemed to respect him. Throughout my career, I have tried to adopt many of his traits. I strongly believe in having open lines of communication between employees, and this is the most important lesson he taught me.

✗ NO: Not really.

Here's a great rule to remember when it comes to interviewing: If you can answer the question in five words or less, you better come up with another answer. While it certainly wouldn't be prudent to talk the interviewer's ear off, short answers that don't reveal much of yourself or your background will not be looked upon favorably. You should always be sure to elaborate on what you say. Describe the management style of someone that you know personally. be specific in your answer, and be sure to explain how you have tried to follow this good example.

Q: Describe a leader you admire.

✔ **YES:** I've always admired the way the president of my current company conducts business. He is very down to earth and knows the name of every employee on staff. He is completely approachable and willing to listen to any idea someone may have—whether it's the receptionist that answers the phone or the vice president of finance. His "just another working guy" mentality really helps keep the spirit of teamwork alive.

✗ **NO:** I've always admired the way that Jerry Garcia was able to bring together an entire community of youth and music lovers and keep them together until his untimely death.

You don't have to know the person in order to imitate their style, though it might seem more realistic if you do. Feel free to give personal or popular examples of leaders you believe are effective. Be careful of offending the interviewer and refrain from citing your admiration of controversial leaders, as it could be detrimental to the overall impression you leave. Talk about why you admire this person and why you think he or she is a great leader. What has he or she done to accomplish so much? What are some of the lessons you have learned from this person, and how are you able to incorporate these tactics into your professional life?

> **Q:** What personal characteristics do you think add to your overall effectiveness?

✔ **YES:** I think that I have a strong ability to create deeper relationships with people than business usually allows for. I am able to know more about a client than just the amount of money he or she brings to my company each year. I get to know my clients on a more personal level, and I keep them in mind all the time. If I read an article that I know one of my clients might enjoy, I'll send the clip along. In doing so, I find that my phone calls are returned much more quickly—and happily—than the next person's might be.

✗ **NO:** I think that my strong ability to manipulate others allows me to nudge people in my direction when they might otherwise go another way. I seem to be able to convince them that they need what I have to offer, and this is a talent that has served me well in my sales career.

What is it about your personal style that makes you unique from the other candidates that the interviewer has met with? What traits do you possess that make you more effective? Without sounding cocky or exploitative, talk about why you think you are able to get cooperation from others.

Problem-Solving Ability

When the going gets tough, do you sink or swim? When faced with difficult problems, are you able to offer up solutions on your own, or do you wait for someone else to tell you what to do? The ability to solve problems is a hot commodity in today's job market; employers want workers they can count on to be there in times of need, and to always be thinking about ways to make a company better. To say "I'm a great problem solver" is one thing; to *show* that you can solve problems quickly is entirely different. Think about the times that you have been under pressure to get something done, and how you have worked to resolve problems. Talk

about the results of your actions and what that meant for your fellow employees as well as the company.

Q: Describe a time when you've used a problem-solving process to obtain successful results.

✔ **YES:** The hotel chain that I work for offers a free night's stay to any customer who has had an unpleasant experience there in the past. As customer service is a top priority of mine, I took it upon myself to follow up with some of these unsatisfied customers. Upon retrieving the names of all those customers who had complained about our hotels in the past few years, I noticed that there were several customers who were arranging hotel stays around the country through abuse of this policy. I suggested that we set up a flagging program in our computer that would allow the clerk or person making reservations to recognize this customer as someone who had complained in the past. Hotel employees were instructed to make mention of this customer's past experience. By stating something as simple as "Mr. Smith, I know that you have had an unpleasant experience with our hotel in the past, and I am happy that you have decided to give us a second chance. If there is anything I can do to make your stay more accommodating, please don't hesitate to contact me." For the customers who have had legitimate complaints in the past, this tactic allows us to be able to address their concerns more closely and make them aware that we are working to correct any problems they have found. For those customers who have chosen to abuse our satisfaction guaranteed policy, they are being warned that their name is on record as having complained in the past, making it less likely that they will do so again after this stay. As a result of this new system, our satisfaction rate has improved tremendously, and fraudulent cases have decreased.

✘ **NO:** The retail store I worked for was experiencing a surge in shoplifting incidents. While we were able to catch and prosecute many of the culprits, we were still not able to catch all of them.

Strange but True

Interview Questions

"How many pizza parlors would you say there are in the United States? How would you go about finding this out?"

After looking over the profiles of most of the convicted shoplifters, I realized that—for the most part—these shoplifters were young girls aged 17 and younger. In order to curb the number of thefts in our store, we put up a sign stating that all girls under the age of 18 must be accompanied by an adult. Since that time, we have definitely seen a drop in the amount of lost inventory.

You are trying to establish yourself as a fair employee who uses logic to solve difficult problems. When choosing a situation to describe, make sure it defines a real problem and a good solution that has helped in solving this issue. Describe, step-by-step, how the process you came up with was able to lead to a successful conclusion. What measures or benchmarks did you use to control or manage the process? What were the results?

Q: How do you usually go about solving a problem?

✔ **YES:** The first step I take is to figure out all the possible causes for the problem. I then think about the outcomes that could arise from my taking action; I consider the best and worst case scenarios as well as the things that are likely to occur. I then try and relate this problem—and its possible causes—to a larger problem. When I have everything laid out in front of me, it is much easier to make a logical connection between cause and effect, and come up with a practical way of resolving the issue.

✘ **NO:** When given a problem to solve, I try to speak with my boss or someone in a higher position to see what he or she would do about it. I figure this person is in an authoritative position for a reason, and I usually try his or her solution out to see how it works. If the plan backfires, I always have someone to go back to for support.

The key here is to show the interviewer your initiative and your ability to make logical decisions. Convince the interviewer that you are able to solve a problem successfully and that you already have a set plan of how to tackle such complex issues.

What criteria do you base your decisions on? Do others seem to have faith in your problem-solving abilities? If you can, give specific examples of times when you were able to wield these problem-solving abilities to a successful conclusion.

Q: How do you measure the success of your work?

✔ **YES:** The best way I can measure my own success is through customer feedback. When my customers call me with a referral, or someone calls to say another one of my customers referred them, I take that as an indication that I am doing a good job. Repeat business has always been more exciting to me than winning a new account. Knowing that my customers have come to rely on me and that they've told their acquaintances about me and my company is really the highest compliment.

✘ **NO:** I look at the company profit. If the company has done well for the year, then I have done well for the year. If the company has not done well, then I have not done well.

One of the most important things to remember here is that the interviewer is interested in how you separate your own work from the work of the company. Regardless of whether or not the company is successful, how do you know whether you yourself were successful? What evidence do you look for to evaluate the success of your own work?

Q: How practical or pragmatic are you?

✔ **YES:** I've always considered myself a very practical person. I have no problem picking up on underlying problems, even when they're not too obvious—or when they're so obvious that people overlook them. I remember one time when an investment banker visited the real estate finance class that I was taking and asked what might cause the Tokyo investment community a problem in attracting local investment dollars. A number of finance MBAs in the class tried to think of some complicated set of reasons. I decided that it would have to do with getting

out of a bad market quickly and that a nonliquid investment would create problems. I said investors would be unsettled if the primary investment is local real estate and inflation has caused the paper value to exaggerate the real street value. As it ended up, that was the answer he wanted.

✗ NO: On a scale of 1 to 10, I'm about a 5!

The interviewer is not looking for a number here or an exact degree of how practical you are. He or she is trying to figure out how well you solve problems. If possible, give the interviewer an example of a time when you used a practical approach to solve a problem. Be sure to highlight your common sense rather than your academic background in this answer. Assure the interviewer that although you have the education they are seeking, you also have the experience and practicality to look at a problem—and solve it—from a very simple angle.

Q: How do you balance your reliance on facts with your reliance on intuition?

✔ YES: Though I believe that facts, obviously, are important, they often neglect point-in-time influences, especially as far as market research is concerned. One incident that I can remember is when I was asked to look at pricing data that was collected just after a major presidential election. The timing of this survey caused me to doubt that consumers would really spend as much for a new car as the survey indicated they would. As a result, we ended up holding on to the last quarter's pricing structure. We sold more cars, as interest rates climbed, while some of our competitors had expensive inventory carryover.

✗ NO: I don't really see any comparison between these two things. Facts are facts, and you can't dispute them.

Though collecting and using fact-based data in any job is important, having a strong intuition about an industry or a subject is also important. The marketplace changes on a daily basis, and you need to be able to keep up with these changes

and modify your way of doing business accordingly. If you can, tell the interviewer about a time when you were able to come up with a successful solution to a problem by using both the facts you had been supplied with and your own intuition. If you had answered this problem by relying strictly on the facts at hand, what could have happened? Demonstrate your ability to "think outside of the box."

Q: Tell me about a time when a problem arose that you failed to anticipate.

✔ **YES:** My boss had asked me to spend a little time trying to find some inventive ways in which we could cut costs in my department. I immediately got to work and found all sorts of ways in which we could cut barely noticeable amounts of money in various areas that would result in an overall 10 percent decrease in costs. What I hadn't realized is that each of the department heads had already been asked to choose one area in which they would be willing to cut costs. The department heads responded in much the same way: There was no area within their department that they were willing or able to cut any costs. Soon after I submitted my solution to my boss, I noticed the apathetic way in which each of the department heads dealt with me. I failed to realize that the same solution had already been attempted and that there were a lot of negative feelings associated with my findings.

✗ **NO:** I really can't recall a time. I am very good at foreseeing the possible outcomes of any situation—including the problems that are likely to arise.

Everyone has failed to anticipate a problem at some time, even the interviewer. The question is, Are you secure enough to fess up to it and see it as a learning experience? Discuss an incident in which you failed to see the warning signs that a problem was likely to occur. What did you learn from this experience? How has your judgment changed as a result of that incident?

Strange but True

Interview Questions

"What is your favorite color? What does that color tell me about your personality?"

Q: Have you ever resolved a long-standing problem?

✔ **YES:** For as long as I could remember, the hotel that I worked for chose to batch our guests' personal faxes to make the task easier on our administrative staff. Several guests complained about this, claiming that they needed these documents sent out immediately. I arranged a lease deal on an outgoing fax machine for our guests to use. This not only freed up time for our administrative staff but also allowed us to protect any incoming information until the appropriate guest could be located.

✘ **NO:** Not that I can remember.

This question isn't asking whether you've ever been able to solve the problem of world hunger. Though it sounds a bit intimidating, it's asking about your ability to solve a long-standing problem, not necessarily a huge one! No matter how small the issue, talk about how you came up with a solution using your good judgment. The problem does not even need to be work related; it could be something you did in school or with a volunteer organization. Make sure that the problem you choose to talk about is one you solved successfully. What motivated you to tackle the problem to begin with? How did you overcome the obstacles? What were the results?

Q: Describe a time you had to make an unpopular decision.

✔ **YES:** Though we had always championed the idea of teamwork and community at my current job, there was an obvious line set between those who were in high-level positions and those who were not. One of the main issues that often arose was that high-level executives had assigned parking spots right near the front door, while others had to walk for five minutes or more to make it to the door. As many of these higher-level people didn't arrive at the office until later, or were often called away on business much of the time, employees would complain about this obvious inequity. I thought that these employees had a legitimate complaint and that the idea of

assigned parking spaces was inconsistent with our policy of an equal work force. Though the matter is forgotten now, I did not have many of the high-level employees on my side with this decision.

✗ NO: We were working on a very tight deadline, and I told the entire staff that because we were so far behind, we would need to either work overtime a few nights that week or come into work for a few hours on Saturday. My team was not very excited about this prospect.

Being an effective leader requires, on some occasions, making unpopular decisions. The interviewer wants to know that on the occasions where you have had to make such decisions, they were in fact necessary. He or she also wants to be assured that these "unpopular" decisions don't occur that often. Talk about your willingness to make these decisions and accept the isolation that is likely to follow as a result. Discuss the way in which short-term sacrifices often result in the successful achievement of long-term goals. Be sure to give a specific example.

Q: Describe a time when a problem wasn't resolved to your satisfaction.

✔ YES: During last year's holiday season, we weren't able to complete a customer's order in time. Our production capacity was not sufficient to deliver the entire order on time. As a result, the customer asked for a discount on his order. I was upset by the fact that we did not take initiative and offer the customer a discount at the same time we informed him that his order would not be ready. The sense of goodwill and genuine regret for not having the order ready would have been greater.

✗ NO: I had been having a lot of trouble with a person in my department who thought it was okay to arrive at work more than 20 minutes late every day. When I spoke to her about this, she said it would not happen again. To this day, she has never made it to work on time.

This question focuses on the candidate's standards of quality. Do you let things slide by when there is an easier or better way to solve the problem, or do you work tirelessly to ensure a satisfactory ending? Describe a situation in which you foresaw long-term complications from a problem that was poorly handled. Did you initiate the resolution of this situation? If the solution still wasn't satisfactory, did you do anything else? If there was nothing else you could do, why not?

Q: Tell me about a time when there was no rule or precedent to help you attack a problem.

✔ **YES:** I was the first employee in both a newly created position and a newly created department. In order to gain an understanding of what my ultimate goals were, I spent the first week speaking with employees to figure out the history that had led to the creation of this position in the first place. Once I better understood the need the company had, I was able to develop a method for setting priorities. I was also able to figure out the steps I would need to take to ensure that this new position and department were worthwhile creations.

✗ **NO:** While my boss was on vacation for the week, a customer called with a question that I was disinclined to answer, even though I thought I could do so. Since there was no one else in the company that could answer the question with authority, I had to try and get in touch with my boss via a barrage of phone calls, e-mails, and even a singing telegram. Eventually, he got the message and called me with the answer the customer was looking for.

The interviewer is trying to determine your confidence level as well as your willingness to accept new challenges. How resourceful are you when it comes to determining how to proceed with something in which there is no set precedent? How well do you operate without the assistance of a formal structure? Talk about a specific situation in which you needed to set priorities and develop a plan of attack for a particular question or

problem. Describe your problem-solving process, especially the steps you took and measures you established in a particularly trying situation.

Q: Describe an opportunity in which you felt the risks far out weighed the rewards.

✔ **YES:** We were given the opportunity to purchase manufacturing equipment at thirty cents on the dollar from a company that had recently dissolved. At the time, we anticipated an overhaul of our manufacturing facility five years down the road. I made the decision that it was too far into the future to spend money, only to have idle capacity for a five-year period. If market conditions had shown more promise for new sales in the initial two-year period, I would have gone ahead with it.

✘ **NO:** My staff had been complaining about the lack of computer power within our department. The computers that we had were old, and the software was outdated. When I approached my boss about purchasing new equipment, the amount of money he offered to help with the problem would have only been enough to purchase new equipment for one of our employees. A friend of mine then told me that he could get the exact same advanced equipment—for all of my employees—at the exact price my boss had offered. The catch? The equipment was stolen. While it was definitely something to consider, I decided that we would be better off buying legitimate equipment and improving one person's work station at a time.

The interviewer wants to be assured that the candidate is able to take reasonable risks but that he or she would not be foolish in these decisions. The best way to answer this question is to offer an example of a time when you were given a decision to make and were able to use good judgment in determining the risks versus the benefits. How was the outcome of your decision preferable to what might have happened? Were you aware of the possible risks? What was the thought process you used to decide against this?

Insider Tips

Career Planning

Career counselors often report that one of the most common problems job seekers run into is that they don't consider whether or not they're suited for a particular position or career. Remember that you're not just choosing a career—but that you're also making a choice about the life you want to lead.

CHAPTER TWELVE

Your Driving Forces

Enthusiasm

Aside from basic skills, one key component to your being hired is to show that you are enthusiastic not just about the prospect of employment but also about the specific company and industry in general. Before heading into an interview, think about the many reasons why you would like this particular job, and why you want to work for this company. Again, offer specific examples when you can. Avoid being overzealous. First-timers often make the mistake of waxing poetic on the many reasons why they were "born" to work in a particular industry. Showing excitement without being fanatical is the key to winning over an employer.

Q: What led you to apply for a position in this industry?

✔ **YES:** I've always wanted to work in an industry that makes tools. One of my hobbies is home improvement projects, so I've collected a number of saws manufactured by your company. I could be an accountant anywhere, but I'd rather work for a company whose products I trust.

✘ **NO:** Actually, it's not so much the industry that I am applying to as it is the position of marketing director. As my expertise lies in marketing—and virtually every company has a marketing team—I am not too concerned about the actual industry I work in. After all, marketing promotions work the same in every industry, right?

Talk about how you first became interested in this specific industry. Discuss the similarities between your current job and the job you are applying for. Be sure to emphasize that you are looking for a career, not just a job! Make sure that your enthusiasm for the industry—and work in general—comes through in all of your answers (where appropriate, of course).

Q: What makes you think you'd be particularly good at this job?

✔ **YES:** My academic career included several classes in business and marketing. Additionally, in my current internship, I have frequently

been given the chance to help promote our products by attending trade shows, helping in the development of flyers and sales catalogs, and sitting in on meetings with the company sales department. I have been commended for my willingness to voice opinions and offer new ideas on how we could better market our products. I am forward thinking, and I always try to keep up with current trends and tendencies. I think that my creativity and strong writing skills would only augment the success I could have as part of your marketing team.

X **NO:** I can't say anything specific. Suffice it to say that when I saw the job description in the newspaper, I knew it was something I could probably do well in.

The question is specifically asking about which skills and characteristics you possess that could aid you in being successful. Think about the kind of person that would be perfectly compatible with the job you are applying for. What skills do you possess that reflect this "perfect candidate"? Discuss ways in which you keep up with the industry. Read the trade magazines and visit various organizational meetings and Web sites to find out about current trends. Make it part of your job to keep current, and make sure the interviewer knows that you are doing this.

Q: How do you stay current?

✔ YES: I pore over the *Wall Street Journal*, the *Times*, *Institutional Investor*, and several mutual fund newsletters. I also have a number of friends who are financial analysts, and we often discuss the business amongst ourselves.

X **NO:** I read the newspaper every day. Though most of my time is spent browsing through the sports pages, I do take a quick glance to see what is happening in the business world as well.

Again, this question relates to the previous one. Show the employer that your interest in a specific job or field does not end at 5 P.M. Talk about the many ways that—even outside of

Job Search Odds and Ends

Fastest-Growing Occupations

Certain professionals will be consistently in higher demand than others. Here are some of the fastest-growing jobs/careers for the coming years:

- Childcare Center Director
- Engineer
- Geneticist
- Industrial Designer
- Intellectual Property Lawyer
- Landscape Architect
- Molecular Biologist
- Online Sales Manager
- Technical Education Teacher
- Technical Support Manager
- Web Advertising Specialist
- Web Site Developer
- Webmaster

work—you keep up with your business. It could be that you spend your lazy Sunday mornings reading trade magazines; there's no shame in sharing this with the interviewer. If you are a member of any professional trade organization, now is the time to talk about it. Do you attend regular meetings or chat frequently with the other members? Show the employer that this position is not just a way to make a living but that it's a way of life for you!

Q: Why is it that you have decided to make this industry your career?

✔ **YES:** The technology in the industry is changing so rapidly that I see lots of room for job enhancement regardless of promotions. I'm particularly interested in the many applications for multimedia as a training tool.

✘ **NO:** I know that the salary range for top professionals in this field extends well into the six-figure bracket. As I hope to save enough money to retire by the time I am 50, this is exactly the kind of money I'll need to make to achieve that goal.

Again, the interviewer wants to make sure that any time and energy spent on training you will be money well spent and that you will remain with the organization for several years to come. Think about the many reasons why you have chosen this specific industry or job as a career and about what it has to offer you in the future. Don't mention money! In fact, a good rule to abide by is not to mention money at all. You want to assure the interviewer that by selecting you for the job, they are selecting a competent and loyal employee who will look forward to many years of continued growth with the company.

Other key factors to keep in mind when answering this question are what expectations you have for the industry as a whole and what aspects of the business excite you. Though it may seem redundant (haven't I already answered several similar questions?), the key to a successful interview is to drill your "themes" into the interviewer's head. If you need to mention on

more than one occasion your deep interest in the industry or your membership in a professional society, so be it. Be sure to offer specific proof of your long held interest in the industry and not just your very recent decision to make it your life's career. Passion for your work is one thing that should never be taken for granted.

Q: Where do you see yourself in five years?

✔ **YES:** I would like to think that in five years I could be managing my own department within the company. As I have served directly under department heads in the past, I think that I have learned valuable lessons as to what it takes to be a good leader. Getting the chance to use these skills and, I hope, to make a difference within the company is where I would like to be.

✘ **NO:** I see myself running my own business. As a leader in the field, I think that working for your company would certainly prepare me for the daunting task of running my own business. I am really hoping to learn the business from the ground up here and then work to apply that to my own company.

Here's one instance in which you don't want your answer to be too specific. If you think you would like to see yourself at a management level, say so, but refrain from giving an exact job title such as senior vice president of financial affairs. Showing that you are achievement motivated is one thing; telling the interviewer that you are out to get others fired is another. Use this question as a way to talk about your greatest skills. Again, be realistic. If you are being hired for the mail room, it is unlikely that you will be running the show within the next five years. Though confidence and a desire to be promoted are all valuable to an employer, an employee who is living in his or her own fixed reality is another story. One way to surely eliminate yourself from consideration for a job is to state unrelated career goals. If you're applying for a job as an accountant, it is not wise to tell the interviewer that in five years you hope to be the host of your own late-night talk show!

Motivation

It is not uncommon–in any industry–for an employee to lose enthusiasm upon being hired. The "thrill of the chase" can relate to the workplace just as easily as it does to the dating scene. One way to set yourself apart from the rest of the applicant pool is to show an employer that you are not only enthusiastic about obtaining a certain position but also determined to rise above it.

Employers are always looking for the next great employee. By demonstrating your desire to achieve, you are showing the employer that you would be a valuable asset to the company. But how can you show motivation? Do your homework! Find out all you can about a company before you attend the interview. Figure out ways in which you could help the company achieve its potential (while squashing the competition) and allude to these ideas during the interview. Again, the idea is to sound excited about the prospect of working for this company, not like a know-it-all. Don't saunter into the room and start telling the CEO of a company what he or she is doing wrong; simply demonstrate that you know the business and that you are bursting with ideas.

> **Q:** Tell me something about yourself that I wouldn't know from reading your resume.

✔ **YES:** Since I was 18 years old, I have managed my own financial portfolio. In addition to the measurable success I have had in the workplace, I count this as one of my greatest achievements. Over the past eight years, I have averaged a 12 percent return.

✘ **NO:** I worked very hard to get a degree in finance.

Remember that you are being asked to tell the interviewer something about yourself that he or she **wouldn't** know from reading your resume. If certain pieces of information were omitted from your resume to keep it all on one page, now is the time to bring them up. For example, if in addition to a part-time job and your full-time studies you were part of an athletic

team or organization, talk about it. While the actual organization might be a bit off the topic, you can usually find a way to weave it into the conversation. By participating in a particular event or becoming part of a certain organization, what did you learn? What are some of the skills you acquired that will help you in your professional endeavors? Do not tell the interviewer something that is completely irrelevant (e.g., "I have ten cats!"). Above all, remember not to repeat anything that can be found from looking at your resume.

Q: Tell me what you know about this company.

✔ **YES:** I served as an intern to a restaurant analyst last summer, so I followed all the steak-house chains closely. What you've done especially well is focus on a limited menu with great consistency among locations; the business traveler trusts your product everywhere in the United States. I'm particularly interested in your real estate finance group and expansion plans.

✗ **NO:** I know that you guys make the best hamburgers in the city!

This is one of those open-ended questions that many interviewees hate! It ranks right up there with "Tell me about yourself." Still, if you have done your homework—like you should have— you should have no problem scoring points with this inquiry. Start out by telling the recruiter how you first became aware of the company. Talk about the personal experiences you've had with the company's product or service—whether it be your own experience or someone else's. Discuss the many reasons why a job with this particular company (and not a competitor) would be ideal. What is this company offering that its competitors are not? While a general knowledge of the company is imperative, avoid reciting the company's mission statement. The recruiter is looking for evidence of a genuine interest in the company (not just a general interest in the industry). Make sure you provide them with the insightful information they are looking for.

Insider Tips

Working Nine to Five

If you look for a new job while you are employed, resist the temptation to give a potential employer your present contact information. If you are afraid you'll miss a call, invest the $20 in an answering machine or the $5 to $10 it costs to set up a voice mail account. If the only e-mail account you have is the one at work, set up a new account with one of the many companies that offer e-mail for free. Forget the fact that if an employer were to call you at work, you would probably feel and sound very awkward. Besides, giving out your work number to potential employers shows a complete lack of respect for and loyalty to your current employer, which paints a not-so-pretty image of you as a potential employee.

Q: Why do you want to work here?

✔ **YES:** About a year ago, your company beat me out for a bid on a project. To find out what it was that had made the organization decide in your favor, I decided to research your products. It was then that I discovered—while many products in the computer industry are becoming increasingly similar—your company strives to be forward thinking. Since then, I have kept a very active interest in your company and the steps forward they have made in the industry as a whole. Your company has maintained a consistently strong service record, and your customer support is unrivaled. I believe that while many bigger companies will come and go, this company will always remain dedicated to the customer. It's that kind of personal attention that I respect, and it's a characteristic that—unfortunately—is hard to find.

✘ **NO:** I live very close by and would love to be able to walk to work. Also, a friend of mine works in your personnel department and has told me that you guys offer a great benefits package. This is exactly the kind of incentive I have been looking for to get me out of the house.

All aspects of the interviewing company should come into play here. In addition to the actual business, you should talk about the other reasons why you would like to become a part of *this* company. For example, if you are applying to work in an office with just three or four employees, you could mention your preference for small companies. Tell the recruiter about the many reasons that made you apply for this position. If you don't know much about the company culture, look at aspects such as the company's reputation or the job description itself to help you come up with an answer. Customer feedback can also be of value in answering this question.

Q: What particular aspect of the company interests you most?

✔ **YES:** I'm particularly interested in your recent joint ventures with two processing companies in Latin America. When my father

was an army officer, we lived in Latin America for three years. I am very interested in what happens with these agreements. What are your plans for the next few years?

NO: There's really no one aspect of the job that interests me. The whole thing sounds intriguing.

This is a great way to showcase your special knowledge of the company. If the company has a Web site, try and gain access to any recent press releases to learn about the latest happenings. If you've researched the company properly, you should have no problem answering this question quickly and authoritatively.

Q: What is your favorite product made by our company?

✔ **YES:** I have been using your model X cellular phone for more than two years now. Although friends and colleagues are constantly having problems with cell phones from other manufacturers, I have never experienced any sort of problems. In fact, whenever I head out to buy a new electronic product, I look for your label; I know that it is synonymous with "quality."

✗ **NO:** Actually, I'd never even heard of your company until I saw the help wanted advertisement, so I don't know any of them. Can I let you know after I am hired?

Whether the company you're applying to is product or service based, describe your related personal experiences. If you are interviewing with a restaurant, talk about your favorite thing on the menu. Think about why you use the company's product/service. If possible, discuss the various other markets that you think the company's product could succeed in. Employers love to hear new ideas from fresh voices; let your voice be one that resonates.

Q: What do you think of our newest advertising campaign?

✔ **YES:** If you are talking about the one with the family at breakfast time, I think it is great. I know that in the past your company has been criticized for offering foods that are high in fat.

This comforting campaign—and the new heart-healthy product—was a great way to step away from that issue. It really shows that you care about your customers and take their comments and concerns seriously.

✗ NO: I don't believe I know it.

Make sure to familiarize yourself with the company's latest happenings, including new products, new advertising campaigns, and any recent press (whether bad or good). Be sure that you know enough about the company's current state to speak in an informed and intelligent manner. Always offer positive comments, and make specific suggestions if you think that they apply.

Q: What do you think our distinct advantage is over our competitors?

✔ YES: I think the smartest way to stay ahead of the industry was with your choice of headquarters location. By operating in a low-cost area and maintaining a low production cost, you are able to spend aggressively on more important aspects such as research and development and advertising. Even when the rest of the industry is showing a dip in sales, your company remains profitable.

✗ NO: I don't really know what you are doing that is better, but I know that I have been buying your products over the competition's for years, so you must be doing something right!

Again, this is the time to showcase your in-depth knowledge of the company, its products, and its operation in general. What things do you think the company does well, particularly when compared to their competitors? Pick one important aspect you see as being a real advantage, and discuss it in an informed and intelligent manner.

Q: Where do you think we're the most vulnerable as a business?

✔ YES: In the midst of my employment, the last company I worked for underwent a merger. Based on your cash position

and strong product presence, your company would be an attractive target for a takeover. Though we did experience some difficulties in my last company, I also know I can weather the storm of such an occurrence.

✗ NO: Just from the communication I've had with your department, I would say that your employees are lacking in many respects. Considering that it took you two months to get back to me after sending in my resume, I would say you could use a personnel overhaul.

Answering this question requires a relatively strong grasp on the business, and a definite knowledge of the firm's competitors. Figure out what the company does *not* do well in relation to its competitors, and talk a bit about this. Discuss the ways in which you would cope if these vulnerabilities were to be fully realized. As an employee with a passion for the business, you should always be thinking of the future of your job.

Q: If you were allowed to run the company, what would you do differently?

✔ YES: I might investigate whether to sell off the light-manufacturing businesses and start an aggressive supplier-relations program.

✗ NO: I would make the company more like school. We would have a three-month summer vacation and catered lunch every day. I would make Friday game day where—instead of working—everyone would be allowed to play games within their departments.

This is another question in which you must avoid stepping on anyone's toes. For example, if you are being interviewed by the human resources director, you probably wouldn't want to say, "I would change the overall structure of the human resources department. The way you are structured right now, I'm surprised anyone gets hired." Rather than concentrate on your own personal experience, look at the company from a business standpoint. If you were given the chance to run this company, what is the most important change you would make? For some people, gaining such

an intricate knowledge is difficult. To answer this question, it really pays to have some insider information. If you know anyone who works for the company—or even in the industry—see if they can help you. Make sure you keep the rules of business in mind. Companies don't turn a profit by letting their employees run wild. Keep your changes informed and intelligent; again, this is not the land of make-believe.

Q: What other firms are you interviewing with, and for what positions?

✔ **YES:** Since I have definitely decided on a career in the publishing industry, I am applying strictly for editorial assistant positions. My most recent interviews have been with Random House, HarperCollins, and Simon & Schuster.

✘ **NO:** I have applied to work at each *Fortune* 500 company for positions ranging from custodian to the vice president of finance.

One mistake that interviewees often make is trying to impress the interviewer with the names of big companies. In the above "NO" example, unless you're applying for the position of CEO, this tactic wouldn't work. As each of the *Fortune* 500 businesses are unrelated as far as industry is concerned, this would be a mass mailing at its worst. Make sure that the companies you mention are all within the same industry as the company you are interviewing with. And don't be afraid of telling the recruiter that you are interviewing with one of their biggest competitors. If anything, it will reinforce that this is exactly the kind of business you want to get into and illustrate that you're committed to finding a job in your field of interest, thus showing you to be a low-risk hire.

Q: Do you think that you are overqualified for this position?

✔ **YES:** Absolutely not! My relative experience and qualifications will only help me to do this job better. Because I have experience in so many different facets of your business, I feel that I

can help aid in the overall success of the company, and not just within my department. For example, my business experience can help me to run the art department in a cost-efficient manner, while my creative background will allow me to find the best freelance talent. As I have been working in the industry for quite some time, I have many business contacts that I can call upon to help me. My qualifications are better for the company, too, since you'll be getting a better return on your investment. Since I am interested in establishing a long-term relationship with my employer, I would expect expanded responsibilities that could make use of even other skills when I have proven myself.

✗ NO: When I first read the job description, I did think that I might have too much experience for the position. But since when has being overqualified been a problem? Because of my extensive experience, I should be able to perform these tasks easily and quickly.

This is one question that intends to catch an interviewee off guard, and often does. The one mistake many people make in answering this question is to automatically take a defensive position. If you do have extensive experience, an interviewer is testing to see whether or not you would quickly become bored in the position. They are also trying to figure out how much confidence you have in your own skills, and how you plan to let your past experience work for you in this company. When answering this question, be sure to address each of your strongest skills and explain how each could benefit the company. Confidence is the key to answering this question.

Q: Describe our competitors as you see them.

✔ YES: As far as I can tell, your competitors have tried to branch out too often and too fast. They have tried to improve upon their main product, and with little success. As a result, they have had a lot of difficulty maintaining a consistent quality. I think that the recent bankruptcy of ABC Company only further illustrates this point. Your company has been smart enough to

Job Search
Odds and Ends

How Should I Address an Employer?

Many people make the mistake of assuming too much familiarity in a cover letter by addressing a hiring manager by his or her first name. When you are contacting a potential employer for the first time, make sure you address him or her with respect. DO: *Dear Mr. Smith;* DON'T: *Dear Jennifer.* If you don't know whether a woman is married or not, address her as *Ms.* not *Miss* or *Mrs.* If you only know the department name to which you are sending your resume, do not address the letter to one particular gender. DO: *Dear Human Resources Manager;* DON'T: *Dear Madam.* Another way to skirt the gender issue—when you're not sure who will be reading your resume—is to use the tried and true *Dear Sir or Madam.*

refrain from looking toward this same type of expansion and instead has focused on creating the best possible product. It is this kind of dedication that I am looking for in an employer.

✗ NO: As far as I can tell, being number one in this industry is a real toss-up. Depending on the public's mood, any one of your competitors could emerge as the best company. You are all making the exact same product, and the price point doesn't differ too much. I see your competitors being at just as much an advantage as this company in taking over the industry.

In addition to researching the company extensively, make sure you have a good idea of its competitors and what they do. Make sure to have more than just a superficial knowledge of this company's competitors; know in which areas the competition is beating out this company and in which they are lagging behind. Give evidence that in addition to a vast knowledge of the company, you know a lot about the industry as a whole. Most importantly, discuss how this company's initiatives are better suited to your personal interests.

Q: What would you say if one of our competitors offered you a position?

✔ YES: I'd probably say no. I'm not too interested in working for the other players in this industry. My desire to work for Nike comes from the many positive experiences I have had with your product. I truly believe in your products and would not consider working for a company whose products I didn't believe in. After all, how could I convince someone to buy a product that I myself wouldn't buy?

✗ NO: I would take it in a heartbeat. I know that this is the industry I want to be in for sure; how I find my way into it does not matter.

It is not always necessary to answer no to this question. Depending on the order of the questions asked, you may have

already told an interviewer that you are applying for a position with his or her competitor. Still, whether you answer this question with a yes or a no, be sure that you let the interviewer know that it is *this* company you would like to work for. Point out the reasons why you would prefer to work for this company even if a competitor offered you a position. Talk about the advantages this company has to offer you both as an employee and as a consumer. Again, the interviewer is trying to determine whether or not your interest in the company and industry is genuine. Talk about why you would choose this company over any other, and prove your interest.

Q: Why are you leaving your current job?

✔ **YES:** Though, at one point, I made the leap from being a bank lender to working in the human resources department, I am hoping to combine these two experiences. Sure, I can work in human resources anywhere, but because of my past experience as a lender, I think that my skills would be well suited to a human resources career within your bank. As I have been on both sides of the traditional job interview, I think I have a strong ability to find those applicants who are most compatible with the job.

✘ **NO:** My current boss and I just don't get along!

Give two or three reasons why you are ready to leave your current job. Focus on discussing the lack of growth or responsibility in your current job, and how you think this new job will challenge you. Regardless of your feelings for your current boss or work environment, refrain from making any negative statements about either. Saying "My boss and I don't really see eye to eye on many points, and I would like to change companies because of that" throws up a red flag to the interviewer that you could possibly have an attitude problem. Your boss isn't there to defend himself or herself, so the interviewer is left to wonder which one of you is the guilty party in all of this.

Q: What are you hoping to get out of your next job?

✔ **YES:** I'd be very interested in taking control of a segment of the company in which we are really lagging behind. Sure, it would be a challenge, but that's exactly what I'm looking for. In my current position, I have been able to increase the sales in my territory by more than 30 percent in just a few years. If I were given the opportunity to work with your company, I believe I could do that again. I also hope to get a very aggressive commission structure if I'm able to turn around a problem territory.

✘ **NO:** I have been with my current company for six months and have not been promoted or received any sort of pay raise. I would like to make more money in my next company, and I would hope that that company would recognize my contributions and promote me much more rapidly.

This question is very similar to the one that asks, Why are you ready to leave your current job? Without being negative about your current job or boss, give one or two examples of your current work experience that explain why you are interested in a new position. For this question, it is best to focus on obtaining a greater challenge. For example, telling the interviewer that there is no potential for advancement in your current position conveys that you are a hard worker who wants to advance; it also implies that you have gone as high as you can go in your current position. Make sure you give some reasons why you believe the job at hand will provide the additional responsibilities you are seeking.

Q: What would your dream job be like?

✔ **YES:** My dream job would allow me to be creative and artistic on a day-to-day basis. It would be fast paced and deadline driven, as I thrive on pressure. I would like to work for a small start-up company with limitless growth potential. I would like to be part of a company from the beginning so that I could help in

the shaping of a new business. I know that your company has been around for about a year now, but I think that your potential for growth is endless. The reason I am so interested in this position is that it would allow me to do all of these things, and then some.

✗ NO: I would love to be an assistant to Martin Scorsese. I would fetch him coffee, rub his feet, or do whatever it was he asked of me.

This is another one of those questions that might tempt you to offer up a bit of your fantasyland to the interviewer. Don't! Talk about a job you would like to have that is either close to or involves the same skills as the job you are applying for. Rather than cite a specific job title, your best bet is to tell the interviewer the tasks that would be involved in your dream job, and how those tasks relate to this job. Tie in the industry, size of the company, or other factors where appropriate.

Q: What motivates you to do this kind of work?

✔ YES: I have been fortunate enough in my schooling to have encountered many wonderful teachers. Each of them has left an indelible mark on me in some way, and I have always longed to do the same for some other child. I want to be the kind of teacher who not only encourages kids to learn but also sets an example that makes others want to teach. The quality of education in this state has been criticized over the past several years, and I want to help change this negative perception.

✗ NO: Since I have a beach house that I like to stay at in the summer, being a teacher affords me the opportunity to work nine months out of the year and then relax the other three.

Here is a great opportunity to show your enthusiasm for an industry, as well as your belief in the products or services of the company. It is always a wise idea to use personal experiences to underscore your enthusiasm. Talk about your natural interests, as the interviewer is trying to find out if they are compatible with the job.

Insider Tips

"My Old Job Was Boring . . ."

Never say that your old job was boring. You can mention that your old job lacked challenges, or something to that effect, but don't make it look as though you are giving up on it. Most jobs will have aspects that are less exciting than others. You don't want an interviewer to question whether the position being offered would be entertaining enough for you.

Job Search
Odds and Ends

Cost-of-Living Salary Calculations

If you're offered a job in a new city and you're contemplating relocation, you'll have to consider the city's cost of living. The easiest way to make comparisons and calculate your real earning potential in the new city is by checking out a Web site such as *www.homefair.com* that offers a "salary comparator." Simply type in the city and country you're moving from, the city and country you're moving to, the salary you currently make, and the salary you would make in the new city. The Web site's salary comparator uses a cost-of-living database to make earnings calculations for you in minutes.

Q: What salary would you expect for this job?

✔ **YES:** Your job description mentions that you would prefer someone with a master's degree in engineering—which I have. Based on the other qualifications you are looking for, I am confident that my skills meet your highest standards for an employee. Therefore, I hope that you would offer me a salary at the higher end of your pay scale. Could you give me some indication of your desired range?

✘ **NO:** I will not start for anything less than $250,000.

This is one of the most loathed questions a recruiter can ask, and it's one that people have an awful lot of trouble answering. As crazy as it sounds, many people, especially recent graduates, are completely uninformed as to how much money is average for a particular job. Before even *thinking* of discussing salary, you should be aware of the average salary range for your particular position in your particular area. Though you don't want to sell yourself short, you also don't want to throw out a dollar amount that is completely unrealistic.

If the interviewer seems unwilling to discuss the specifics of what the company expects to pay, talk about your current salary a little bit. "I make $50,000 per year in my current position and hope to make at least that. However, I would be completely willing to negotiate should the position be offered to me." If you're fresh out of college or new to the job market, be sure to research the average salary for your job title as well as salaries in areas of interest to you. That way, if pressed for a salary range, you can come back with the national and/or local averages. A good rule to follow is to always say that you are willing to negotiate; besides emphasizing your excitement about the opportunity, you can help to put yourself back in the running if the salary amount you suggested was much more than the company is willing to pay.

Q: What new or unique skills could you bring to the job that other candidates aren't likely to offer?

✔ **YES:** Because the company I currently work for is one of the oldest players in the industry, I think I could bring the history and experience that goes along with that. I can help this company avoid making some of the same mistakes we have made in our established markets. For example, if I were to start work today, I would work at retaining your core customer base before trying to secure new accounts. It is this kind of experience that you are not likely to find in many other candidates.

✘ **NO:** I am an expert juggler. How many other accountants can you say that about?

This question addresses your desire to add "true value" to a job (beyond what is expected of an employee). Imagine that you are being considered for the position alongside one other person with the exact same educational and professional qualifications. What are the things that would make you the better hire? Steer clear of vague answers such as "I am multitask oriented" and "I wear many hats." These answers tell the recruiter absolutely nothing about your skills and abilities.

Q: What interests you most about this job?

✔ **YES:** I would love the opportunity to work under John Doe, a man who really helped to build the financial services practice under bank deregulation. I have worked closely with Mr. Doe on projects before, and I completely respect him and his opinions. I think that in addition to getting along with your boss, it is important to respect that person, and to believe in him or her. My esteem for Mr. Doe is one of the main reasons I chose to apply for this job.

✘ **NO:** The whole job seems very interesting to me. I am interested in learning more about each part of it.

Point out the new responsibilities you be assuming in this job, as well as the reasons why you are already well suited for it. Mention similarities to some of your past jobs in which you have enjoyed professional success. DO NOT SPEAK IN GENERALITIES!

Q: What would you like to accomplish in this job that you weren't able to accomplish in your current position?

✔ **YES:** The company that I work for right now is rather small. That said, the budget we had for marketing our products was fairly limited. For the most part, our marketing efforts were limited to print ads and other traditional resources. I know that your company dedicates much of its time and energy to interactive media, targeting the 8- to 25-year-old category. This is a step that I am looking forward to taking, and one that I think I have many good ideas for.

✗ **NO:** My current position has not allowed me to use my creativity. Whatever ideas I have put forth are always rejected. It is getting to the point where I withhold my ideas just so I don't have to hear the word *no*. I hope that your company would be more accepting of me and my ideas.

Answer here in the same way you'd answer the question, Why are you ready to leave your current job? Don't say anything negative, and be sure your answer reflects professional goals! Talk about the goals you have set for yourself and how this job would help you attain them. Discuss the things you enjoy and have an aptitude for, but do not dwell on the limitations imposed by your current or previous job.

Q: How have your career motivations changed over the past few years?

✔ **YES:** When I first started out, I worked in sales, which is where I was sure I wanted to be. As I worked very closely with the marketing department, I realized that perhaps that was where my talents were. I found out that I could use my creativity and

strong writing skills to really help out in the marketing end of things. My boss also quickly realized this and immediately offered me a position within the company marketing department. Since then, my interest in marketing has only increased. I know that as is the case with many companies, your sales and marketing departments rely heavily upon one another to make each other work. Though I will always love the thrill of salesmanship, I cannot deny that marketing is where I need to be. Working for your company would allow me to keep a close eye on both of these interests and, I hope, help in the productivity of each of these departments.

✗ NO: Since starting out in the workplace just three years ago, I have changed jobs seven times, and I have changed careers five times. I have done everything from waitress to work as a veterinarian assistant. With so much experience behind me, I think I would be a great asset to your public relations team.

Regardless of whether or not you have changed careers completely, you have probably learned a lot about yourself and your talents since entering the work force. Talk about the things that you have learned from your past work experience, especially where your skills and natural instincts lie. Make sure that your current motivation relates to the job you are interviewing for. Avoid seeming fickle. An employer will not want to take a chance on an employee who can't seem to make up his or her mind about what they want to do. Even if you've had various jobs, talking about the goal you have always had in mind will put a positive spin on your varied past.

Q: Why should we hire you?

✔ YES: My uncle had a company that was a small-scale manufacturer in the industry, and although he later sold the business, I worked there for five summers doing all sorts of odd jobs. For that reason I believe I know this business from the ground up, and you can be assured that I know what I'd be getting into as a plant manager here.

Strange but True

Interview Questions

"Do you consider yourself a loose cannon?"

✗ NO: You're looking for an employee; I'm looking for a job. According to my calculations, one plus one equals me being hired!

Why *should* a company hire you? This question, which is usually the last one asked in a formal interview, is your chance to sum up your skills and value as an employee *without* repeating your resume or employment history. Here's your chance to offer one or two examples that explain why you want to work for this particular company, and why they would want you to work for them. What's the most compelling example you can give to prove your interest? Though this question often remains unasked, it's always in the back of a recruiters mind. If you're lucky enough to get through the interview without hearing it, you should still try and find an opportunity to use your prepared response sometime during the interview, perhaps in your closing remarks.

Creativity and Leadership Skills

In keeping with the idea of motivation, one of the ways in which an employer will try and gauge your potential will be to ask you questions that reveal your capacity for creativity along with your leadership skills. What does it take to make a good leader? In addition to creativity, it requires someone who is resourceful and not afraid to take initiative. Offering ideas on what you would do if hired is a great way to show that you have *already* taken initiative. Questions regarding these themes should also be answered with examples of how you have proven to be effective in the past.

Q: What color is your brain?

✔ YES: Though I would like to think there is a bit of every color in my brain, I tend to think it is mostly yellow. I have always been somewhat of a leader. I'm extremely detail oriented and committed to all that I do. I pride myself on thinking things through before acting and on almost always making the right decision.

✗ NO: Black!

You should prepare yourself for zany inquiries like this one. The interviewer is not trying to stump you here, he or she is just trying to find out what makes you tick. Recruiters are well aware of the fact that people spend several hours preparing for interview questions that may be asked of them; they're trying to see what will happen when you *have not* prepared an answer. The key is to remain focused and confident in what you are saying. The last thing an interviewer wants to hear is "I don't know; maybe it's pink—just because I like that color!" Try to remain calm under pressure and be creative. One key thing to remember: Be sure to explain why you answered the way you did.

Q: If you got on an elevator and everyone was facing the back, what would you do?

✔ **YES:** Unless there were some sort of sign instructing me otherwise, I would assume the normal position. In an attempt to get others to follow suit, I might even announce that it was much more comfortable to face forward.

✗ **NO:** I'd wait for the next elevator.

If you're interviewing for a position in a creative field like advertising or graphic design, you should anticipate being asked some crazy questions like this one. Rather than ask a direct questions such as How creative are you?, an interviewer can test you and see for himself or herself. They ask such questions to test how inventive you might be in a real-life situation.

Q: What's the most innovative project you've ever worked on?

✔ **YES:** When I worked with JLM Company last summer, I noticed that when sales inquiries would come into the office, they would be distributed haphazardly amongst the marketing assistants. Realizing that there had to be a better, more efficient way of logging these inquiries, I took it upon myself to set up a system. I organized these inquiries according to region and distributed them to the marketing assistants based on their regions. This approach

not only enabled our marketing team to come up with better and more creative solutions to our sales problems but also addressed the specific concerns of our pre-existing customers.

✗ NO: When I was in the second grade, we were asked to come up with an idea for a science project. While most of the students brought in plants and leaves as their project, I created an ant farm. To this day, I consider it one of my greatest accomplishments.

Give examples of your initiative and willingness to contribute new ideas. Discuss how your leadership skills have helped you accomplish your goals. Give a specific example that shows a creative, new, or unusual approach you took to reaching your goals.

Q: Describe a time when you've been able to overcome an obstacle in a creative manner.

✔ YES: For months, the publishing company I worked for had been trying to get an appointment with a particular *Fortune* 500 company to talk about a possible advertising campaign. After several sales representatives tried to no avail, I volunteered to take a crack at the task. Rather than contact the vice president of advertising herself, I decided to target her assistant. I was able to schedule an appointment with the assistant and give him my sales pitch instead. I must have made quite an impression, because the assistant immediately scheduled me for a meeting with the VP herself for that very day. Two weeks later, we got the order, and the deal was made.

✗ NO: When I worked in the accounting department of a doctor's office, I was placed in charge of all the delinquent accounts. After various attempts to contact these patients and work out a payment schedule, I thought of a better way to do it. I created a false letterhead to make it seem like I was writing from a lawyer's office and informed all the guilty parties that if they didn't pay within a month of receiving the letter, we would bring them to court. Within weeks, nearly all of the accounts were paid in full.

A smart way to answer this question is to focus on how you overcome problems with the help and support of your coworkers. Show

that in addition to being a creatively independent thinker you are concerned about the company and your team as a whole. Also, illustrate your strength as a leader. Think about how you have approached a problem differently from how others might approach it, and how you have achieved success in doing so. Emphasize your creative solution along with its positive results.

Q: Consider the following scenario:

You are working late one evening and are the last person in the office. You answer an urgent telephone call to your supervisor from a sales representative who's in the middle of a meeting with a potential client. The sales rep needs an answer to one important question to close the sale. Tomorrow will be too late. You have the expertise to answer the question, but it's beyond your normal level of authority. How would you respond?

✔ **YES:** First and foremost, I would be sure to document the situation so that I could inform my supervisor of everything that happened the next day. I would then answer the question, based on my own knowledge and the information provided. In addition to leaving my supervisor a detailed note about the occurrence, I would be sure to schedule a meeting with him or her the next day so that we could discuss the matter in further detail. In addition to explaining my decision and the answer I gave to the sales representative, I would ask my supervisor whether or not he or she thinks I made the right decision, and what he or she would prefer I do were the same situation to occur again.

✘ **NO:** After calling my supervisor's home number, cell phone, and beeper, I would tell the rep that I could not help him and that he would have to lose the sale.

Display confidence in your abilities and show that you can be counted on in emergency situations. Keeping the supervisor in mind throughout the entire situation illustrates the candidate's respect and loyalty to his or her superiors. Your answer should indicate that you're not afraid to be the decision-maker in a tough

Insider Tips

Design a Letterhead

If you have a computer, you can design a letterhead for yourself and save it in a file to use for cover letters and other correspondence. Include your name, home address, telephone number, and e-mail address (if you have one). Experiment to find an attractive design that's different from that of your resume. If you want typefaces other than the default fonts that come with the computer, a CD-ROM containing several thousand fonts is available in software stores for about $15. However, avoid anything too flashy for business correspondence.

situation, even if the situation's beyond your normal level of authority. Be sure to talk about your responsibility for making this decision, your competence in making all the information available to your supervisor, and your initiative in talking it out to make sure that the decision you made was the preferable one.

Q: What do you think are some of the factors that make companies with good products fail?

✔ **YES:** There are several reasons for this to happen, especially with the advent of the Internet. The entire idea of supply and demand has become an unpredictable equation. With many people doing business solely on the Internet, they can eliminate much of the traditional operating costs and offer their customers products and services at the very lowest prices. In addition, regardless of the product you are looking for, it is likely that there are plenty of suppliers out there. Those companies that have the money and know-how have proven to be successful in the marketplace, while smaller or more inexperienced companies, though their product may be of a higher quality, have not. This could be said for any type of business really, whether virtual or real. If you don't have the right people promoting and/or selling your products and you are not targeting the right people, your product is going to suffer. Only by getting the employees involved with the product and excited about it can success occur. A company is only as strong as its employees.

✗ **NO:** I think it's all a matter of luck. It's a question of being in the right place at the right time. That is what makes some companies successful and others not so successful. Your company was very lucky in that respect.

This question specifically target's the candidate's vision as a leader, as well as his or her business savvy. If you are asked this question, you'll do well to discuss a specific example of a product or idea that failed because of poor enthusiasm from employees or other consumers. Without being overly critical, you should discuss what you would have done differently. You

do not have to target this company specifically in your example, and it's probably a good idea *not to*. Just make sure that when answering, you give an explanation that is articulate and informed, and illustrates your ability to see and improve the overall picture.

Q: How resourceful are you?

✔ **YES:** I consider myself extremely resourceful. While product launches at my current company are generally the domain of our chief engineer, the CEO decided to let me conduct one, as I had shown much creativity in other projects. While it had long been the case that the chief engineer would simply send out a press release describing the new product's virtues, I decided it was time for a change. I contacted three of our largest customers and asked them to try out the new product and let me know what they thought. With an overwhelmingly positive response to the new line, I then asked permission to videotape these real-life testimonials. The customers agreed, and rather than send out just a press release, we were able to distribute a videotape as well. The result was a far higher level of credibility for the company and product, and we exceeded our six-month sales quota. Personal endorsements have now become a cornerstone of all of our marketing campaigns.

✘ **NO:** I would say that I am very resourceful, definitely.

This question specifically targets the candidate's level of creativity and initiative. Your best bet in answering this question is to provide an example of how you've altered the traditional way of doing things at some point and attained the same—if not better—results. Focus on how you obtained crucial information or how you changed your personal style to get someone to cooperate. As always, make sure to sound confident without being cocky, and don't exaggerate the situation just to have a great answer to the question. Employers will find out if you are lying, and if you are, you can rest assured you *will not* be hired!

Q: Give me proof of your persuasiveness.

✔ **YES:** As a summer intern, I was asked to conduct a bench-marking study of all the communication expenditures for a major utility. My job consisted of speaking with various people from each department and getting the general consensus on the matter. This was a very large company full of employees who had been there for 20 and 30 years or more, and unfortunately everyone seemed very resentful of me. Finally, after a complete lack of cooperation from virtually everyone I talked to, I decided that the best way to approach the situation was to have individual meetings with each of the employees I wished to speak to. This more private setting not only allowed me the chance to explain to each of the employees the worth of the project but also allowed them to voice their thoughts more freely than they might when surrounded by coworkers and department heads. Each employee was given the chance to understand that what I was doing would ultimately be beneficial to his or her department, as well as the company as a whole. Once the employees began to understand this, they became much more cooperative. Some of them even offered their assistance. After taking this step, the project went along flawlessly. In the end, I received a bonus for my efforts, as well as a commendation from the CEO, and many of the employees.

✘ **NO:** I persuaded you to ask me in for this interview, didn't I? With very little experience in the field, I think that the fact that I'm sitting here is proof of my persuasiveness.

Though this question is definitely meant to target your leadership skills, you should try and use an example in which you were not the designated leader. After all, if you're the actual leader of a group or project, it is the *duty* of these people to follow you—and it doesn't prove your persuasiveness. Talking about a time when people cooperated with you of their own volition is much more impressive. Talk about your desired goal, how you went about achieving it, and the overall outcome. Were you commended for your work? Why do you think people trusted and believed in you? How would you translate those characteristics into this position?

Q: If I were to speak with your current supervisor, what do you think he or she would say about your initiative?

✔ **YES:** When I enter a new workplace, I find that I am full of ideas on how to make certain processes or tasks run more smoothly. When I first arrived at my current position, I figured out lots of new and innovative ways to cut down on the amount of data entry that needed to be done for my position, allowing for more time to be spent in other, more important areas. While I think that initially my current supervisor was put off a bit by my willingness and enthusiasm in contributing new ideas, she eventually began to anticipate these new ideas. In fact, she suggested that I begin writing up a monthly proposal of all my ideas so that we could begin discussing the issues on a more formal basis. After proposing my idea for a new inventory system, we were able to reduce the total value of the inventory we had to carry by 23 percent the first year alone. I think that my supervisor would use me as an example of someone who's constantly taking the initiative.

✘ **NO:** As he has not given me much of a chance to show my initiative, I don't think there is much he would say.

Think of a time (or times) when you have volunteered to work on a project or to help solve an existing problem in an attempt to avoid an abundance of unnecessary work. How efficient were your solutions, and how well were they received? How did you approach your supervisor with the idea, and what was his or her reaction? Focus on the creativity of the idea, the approach you took to making it happen, and the result you obtained.

Q: Describe an improvement you personally initiated.

✔ **YES:** When I began work for my previous employer, I was amazed at how unorganized the resume system was. Several filing cabinets were chock full of resumes from as far back as five years. With a bit of human resources experience in my background, I decided to initiate a resume cleanup program. When

Insider Tips

Strategic Tactics

Adjust the speed of your speech with that of the interviewer's. People tend to talk at the speed at which they like to be spoken to. If you can adjust your speech rate to that of the recruiter without sounding unnatural, the recruiter will probably feel more comfortable and have a more favorable impression of you.

new resumes came into the office, they were immediately reviewed and a recommendation made. I began scanning each resume into our main computer and organizing each according to name and date. I spent an entire weekend in the office scanning and organizing these resumes, though I was happy to do so. When a new position would arise, rather than take the several days it required to leaf through the hundreds of resumes we had on file, department managers could go to the main computer and search out the qualifications they were looking for. This new system not only saved our hiring managers time but also cut the cost of having to place a help wanted ad in the local newspaper or hire a recruiting firm to find new employees. With so many resumes to choose from, there were plenty of qualified individuals sitting right there all along.

✗ NO: Though I have not initiated any real changes on my own, I have supported the ideas of others—many of which I thought of beforehand.

Here's your chance to give proof of your dedication to your work and your ability to see the entire picture. Prove that if given the chance, you can be instrumental in making significant changes to the company or to the way things are done. Give proof of your effectiveness in making things happen; express your desire to do the same for this company. Sometimes this same question can be asked in a more specific manner. For example, Describe a time in your work experience when you thought an existing process or manner of doing things could have been done better, and what you did about it.

Q: Describe a time when you had to alter your leadership style.

✔ YES: In my current position, I am put in charge of approximately one new project per month. Each month, I am assigned a new group of employees—usually a group of new recruits—to help them learn how to see a project through to completion. My usual style is to look the project over beforehand, figure out the best solution, and begin delegating tasks. About a year ago, the

assigned group began to question my initial plan to complete the project. They proposed some alternate ideas, and I was quite impressed by their suggestions. While it had always been my style to assume that my idea was the right way to approach a project, this team taught me differently. Since then, the first step I take when beginning any new project is to talk with the group and figure out a solution—together.

✗ NO: When I first started my last position, I saw all sorts of things that could have been done differently. Immediately, I started talking to other employees about initiating these changes. Though some were receptive to the ideas, they suggested I talk to our supervisor about them. When I told the supervisor my ideas, he said no to every one of them. While I tried to rally the group to support these changes, they sided with the supervisor. Rather than continuing to fight or to explain why my way was better, I just kept quiet for the rest of my employment.

Assure the employer of your willingness and ability to create strong working relationships by making different kinds of people comfortable with your authority. Your answer should indicate a time when you encountered a person or group that questioned your leadership style, and how you worked to change it. Be specific. What initiatives did you take to improve a less-than-ideal situation? What would the other people involved say about you now? Don't make yourself out to be a tyrant, but don't seem like a wimp either. Indicate that the reasons for your change in style were a result of your keen ability to deal with people.

Q: Tell me about a situation in which you were able to persuade others to adopt your idea.

✔ YES: When I began working for my current employer, I realized that the number of repeat customers we had was very low. Coming from a company that depended heavily upon repeat business from their core customers to make up about 50 percent of their annual revenue, I knew that this was certainly an area

that needed improvement. I approached my boss about spending a little bit of time contacting previous customers and trying to obtain feedback about their experiences. Though he considered it a waste of time, he agreed to let me spend one week initiating the project. After hundreds of phone calls, letters, and e-mails, I realized that the customers were not coming back because they found our company to be inattentive and hard to reach. Many claimed that they called the customer service department several times a day and did not get an answer. From that point on, I tried to pitch in whenever I could. If I heard the phone ringing, I would grab it immediately. Other supervisors began to see my dedication, and they too decided to help. Eventually, we were able to hire a full staff to support this department so that each and every one of our customers could be heard. Since that time, we have seen an increase in sales of approximately 40 percent, much of that being attributed to repeat customers.

✗ NO: When I was hired on as the sales manager at my current company, the first thing I noticed was the lack of enthusiasm amongst the sales representatives I would be supervising. Though they came to work and did what was asked of them, they didn't seem to have any real enthusiasm for what they were doing. While I was in the office until 7 P.M. each night, they were leaving at 5 P.M. I decided to have a meeting with the department members to give them a chance to hear my philosophy on sales, which is this: If you are able to leave the office at the end of the day, you're not doing your job correctly. And if you aren't doing your job correctly, you better start looking for a new company. From that point on, I don't recall *anyone* leaving at 5 P.M. I think that by explaining my position, I was able to persuade them all that my way of thinking was the right way of thinking.

This question is one commonly asked in interviews for sales positions. The employer is interested in whether or not you can rally support for your ideas and make people comfortable adopting them. It is also a test of your initiative. If you answer that you can't think of a time, you are describing yourself as a

follower with no real ideas of your own. Make sure that it is your own gift of persuasion that got your coworkers to adopt the idea, and not some form of tyranny.

Q: How do you think a past subordinate would describe your leadership style?

✔ **YES:** I think that those who have worked under me have considered it a positive experience. I look at my role as a supervisor as the chance to have a say in something and contribute to the success of the company. I do not believe it is my place to have the final ruling. I am not one of those people who constantly reminds you that "I'm in charge!" Before making decisions, I consult with my team to see what kinds of ideas they can come up with. This kind of leadership has been the key to much success in the past, and it's the model I plan to use throughout my career. Colleagues and employees have both commented to me on the positive work atmosphere that I create; I take that as the highest compliment.

✘ **NO:** Former and current subordinates alike probably think that I'm a bit difficult to work for, but I would hope that they can still learn something from my expertise. Though most of my colleagues take a more open approach to their departments, I think they would agree that my methods have been successful in reaching set goals.

By asking this question, the interviewer is trying to determine what your references will say if and when they are called upon. Make sure that when describing yourself, you are objective and realistic without embellishing or being overly modest. Describe candidly your leadership style; give specific examples that reflect your personal approach. Even if your style is to retain ultimate control, what are its positive aspects? Keep in mind that the employer may very likely call your colleagues to find out the truth from them. Rather than make excuses for your style, explain your leadership approach and why it works for you. If you can, give examples of how this style has led to success.

Q: Do you believe that past job appraisals have adequately reflected your abilities as a leader?

✔ **YES:** I think that the many goals I have surpassed and the various projects I have seen through to successful completion are proof of my strong leadership skills. I am sure that any job appraisal would mention the way in which I look to my team for support, as well as how I take the time to clearly define our objectives to all those around me. By creating a certain amount of camaraderie, I have been able to gain the confidence and respect of my coworkers, which, in my opinion, is the real key to success.

✗ **NO:** As the first chance I had to really take on the role of leader ended rather disastrously, I would imagine my appraisal would be rather poor. Still, though the project failed, I feel that my performance was fine. I was given a very difficult team of subordinates, which was the real cause of my problems.

If you've ever had an experience where—under your supervision—a project failed, this is the time to explain that struggle. Even if a project failed, how did you work to affect this project in a positive manner? What were the steps that you took to ensure its success anyway? Just because a project did not turn out as well as you had hoped for does not mean that your job appraisal should be negative. Avoid taking offense to this question or blaming a project gone awry on someone else. Regardless of your team, you were the leader. Talk about the ways in which you would translate your past successes *and* failures to this job. What lessons have you learned? Which pitfalls do you know to avoid in the future?

Q: Describe the situations in which you feel most comfortable as a leader.

✔ **YES:** I think that one of my talents is the ability to take complex issues and break them into their simplest parts. For this reason, I have always been very good at solving problems that

involve facts and figures. As those that work around me are quite aware of this, they usually allow me to emerge as the leader in situations in which there is a complex problem; they look to me to find a solution and instruct them on how to proceed, and I am happy to do so. I am a highly effective leader in these situations. In situations in which there are political or emotional factors to consider, I usually prefer that someone else take the lead. In such situations, I simply resolve to be a good team player. In all other situations, I normally surface as a leader.

✗ NO: The only time I feel comfortable leading is when I have the ultimate say in a matter.

The situations in which you feel most *comfortable* being a leader say an awful lot about you. Do you feel comfortable leading a situation only when it is specifically asked of you, or do you assert yourself in situations in which you think your expertise could help bring a project to a successful conclusion? Talk a little bit about the projects you have led and how other people have trusted you. Why do you think people are willing to follow you in situations such as these? The best way to answer this question is to discuss the times you were recognized as the leader because of your expertise in something, not because you were appointed "project leader." If you're asked to describe situations in which you are a better contributor than leader, you can define types of problems that you're less comfortable working on or situations in which you feel you're too opinionated or biased to lead without controlling the group unfairly. Then end by describing instances when you've played the leader well.

Q: Describe how comfortable you are working with people of higher rank versus working with employees of lower rank.

✔ YES: I am on a friendly basis with just about everyone I come into contact with throughout the course of my workday. I recently learned that one of the receptionists and I work out at the same gym, so we carpool after work and are becoming friends because of that. On the other hand, the general manager and I also share several common

Insider Tips

Strategic Tactics

Adapt your answers to match the type of company for which you're interviewing. For example, if you're interviewing for a job at a large product-marketing company that emphasizes group decision-making and spends much of its energy focused on battles for market share with its competitors, you might want to talk about how much you enjoy team sports—especially being part of a team and competing to win.

Strange but True

Interview Behavior

In addition to the requested resume, cover letter, and writing sample the job applicant had been asked to bring, he decided to bring along his pet ferret, claiming that he "gets lonesome when no one is at home."

interests. We have golfed together on a few occasions and have spent many a lunch discussing our various common interests. I pride myself on getting to know those around me personally while, at the same time, building strong working relationships.

✗ NO: I don't really pay much attention to the assistants and other people of lower rank in my department. My boss, on the other hand, is someone I respect immensely. I am always offering to help him out, and I think that because I have spent so many weekends at work for him, he genuinely likes me.

Be very specific here in discussing your relationships. Talk about how you have been able to build strong relationships with all those around you. Don't talk as if those who work under you are below you socially, and don't seem too obsequious when talking about your boss. Though those of higher rank should always command respect, you shouldn't let them walk all over you. By discussing all they ways in which you "help out" your boss, you may be setting yourself up as the company's next doormat.

Professionalism

Some of the best-known businesspeople in the world have been known to crack under pressure. Sure, it can happen to anyone, but it's not exactly a trait that employers are seeking out. An employer wants to know that when they hire you, they are hiring a level-headed, hardworking individual who will do whatever it takes to make sure that a project gets done—and gets done well! Talk about the ways in which you have seen a project through to completion in the past, and about how you will work to do so with this company.

Q: Give an example of how you saw a project through, despite various obstacles.

✔ YES: My promotion from account representative to account manager required that I pass on many of my oldest accounts to the new account representative. After two years of dealing directly with

me, some of these accounts did not take kindly to a new face. Some even threatened to move their accounts if I could not be part of their projects. While I had plenty of work to do adjusting to my new job, I assigned myself the role of "account advisor" to all of the accounts who were having problems adjusting. I took the time to visit each of these accounts personally, with the new account rep, and discuss the changes that were taking place within our company. I assured each of the accounts that I would be there for them if they needed answers but that they should refer to the new rep with any new business. After a few months of phone calls, they eventually began to stop. The accounts realized that my replacement had a lot of talent, and they began to trust in his abilities. To this day, each of those accounts is still with my company.

✗ NO: After just a few months with my current company, we underwent a large restructuring program. Frustrated with the way the "new" company was being run, most of the employees in my own department began to look for and accept new jobs. With a huge project on our hands and less than half the antici- pated work force, I was asked to make huge sacrifices in order to complete this project. I worked late almost every night for a month, came in one weekend, skipped lunch, you name it. In the end, the project turned out okay—but because I don't want to have to go through this again, I am looking for a new job.

The goal in your answer is to demonstrate your competence and willingness to do well, even when the pressure's on. Don't dwell on the obstacles themselves; the interviewer doesn't care about the problems of your current or former company. Focus your answer on how you approached these obstacles, and the results that you got.

Q: Tell me about a time when you showed real determination.

✔ YES: The majority of my coworkers at my current company are over the age of 40. That said, many of them had never had to use the Internet and were unfamiliar with online communication.

When my company went online, nobody seemed to appreciate what this could do for the face of our business. Most of the employees weren't sure what to do. I was convinced that if everyone took the time to learn about the Internet, they would all find it a much easier way to do business. I began a promotion in which each morning I would send out via e-mail a trivia contest. The first person to get all answers right and send them back via e-mail, would win a prize. As the employees became more comfortable using e-mail to enter the trivia contest, they began using the Internet to help them conduct business as well.

✗ NO: When I was in college, there was this really attractive girl who would never go out with me. I must have asked her 50 times in the course of one semester, and each time she said no. I began sending her letters and gifts and calling her on the phone. Finally, after months of trying, she finally agreed to go out with me.

Talk about a time when you persevered to accomplish a goal. You can use either a professional or a personal goal here, as long as it reflects an interest in developing new skills. Demonstrate your ability to gather resources, predict obstacles, and manage stress. Talk about the results you obtained.

Q: Tell me about a time when you showed real diligence or perseverance.

✔ YES: I was working on an installation project when about half way through to completion, the client decided that she wanted something different. While for many this would cause quite an obstacle, my partner and I agreed that we could still get the work done by the original completion date. We had to put in about 70 hours a week for the next few months, but we did it to make sure that the client was happy and the project went according to plan.

✗ NO: I had been working for my company for a few months and thought that I had contributed a lot to the company and, therefore, deserved some sort of raise. I badgered the boss day

and night until eventually he gave in. He gave me a raise and said that it was because I had been able to wear him down.

Talk about your professional character. Describe your focus, diligence, and accountability. Demonstrate how you gather resources, manage your time wisely, or are willing to go the extra mile. Use a specific example from your professional, educational, or personal history. Make sure you don't paint a somewhat problematic picture of yourself. There's a big difference between being determined and just plain annoying and tiring.

Q: What is the most difficult task you have ever been given?

✔ **YES:** I was given the task of cutting costs by at least 5 percent within my sales division. Obviously, none of the managers I had to talk to about this thought that it was their department that needed to cut costs, and they didn't see any place where it could be done short of firing people. Remaining objective, I decided that it was up to each of the department heads to agree to an equal percentage of cost cuts. In the end, each department head agreed to a 25 percent reduction in travel expenses. Though each department required heavy traveling, they made it a point to book flights at least two weeks in advance and to combine trips. In the end, the pinch was barely felt, and I was able to accomplish my goal.

✘ **NO:** I was in charge of sending out letters to all those employees who we had interviewed but had not hired. Sending out rejection after rejection became very difficult for me.

Make sure to talk about a task that from a business standpoint was difficult to accomplish. Describing a situation in which you had difficulty doing something because of personal reasons (e.g., firing someone) does not indicate that you are a strong leader. For recent graduates, it is okay to talk about an educational task or project that was difficult for you to do. Talk about how you went about performing this task, the steps you took, and the end result.

Q: Do you think that your current boss would describe you as someone who goes the extra mile?

✔ **YES:** Absolutely! I have been with the company for three years, and in each of my past reviews, she has pointed that fact out. It seems as though I am always the first one in the office each morning and the last one to leave. I am not happy until my job is done, and done well. This is one of the things I think my current boss appreciates the most.

✘ **NO:** I think, maybe, she would. On the few occasions that we have been asked to put in a little bit of overtime, I have not complained.

Someone who "goes the extra mile," by definition, is someone that puts in an extra effort "just because." These are people who work later hours, take on extra work, and so forth, without being asked or told it is mandatory. Employees like this are loyal to their employer and, therefore, a great asset to any company. Be prepared to offer proof that you are this type of employee. Talk about a time when you were willing to help tackle a tough problem, and demonstrated your ability and willingness to work hard in doing so. If you do talk about your willingness to put in extra hours, make sure that the interviewer realizes this was done as a result of enthusiasm and hard work, and not the result of poor time management on the part of you or your supervisor.

Q: How many days were you absent from work in the past year, and why?

✔ **YES:** I was absent from work three days last year. I caught the flu early in the year and was forced to miss two days, and I experienced a death in the family just last month and took a day off.

✘ **NO:** I used up all of my sick time last year because I am prone to illness, especially during the winter months.

A history of absenteeism, tardiness, or any indication of a weak work ethic can be detrimental to your candidacy. Answering this question should be an easy way to score points in your favor. Even if you used up all of your sick and/or personal days, tell

the interviewer the reason. Be honest (lying will be found out). If you think your poor attendance may be a source of bad references, be prepared to give a detailed and exonerating explanation of why you have missed so much work in the past. Most importantly, convince the interviewer of your dependability and assure him or her that punctuality and/or absenteeism is not something they should worry about.

Q: Are you punctual?

✔ **YES:** Yes. In the past year, I have only been late to work on one or two occasions, and each time I have called my supervisor ahead of time to let him know. On each occasion, it was a matter of traffic delays.

✗ **NO:** I tend to get to the office about 10 minutes or so late every day, but I make it up at the end of the day.

This is really just an alternate version of the previous question. The problem here is that whereas there is a definitive answer to the earlier question ("I was out three days."), this question is much more open ended. Again, to say yes to this question when you know that you are always tardy will certainly come back to haunt you.

Q: Tell me about a time when you feel you didn't perform to your full potential.

✔ **YES:** The first time I had to give a presentation to our board, I failed to anticipate some of their questions. I was unprepared for anything other than what I wanted to report. Now my director and I brainstorm all the what-ifs in advance.

✗ **NO:** When I first began working for my current company, I was full of all sorts of ideas that I thought would be helpful to the company. Each time I would submit one of these ideas to my supervisor, he would reject it without an explanation. Finally, I began to think that no idea would ever be good enough for him. As a result, I have not submitted a new idea in months.

This is one question that actually forces the candidate to confront a negative experience in his or her past. How you answer this and the example you give are of the utmost importance. The best way to field such a question is to talk about a mistake you made early in your career, making it easy to lay the blame on a lack of experience. Talking about current mistakes will depict you as incompetent. After briefly describing the situation, finish the story with the better judgment you have shown since then in facing similar experiences. Look to that mistake as a learning experience, and tell the interviewer what it has taught you.

> **Q: We have found that all of our employees fall into one of two categories: concept oriented or task oriented. Which of these categories do you think you would fit into?**

✔ **YES:** When given a project, I like to be involved in every step. From initial solutions to final product, I like to be able to use my creativity and strong problem-solving abilities. That said, I would definitely consider myself more concept oriented.

✘ **NO:** Since I was a philosophy major, I think that I am definitely a more concept-oriented person. This would probably help to make me a unique member of your manufacturing team.

Don't slight the question by coming up with an all-encompassing answer ("I've got a little bit of both in me!") Choose a side and stay there. Describe some of your personal characteristics that made you choose this orientation. Most importantly, be sure that the answer you choose coincides with the job description. If you are to be engaged in manual labor 40 hours a week, it is not likely that your orientation toward concepts will help you in any way. Similarly, if your job entails a lot of creativity, being task oriented is not necessarily the best way to be. Whatever answer you come up with, make sure to relate it to the job in some way.

Q: What would your supervisor tell me about your attention to detail?

✔ YES: As my supervisor relies heavily on me to think projects through with her, I am confident that she would praise my attention to detail. I know how easy it can be for someone to overlook the smallest details of a project, and I pride myself on catching these mistakes before they find their way into the final results.

✗ NO: In the past, there have been some questions as to the speed at which I deliver my work. It seems that in my haste to get projects completed on deadline, I have missed some small details that have affected the overall result of the project. Not one of these oversights has ever resulted in a major problem. I look at it this way: What I lack in attention to detail, I make up for in the speed of my work.

Regardless of the job you hold or the industry you belong to, a strong attention to detail is a great asset. Throughout the day, there are so many small details that often get overlooked that it is comforting for employers to know they have employees they can count on. If your attention to detail track record is not the best, don't try and push off the importance of this trait by discussing another one of your strengths. Instead, admit that you have let mistakes get past you before, but talk about how you are working to stop this. If you do, in fact, have a strong attention to detail, talk about an experience when this really helped you in some way.

Q: How do you manage stress in your daily work?

✔ YES: Unless I have a ton of work to do that I just can't get away from, I make sure that when I take my lunch hour, I actually leave my office. Just that simple change of scenery, even for a few minutes, is enough to keep me energized for the rest of the day.

✗ NO: I'm a big believer in the 20-minute power nap. Each afternoon, assuming there's not a lot of priority work to get done, I slip into my office and take a 20-minute snooze. I wake up feeling like I can take on the world!

This is a simple enough question to answer. The interviewer is interested in whether you have a tendency to crack under pressure. He or she wants to know how you manage high-pressure situations. If you have a simple daily ritual that helps you maintain your composure, even in stressful situations, tell them about it. It may also be helpful to describe a stressful project you've worked on and the specific actions you took to get it done without losing your head. If you think that your ways of relieving stress—yelling at those who hold lower positions, taking in a movie in the midst of the work day—would be frowned upon by your current boss or a future one, do yourself a favor and keep it to yourself. The key is to talk about how you keep *professional* when under a lot of pressure.

Q: In your current job, how do you prioritize?

✔ YES: My normal plan of action is to work with my two largest accounts in the first part of the day. That way, if there are any major interruptions, I know that my key accounts are well taken care of.

✗ NO: I'm very much of the "first come, first serve" philosophy. I don't spend much time prioritizing my work; whoever can get a hold of me first will have my attention.

This question relates to key aspects of your professional style: your organization and your ability to manage your time. It also touches upon your ability to know which tasks are the most important and which projects can wait until later. Talk about the way in which you attack each new day. If there is no pressing project, how do you know what to do first? Demonstrate your ability to gather resources, predict obstacles,

and manage the typical stress that occurs. Talk about the ways in which you have become a better time manager over the past few months or years. Above all, point out that you come to work with an organized plan every day and don't just rely on jobs to come your way.

Q: Describe a professional skill you've been able to acquire in your current position or at your current company.

✔ **YES:** While I had used computers quite extensively in my previous positions, I had never been introduced to database technology. As my current company relies heavily upon several different databases to store all of our work, I have become quite an expert in programs such as ACT. What used to take me hours of research and typing can now be completed with just a few clicks of the mouse.

✗ **NO:** In the past, I have had less than perfect customer service skills. I have even been reprimanded for being impolite on the phone. I have always found it much easier to deal with people face to face.

The best way to answer this question is to talk about a new skill that you have learned—and worked toward mastering—while at your current job. Though it is okay to talk about a skill that you have been able to improve upon in your current job, you don't want to raise any unnecessary flags in the interviewer's mind. You certainly don't want to draw attention to negative aspects of your professional abilities, even if they're in the past and even if it's something you've worked toward overcoming. The point of this question is to disprove the theory that you can't teach an old dog new tricks (no matter how old or young you are). You want to make sure that the interviewer sees you as a desirable candidate, and one who is able and ready to take on new tasks with enthusiasm. You could tell your interviewer about any new software applications you've learned, professional seminars you've attended, or adult-education classes you've taken.

Insider Tips

Imperfect Performances

Don't expect to give a perfect performance, especially in your first few interviews. If you have a terrible interview, don't let it shake your confidence! Remember that everyone has a bad interview experience sooner or later. Learn from it, work on your performance, and keep looking for other opportunities.

Q: Why is service such an important issue?

✔ **YES:** Asking why service is important would be the same as asking why customers are important; it is the heart and soul of any business. You can't have a business without customers, and you can't maintain customers without a strong dedication to service. If a customer isn't receiving a level of service that meets or exceeds his or her expectations, you can be sure that customer will be taking their business elsewhere. And it's likely that he or she will relay that information to other would-be customers. On the other hand, if you are dedicated to providing the best service you can, customers will keep coming back for more, and they'll still tell others about you. In many instances service may be the one thing that distinguishes a company from the competition. A bad reputation for service may compromise a company's position in the marketplace.

✘ **NO:** Service is important because it really is what a company's reputation is built on. Still, while service *is* important, it is still the product that can make or break a company. I know plenty of companies that have a great product but poor service, and I keep going back for more.

A question like this is used to gauge your business sense. The interviewer is trying to determine whether or not you understand the importance of good customer service in establishing a positive image in the marketplace. If you can, talk about the ways in which you or your company has taken steps to ensure good customer service, and how that has benefited you or your company. Show that you understand the impact of repeat business, and convince the interviewer that you will work hard to uphold a standard of good service.

Q: Tell me about a time when you had to deal with an angry customer. How did you handle the situation?

✔ **YES:** As you can imagine, in the retail world, you are forced to deal with irate customers from time to time, regardless of how strong your product or customer service is. I specifically remember one occasion in which a customer was angry because the item he had purchased

was not working properly once he got it home. The best way to handle these situations, in my opinion, is to always remember that there is a simple solution. Products can be fixed, exchanged, or refunded. I try to think of myself in terms of the consumer. When discussing the problem with the customer, I speak in a calm, even voice, thus prompting the customer to do the same. The main issue to be concerned with is solving the problem at hand, and you need to be professional enough to get that done.

✗ NO: In my current position as a retail manager, I would say that we get an irate customer in the store at least once or twice a week. While at first I was taken aback by the sometimes abusive behavior of these people, I have come to accept it as part of my job. Now, when angry customers call or come in, I am quick to stop them from going on and on about the problem they are having. If they are not happy with the product, fine! I lay out their options—refund or exchange—and let them make the choice. You just have to become immune to the anger.

How you react to an unsatisfied customer is very important in most positions, and especially important if you work in a service industry. The interviewer will be looking for evidence of your aptitude for work that involves a great deal of contact with the public, even in situations in which the public isn't being too nice. Give an example of a time when you were faced with a difficult person and how you handled it. Be sure to explain the result of that situation, if in fact something positive came out of it (e.g., the customer reordered a week later). Your answer should illustrate your maturity, diplomacy, and awareness of the needs and feelings of others. Though you shouldn't take such things personally, you should be able to show compassion to the customers who are in need of pacification.

Q: Are there any issues in your personal life that might in some way affect your professional career?

✔ YES: I really pride myself on my keen ability to separate my personal life from my work life. When I'm in the office, I am an

employee of the company. This is not the time for me to deal with or worry about issues in my personal life.

✗ NO: Because I have two growing children, there is always the possibility that I could be called out of work at a moment's notice. My kids are also very active; they each play sports throughout the year, and I do like to leave early on occasion to go and cheer them on.

The interviewer wants to make sure that you're not going to be bringing your home life to work with you. If you are dealing with stressful personal issues (e.g., a divorce), the company wants to be sure that your time spent at work will be concentrated on work only. Though certain questions about your beliefs or your family are illegal, the interviewer wants to know whether you will be able to perform the duties this job calls for. In the health services industry, for example, personal issues that have not been worked through properly could easily affect your judgment in assessing patients, planning treatments, and making recommendations. Make sure the interviewer knows that you are a fully integrated individual and that your professional life and personal life always remain separate.

Q: Tell me about a time when your diplomacy skills were really put to the test.

✔ YES: I recall one incident in which a customer came into the store I work for and demanded her money back on an evening dress that had apparently been worn. Because this kind of situation happens often—people want a fancy dress to wear for one night only—we have a strict policy that says once the tags are removed, there are no refunds. The woman claimed that the dress had become very worn looking after being sent to the dry cleaner and that they had claimed it was a faulty fabric. Rather than argue with the woman about the policy and about the fact that the tags had been removed, I happily refunded her money, though I didn't believe that she was being honest. In the end, I decided it was more important to keep the other customers

from hearing her complain and then doubting the quality of our merchandise.

✗ NO: When my boss asked that I become a sort of "office spy" for him, I was very hesitant. I had built strong relationships with many of my coworkers and did not want to be the one to report back to the boss about who was not doing their work. Still, feeling that my own job might be in jeopardy, I agreed. I was able to get the information my boss needed very easily from my coworkers and report back to him within a week. In the end, my ability to blend in with my coworkers and my close relationship with my boss allowed me to be promoted to the position I am in now.

Diplomacy involves using tact, finesse, and good judgment to reach an end that is ultimately beneficial to the entire company. Being "diplomatic" for selfish reasons is closer to back-handedness. In answering this question, make sure you demonstrate a pragmatic sensibility. Talk about a problem situation with a client or a work associate that you resolved by remaining objective. How did you show empathy and build rapport? What was the end result? How did this help all those involved, including yourself?

Q: How do you manage your work week while making realistic deadlines?

✔ YES: Unless there is an extremely pressing issue, I always reserve two hours of dead time every day so that I can take care of any unanticipated problems that may occur. I used to have each minute of my day allotted to certain projects, but I found that that didn't allow for unexpected phone calls, problems, or situations. By planning for only 6 or 7 hours of work time, I am able to manage my own projects, and quickly respond to the needs of my boss and staff.

✗ NO: My strategy is to work until what needs to get done does! If I am approaching a deadline and that means I need to work throughout the weekend or stay late a few nights, fine.

Job Search
Odds and Ends

Taboo Topic

Though many employees disagree, more and more companies are trying to establish a no-dating clause within their company. The reason they do this is not to prevent you from having any fun but to ensure that you are able to draw a line between your professional life and your personal life. As Shakespeare tells us, the course of true love does not run smoothly. This holds true for romances that originate and blossom in the workplace. Ask anyone who's tried it, and they'll most likely tell you the same. One way to tarnish your image in the eyes of an employer is to mention an interoffice romance.

Your ability to manage your time is at the heart of this question. While a willingness to put in overtime and come into work on your days off is highly desirable, the ability to manage your time wisely so that you *don't* have to do that is what this interviewer is after. The best way to answer this question is to describe—in detail—how you establish priorities, set deadlines, and determine schedules.

Q: Tell me about a time you had to extend a deadline.

✔ **YES:** Two weeks into a project, it became clear that the client expected much more than we had originally decided on. Rather than refuse his requests, we showed him a price structure similar to a menu, from which he could choose more features at a higher cost and in a longer time frame. He opted for something in the middle that he understood would cause a three-week adjustment to the schedule. We then renegotiated the original contract, and both parties were more than satisfied with the final results.

✘ **NO:** I had figured that the project I was given would take me about two months to complete. As I got closer and closer to the end of the second month, I realized that I was going to need at least another two to three weeks to get the project done. I informed the client of my decision, and though he wasn't really happy about it, I think he was genuinely impressed with the end result.

The last thing an employer wants to hear about in this answer is your poor work ethic, your lack of proper time management skills, or your inability to set realistic deadlines. Talk about your accountability and your willingness to adjust a deadline if you think it will add to the overall quality of a project. Think about what could have happened had you not adjusted this deadline. Would the overall goal have been compromised? After deciding to adjust the deadline, how were you able to improve upon the project?

Q: What personal skill or work habit have you struggled to improve?

✔ **YES:** I think that one habit I have worked very hard to overcome is my inability to say no. I used to be helpful to the point of overextension. It didn't matter that I already had a full plate or whether or not I thought I could do a good job on a project; I would simply always say yes when employees asked me for help. Now, when someone asks me to do something for him or her, I counter with something I'd like help on in return. Since doing so, cooperation in my office has improved considerably.

✘ **NO:** I have always had a bit of a problem with authority. From the time I started school until the time I entered the workplace, I've always had a problem with people telling me what to do. Eventually, I began to realize that there is a definite chain of command in the workplace. In order to get to the place where *I* get to do the bossing around, I need to listen to my current supervisors. I think my current boss would agree that I have improved as far as my respect toward her.

Here's another one of those questions that forces you to confront a negative aspect of your professional character. The interviewer wants to hear about a particular skill that you have had trouble acquiring, or something about yourself that you have had to change for the betterment of the workplace. The smartest way to answer this question is to find an example from your earliest days in the workplace so that any sort of negative quality can be attributed to your lack of experience. Talking about a problem that you have been trying to overcome in your current job will only show the interviewer that that trait could follow you to your new place of business. In the end, make sure you leave no question in the interviewer's mind as to whether that particular work habit is still an obstacle.

Q: What books do you keep on your desk?

✔ **YES:** The two most important books on my desk are my dictionary and thesaurus. Though I would consider myself a very strong writer,

I am always looking for new words to use so that my writing does not become stale. I also keep a copy of Strunk and White's *The Elements of Style*, which is a good reference for looking up all the grammar rules that you learned in high school and college but forgot.

✗ **NO:** I'm a big fan of Jay McInerney, and you can always find one of his books on my desk. When I get a chance during the day, I like to try and cram in a few chapters. *Bright Lights, Big City* is by far my favorite of his novels.

In asking this question, the interviewer is not interested in whether you have any interest in joining his book club. He or she is trying to determine whether or not you take your profession seriously. If you've ever worked in an office, you know that there are two kinds of workers: those with an amazingly cluttered desk and those with an amazingly neat desk (as a side note, it's those with the amazingly neat desk that you sometimes have to worry about). Amongst this mess, what are the tools you use most frequently during the workday? For an editor, or someone who does a lot of writing, a dictionary or a similar reference book is a good thing to have handy. For someone who does a lot of cold calling, perhaps a phone book would be of some use. In any case, answering this question by telling the recruiter your top ten favorite authors of all time is certainly not the way to go.

CHAPTER THIRTEEN

It's All about You!

Your Accomplishments

Accomplishments are one way to measure your success in the workplace. Think of all the times you have risen above and beyond your typical job description and done something great for the company. Don't bore the interviewer to death with your heroic tales; focus specifically on the actions you took and the results you obtained. The best thing about accomplishments is that they can be examples from your professional career, academic years, or personal experiences.

Q: Tell me about a major accomplishment in your life.

✔ **YES:** As the publicity director of a tiny, alternative publishing house, it can be difficult to get major sources to review our books. Because the subjects we cover are often far from the mainstream, many television shows and review publications find our topics a bit too controversial. Last year, we published a book that I really thought could have been a number one bestseller. Though I always put forth a lot of effort to publicize all of the books we published, I was particularly interested in seeing this little gem find its way from obscurity to popularity. As a result of all my efforts, coverage of this book really reached sky high. The book became a *New York Times* bestseller, and both the author and the book have become household names.

✗ **NO:** I saved my last company from financial ruin.

Talk to the interviewer about an accomplishment in your life that you are most proud of. The accomplishment can be work related, but it doesn't have to be. Be honest and be specific. Don't just throw out a general statement ("I won an award"); describe the steps you took to accomplish this goal and how all your hard work paid off in the end. Don't exaggerate or boast, as interviewers have ways of finding out whether or not you are telling the truth. Don't be long winded. Instead, focus on your actual accomplishments and the steps you took to get there. The interviewer wants to know whether or not you will be able

to contribute something to this company; this is a great opportunity to prove that you can.

Q: Tell me about a contribution you've made to a team accomplishment.

✔ **YES:** In my current company, all projects are worked on by an entire work group. My last work group was comprised of five very intelligent and very creative people. However, the overall technical skills were a bit lacking. People knew how they wanted our presentation to look, but they didn't know how to go about achieving that. I am an avid computer user and have taken several classes in graphic design. I think that the group's creativity, coupled with my technical skills, allowed us to come up with a really fantastic presentation that the client accepted without hesitation.

✗ **NO:** Though I sometimes work in groups, I do prefer to work independently. When the situation arises that I am placed within a group setting, however, I think that I am very effective in immediately asserting myself as the leader. As I am used to having the final say in each step of a project, I bring this individualized, can-do attitude to the group. I am always volunteering to do the brunt of the work, and in most cases, the group goes along with this.

Even if you spend most of your time working independently—or work independently because you choose to—the interviewer wants to be reassured that you can and do deal with other people well. When placed within a group setting, do you immediately try to take control, or do you offer up a certain expertise? Think about the kinds of tasks you've performed before in group settings, and the skills that you have mastered. What would the other members of your team say about your contributions? Would they want to work with you again? Would they consider your skills vital to the team's success? Offer proof, using specific examples, that you delivered more than the team

Insider Tips

Reading Trade Literature

You should make a habit of reading the trade literature of the industry you are focusing on; you should also read some background books about the field. Remember, your aim is to sound like an industry insider; you'll need to be familiar with industry-related topics while you're networking and interviewing.

expected and that the team would compliment your contributions to the group's efforts.

Q: Are there any special contributions you feel you've made to your employer?

✔ **YES:** For the past four years, I have run a Walk for Hunger campaign at my company. I believe that it is a very important cause, and I know it can be very difficult for a company to find volunteers, so I stepped in to help. Each year has been more successful than the last, and coworkers have told me it's one of the things they look forward to most throughout the course of the year, which obviously makes me very happy.

✗ **NO:** I think that I have made a special contribution to my company every day that I have been there. Even if they don't realize it now, these contributions will certainly be missed upon my departure.

Convince the interviewer that you are ready to go the extra mile for your employer. Tell him or her about a specific time when you delivered more than the employer expected, "just because." Let the interviewer know that you deliver more than your employer expects. If you were hired, what situations would you handle especially well? What unique contributions can you make to the organization? How would you go the extra mile?

Q: If you were hired here today, what is the first thing you would do?

✔ **YES:** I would help to increase your business within the software market. Though your company is mainly known for its printed products, I believe that your software is one of your greatest assets. I have spent the past four years working as a sales manager for a software developer, so I have a great understanding of how to market these products more effectively.

✗ **NO:** I would call up my wife and tell her to put on something nice, because I'm taking her out to dinner to celebrate!

In addition to your showing your enthusiasm for a job, this question tests your knowledge of a company and its products. Give the interviewer clear, tangible evidence that the company will benefit immediately upon hiring you. Focus your answer on the action you would take, and—above all—make sure your goals are realistic. Is there an area you think could use some improvement? Discuss the steps you would take to achieve maximum results. Do you have a creative way in which you could improve some aspect of the company? Talk about it. If you can, relate what you would like to accomplish in this company to past achievements and experience.

Q: Tell me about an accomplishment you had a difficult time achieving.

✔ **YES:** When I first began working for my current company, part of my job required meeting with our technical support staff once a week to find out about any technical problems or issues we were facing. As part of the human resources team, it was my duty to voice any concerns these people had to the right people and get the problems fixed. I didn't have very much experience with computers and was quite embarrassed that—for the most part—I didn't understand their complaints. I didn't know what a modem was, and I certainly didn't know how to increase the speed of one. I decided that in order to do a great job, I would need to learn more about what it was that each of our departments did. Whenever I could find the time, I would go down to the technical department and sit in for a while. When I had questions, I would ask them. The staff was always very happy to answer and seemed pleased that I had taken so much interest in learning more about their job. Although I definitely struggled for the first month or so, I now can converse about the technical problems with the best of them, and employee satisfaction has never been higher.

✗ **NO:** I was asked to complete an end-of-the-year marketing report with the assistance of one of our department's newest hires. After just a few minutes of working with this person, I knew our

partnership would not be a happy one. My assistant was a recent college graduate who wanted to use all of her recently acquired in-class studies to complete the report in a more efficient manner. When I tried to explain the way that had worked best for me for the past several years, she assured me that her way was better. For the next two weeks, all I heard from this young woman was how everything I did was wrong. Though the report was completed on time and done well, it was not easy dealing with this new partnership.

Be careful what you are implying when you answer this question. Citing an instance in which the problem was a coworker can make you sound as though you're not much of a team player, or that you're a bit of a know-it-all. Talk to the interviewer about a time when you've accomplished something despite obstacles, lack of training, or inadequate experience. Focus on your ability to overcome this problem and achieve successful results in the end. Express your willingness to accept your challenges, and your ability to triumph over them.

Q: Tell me about something you accomplished that required strict discipline.

✔ **YES:** When I was a full-time graduate student, my one goal was to avoid accruing any more student loan debt. In addition to working toward an advanced degree in journalism, I spent 20 hours a week as an unpaid intern at a local magazine and another 25 hours a week as a waitress. Juggling these three very hectic, very demanding schedules was certainly a challenge, but it makes me appreciate all that I have achieved that much more now.

✘ **NO:** I decided that I needed to lose 10 pounds for a friend's wedding that was less than two months away. Though I had to stop snacking during the day and cut desserts out of my diet, I did it and was able to shed the weight by the time the big day came around.

Here's another opportunity for you to discuss a skill you have had to work hard to develop, and have been successful doing. This is also an opportunity to discuss a time when the amount of work you had and the time in which you needed to finish it were a challenge. Discuss your strong time management skills and how you are able to prioritize to accomplish a goal. How did you remain focused? What were the end results? What did you learn from the experience?

Q: What situations do your colleagues rely on you to handle?

✔ **YES:** Whenever we're faced with a difficult or dissatisfied client, my coworkers come to me to deal with it. Unlike many other people in my position, I never lose my temper in front of customers. This is extremely important, especially when dealing with an irate client.

✘ **NO:** I'm not sure if there's one real expertise that I am relied on for. We work together as a team, and that is the way all situations are handled.

Even within a strictly team setting, there are obviously situations that you are better at handling than your colleagues. Even though you may not be singled out to deal with each of these situations, tell the interviewer about the situations that you excel in. Which situations are you more qualified for (or better at handling) than your peers? This question provides a good opportunity for the candidate to showcase his or her dependability, strength of character, and professionalism.

Q: Tell me about a quantifiable outcome of one of your efforts.

✔ **YES:** I reorganized inventory planning and was able to automate the inventory-reorder function. A task that used to take 40 hours to complete now only takes five!

✘ **NO:** I was able to do a good enough job on a project that my salary was raised from $45,000 to $50,000.

Insider Tips

Let Your Personality Shine Through

Though it's good to practice answers to possible questions, be sure to allow your personality to surface. The interviewer will take notice of whether you are being straightforward or are trying to give the "expected" answer.

One thing that is true—in business especially—is the fact that numbers don't lie. One of the easiest ways to showcase your accomplishments is to quantify them. But remember, unless you're talking about sales dollars or company profits, don't talk dollar amounts. Describe a specific accomplishment, the outcome of which produced a clear benefit. Offer proof, using real examples, that you deliver more than what's expected.

Q: Tell me about a project you completed ahead of schedule.

✔ **YES:** I was in charge of a new product rollout. In general we completed each phase without a major setback—which was partially luck—but I also systematically called two days ahead of every deadline to check the status with all groups involved. I believe that is what made the real difference. The launch took place two weeks ahead of plan—a very significant period of time in our industry, where shelf life for products is generally less than one year.

✘ **NO:** My boss had asked me to complete a project for him, and he suggested that—after rereading the report and editing it—it would take at least two days to complete. Rather than reread the report, I made sure to read it through very carefully the first time around. In doing so, I was able to complete the project in only a day, which was a new company record.

In discussing how you were able to complete a project ahead of schedule, make sure that you are not forcing the interviewer to question the integrity of the project, or the attention to detail you displayed while working on it. Focus on how you set goals and schedules, measured results, and championed the outcome of a project. This question is aimed at your diligence in accomplishing tasks and, assuming the project required group effort, at your leadership skills.

Your Career Goals

Where do you want to be two years from now? is a question that relates specifically to your career goals, and you should make sure that your answer coincides with the typical career path you are about to embark on. If interviewing for the position of front desk clerk, for example, you should not tell the interviewer that in two years you hope to be running the company. Keep your goals realistic, and always make sure that—within the given time period you are asked about—they are attainable.

Q: Where do you hope that your career will have progressed to in the next few years?

✔ **YES:** Over the next few years I would like to be at the point where I have bottom-line budget responsibility and charge of a production unit in which I have labor-relations, quality-control, design, and manufacturing responsibilities. I believe this job will go a long way toward helping me meet my career goals.

✘ **NO:** I hope that in the next few years, my talents will really be recognized and that I will be rewarded accordingly.

Avoid the temptation to suggest job titles; this makes you seem unbending and unrealistic, since you don't know or control the system of promotion. Likewise, you don't know how long it might have taken your interviewer to reach certain levels, and you wouldn't want to insult him or her. On the other hand, you don't want to be *too* general either. The best way to answer this question is to discuss the new experiences you would like to have in the next few years and the responsibilities you would like to have acquired.

Q: What are your long-term career plans?

✔ **YES:** My long-term career goals are to become known as an industry expert and to have earned a respectable management position with responsibility for a major piece of the business. I'd

like to think I'll have experience in many parts of the business over time.

✗ NO: In the end, I would like to be able to retire by the age of 45.

You don't want to spout off various job titles or a specific position. You never know what kinds of duties and jobs will be obsolete by the time you reach the end of your career, especially in fields that are always changing (e.g., computers). Instead, focus on the experiences you would like to have in your career, and the things you would like to be responsible for. Even though this question *does* ask about your long-term goals, be sure to stay realistic and keep your goals along the same career path.

Q: Since this will be your first job, how do you know you'll like the career path?

✔ YES: Although it's true that I've never worked in this industry before, I've talked to many friends and alums at my school who've been successful here. I always ask them the questions, What's the most frustrating thing about your job? and What's the most rewarding thing about your job? From the information I've gained, I'm confident that I'll be able to adapt quickly to your culture and will find the next few years rewarding, based on my goals and values.

✗ NO: Based on what I know about the industry, I am pretty sure I will like it here. If not, I'm still young enough to change careers. Doesn't the average person change careers five times anyway?

Unless you've done your research and/or are really familiar with the industry, this can be a difficult question to answer. Before going into an interview, be sure you know what kind of job—or even job title—you would be next in line for. By taking the position you are applying for, what would be the next logical step, according to your industry's general career path? If you have

had any experience in the field—an internship, for example—make sure to mention that. You should also feel free to discuss the conversations you've had with professionals within the industry, and how you've gained a better understanding of the job *and* the career path through those people. Point out why you are interested in this career, how you've learned more about the industry, and how you are able to keep current with the industry trends.

Q: What makes you think that this job is right for you at this point in your career?

✔ **YES:** Though I have never had the title of manager, I think that my past experiences up until now could have only led me in this direction. I have spent the past five years working as a corporate trainer for two separate *Fortune* 500 companies. My job requires that I learn the functions and responsibilities of each of the company's departments well enough that I can then teach others how to do the job. More than learning the business basics of just about every department in a major corporation—from sales and marketing to accounting—I have also learned how to deal with people effectively in an authoritative position. I still get phone calls from employees I have trained in the past—asking me questions, and telling me about their own promotions. I think that if you asked any of these people, they would agree that I would make a great manager.

✗ **NO:** I figure that I've had enough experience in so many areas of business that I'd be a good match to pretty much any position. I chose this one because I like the idea of doing a lot of traveling and using my sales background.

In addition to addressing your applicable skills and the logical progression that brought you to apply for this job, be sure to address your desire to work for *this* company in *this* position. Showcase the knowledge you have of this company and what the specific job entails. Describe the experiences you want to pursue that build on your current skills and interests. Be as

Insider Tips

Handling Prepared Responses

Once the interview begins, your focus must be on interacting well with the interviewer—as opposed to trying to recall the exact responses you prepared earlier. If you prepared for the interview well, your conduct and responses will convey to the interviewer the image that you want to project without effort.

specific as you can, based on what you know about the current or future direction of the position and the department. Demonstrate why this position fits with your personal career goals. Talk about how you can create job growth for yourself.

Q: What new challenges would you enjoy taking on?

✔ **YES:** I've worked in various positions in the hospitality industry for over eight years and have progressively worked in larger, more prestigious hotels. I've learned both the food-and-beverage side of the business as well as the hotel-management side. Armed with that background, I now believe I'm ready to take part in the convention and conference area.

✗ **NO:** I would enjoy taking on all of the challenges this position would have to offer me.

Based on the skills you have learned and enjoyed using in your current position, describe the new challenges that you would like to take on and that you feel capable of handling. Be as specific as you can, considering what you know about the current or future direction of the position, department, and company as a whole. Think about the duties required of the job at hand and which ones might provide you with a bit of a challenge.

Q: If you could start all over again, what direction would your career take?

✔ **YES:** I've always enjoyed consumer sales as I've moved up in my career. Looking back, I wish I'd gotten a bit more experience in market research earlier in my career, because it's important to understand the types of quantitative models and technical-research techniques that are now important for a regional sales manager to know.

✗ **NO:** I really wish that I had never given up playing the trumpet in fourth grade. I think that with enough practice, I could have been one of the best.

The interviewer is trying to figure out if the career path you have chosen to take (including this interview) is the ideal one for you. Is it this industry alone that you are passionate about, or does your heart lie somewhere else? In answering this question, offer some insight as to how your goals may have changed a bit, given the information you have now. The best way to answer this question is to think of a separate but related task that you enjoy and to talk about how you may have chosen to do something with that. Be honest and insightful, but reassure the interviewer that the only place you want to be is with this company.

Q: How long do you think you'd continue to grow in this job?

✔ **YES:** I define job growth as the process of acquiring new skills, new knowledge, and new insights into the industry. That said, as long as I can measure this type of growth, I consider myself successful. I'm a believer in stretching a job by reaching out to learn more about other areas that are peripheral to the job I'm in.

✘ **NO:** I think that one year would be about the limit, given the position and its responsibilities.

This is a variation on the question, Where do you want to be in five years? Again, when answering, be as specific as you can based on all you know about the position. Make sure that any goals or time frames you state are realistic and well thought out. Don't mention a job title you'd want next, or the interviewer will wonder if you're already preoccupied with moving on.

Q: What career path interests you within the company?

✔ **YES:** I'd like to work toward becoming a senior project manager within your commercial real estate firm. My background includes several areas within commercial real estate, including working in architectural design, with governmental departments and agencies, with banks in the finance area, and, finally, in sales and

Insider Tips

A Clear Direction

Employers like job candidates who have real interests and a clear direction. They know that if you're interested in a particular industry, company, or job, you're more likely to enjoy the position, perform well, and stay with the company. Employers *don't* like to hear that you aren't at all discriminating—that you'll take whatever job they have available.

Strange but True

Interview Scenarios

A job applicant was led into a very small room. He sat in the middle of the room and the two partners sat on either side of him. At once, they both began bombarding the job applicant with questions, purposely not giving him the chance to answer. When they did finally allow him a chance to answer, the question was, "Is today Tuesday?"

The job applicant responded, "No, today is Friday."

The partner asked, "Why?"

leasing. I'd like to pull all this background together in the next few years and eventually have project management responsibility.

✗ **NO:** If I were hired for this position, what would be the next normal promotion?

In addition to demonstrating your knowledge of the company, or the typical career path with the industry, the interviewer is interested in how realistic you are. Use the knowledge you have of this industry, and this company in particular, to talk about the path you are interested in following. If you're unfamiliar with the typical career path, it's okay to ask a question such as What's the typical career path for someone with my skills? Focus principally on businesses or divisions of the company that interest you, as well as skills and challenges you hope to master in the next few years.

Q: How does this job compare to the other positions you are pursuing?

✔ **YES:** Since I've narrowed my job search to only those large securities firms within the finance industry, this job is very close to the other types of positions I am currently interviewing for. The basic skills necessary with all of these firms are similar: strong quantitative and analytical abilities, the ability to make decisions quickly, and good interpersonal skills to react to a customer's needs.

✗ **NO:** Right now, I am pursuing opportunities in a few different fields. In addition to marketing opportunities, I have looked into sales, public relations, editorial, and recruiting jobs. While some of these jobs do require similar skills—strong writing skills, good interpersonal skills, and attention-to-detail—they are all very different industries.

While the interviewer does not want to hear all about your most recent interviews with their biggest competitors—and how promising they look—they do want to be assured that you are settled on a career path. They want to make sure that you are not

picking job titles and/or companies out of a hat. Some consistency or thread of commonality among your other prospects is important here. Your choices must reflect your career aspirations. Talk about the common skills that are clearly needed in all the jobs you're pursuing.

Q: Have you progressed in your career as you expected?

✔ **YES:** My six years with a major gas company have included solid experience in price analysis, capital budgets, and financial planning. I now believe I'm ready to take on departmental responsibility for the entire finance function within a finance company.

✘ **NO:** When I originally got into the publishing industry more than a year ago, I did not expect to still be an editorial assistant at this point. I guess you could say I have been a bit disappointed in my progress.

Think about your past career experiences. Have you accomplished as much as you had hoped to at this point? If not, why do you think that is? Talk about the many learning experiences you've had and what these have taught you about the industry. Be realistic in admitting the areas where you need more experience. Honesty—without demonstrating either pessimism or unrealistic expectations—is important when answering this question.

Q: Have you ever taken a position that didn't fit into your long-term plan?

✔ YES: Though I had always been drawn to a high-tech career, I was offered a very lucrative position in real estate back in the 1980s. Though I knew that real estate was not my life work, I decided to take the job for financial security for me and my family. Before long, I realized that the work wasn't fulfilling or challenging enough to keep me happy. I stayed with the company for two years but, as I had remained close to many of my original contacts in the high-tech industry, was lucky enough to be able to pick up where I'd left off. I've since

moved up in the ranks, and my long-term plans include staying in this industry and assuming greater responsibility in the area of computer programming and networking.

✗ NO: Yes.

Don't be afraid to answer no to this question. Many members of the work force have been lucky enough to develop a strong and compatible career path right off the bat, and stick to it throughout their careers. If this is the case with you, don't be afraid to tell the interviewer so. If you have taken a job that didn't quite fit in with what you hoped to accomplish, talk about the reasons that lead to this acceptance. The interviewer is trying to determine how wisely the candidate can pick jobs to match his or her interests and aspirations. If you've been sidetracked by some job, you'll probably have to convince the recruiter that you are on the right track pursuing this position.

Your Personal Interests

Though questions about personal interests are becoming less and less common (some of these questions can—inadvertently—lead to illegal information), you still may be asked about your various personal interests and hobbies. Why would an employer want to know how you spend your weekends? Finding out what you do in your leisure time is a good and quick way to get to know you as a *person*, not just a job applicant. Make sure not to drone on too long about your outside activities. Becoming more excited and animated about your weekend plans than you are about a potential job opportunity may only serve to lessen an interviewer's opinion of you as an employee.

Other questions that may go through an interviewer's mind while he or she asks you about your outside interests are whether you have a balanced lifestyle, whether your personality is reflected in the type of job you choose, and whether your personal and professional interests seem compatible. (See, there is a science to this whole thing!)

Q: Other than work, tell me about an activity you've remained interested in over several years.

✔ **YES:** I've been involved in fundraising for cancer research ever since my grandmother died from the disease. In the back of my mind, I guess I'm hoping that the research can lead to findings in time to save the life of someone else in my family.

✘ **NO:** I have varied interests and have taken part in many activities over the years. Unfortunately, there's no one thing that has been able to keep my attention for too long.

The interviewer is questioning whether or not you are a fickle person. Do you take a strong interest in things and stick to them, or do you seem to have a problem with commitment? (No, marriages and other relationships don't count.) Prove to the interviewer that you are a solid person who doesn't just jump into something to jump right back out. Talk about your hobbies and favorite activities. Think about the other questions the interviewer is considering: Are your interests compatible with the job you are applying for? Would they be of value in any way to the company?

Q: What do you do in your spare time?

✔ **YES:** I am a real sports fanatic. Whether watching or playing, I enjoy the excitement that sports such as baseball, basketball, and tennis have to offer. I especially enjoy team sports. Knowing that a group of people are working so closely together to achieve a specific goal is inspiring to me in many ways. I know that many of your clients are high-profile sports clubs and companies, and I think that because of my dedication to sports of all kinds, I could definitely bring a unique perspective and insight to the company.

✘ **NO:** I like to cram in as much television watching as I can on the weekends. It is for this reason that I think I would be a great asset to your advertising team. I watch about 30 to 40

Strange but True

Interview Questions

"There are three lights in a basement and three switches at the top of the stairs. You can't see these lights from the top of the stairs. You can only go to the basement once to figure out which switch goes to which light. How do you figure it out?"

hours of television per week and can certainly keep you informed of the kinds of commercials that are popping up.

The interviewer wants evidence that you're well rounded, not just one dimensional. He or she is also looking for shared interests or common ground. Make sure that the personal life you describe is an active and fulfilling one. Though the interviewer wants to know that you will be dedicated to your job, he or she does not want to think that this is the only creative outlet you have. You should always, in some way, relate your answer to the job description.

Q: **Tell me about a time when you were in a recreational setting and got an idea that helped in your work.**

✔ **YES:** I was on vacation in Mexico and saw a woman with a homemade seesaw she was using to lift her laundry basket when she needed something out of it. It gave me an idea for a new type of scaffolding, which I designed when I got back to work. Now our brick masons have a rotating bench that keeps their materials at waist level, which reduces back fatigue.

✘ **NO:** I had been given the chance to brainstorm some new ideas for an innovative book series. During a weekend trip to the local bookstore, I noticed that our biggest competitor had just launched a great new series that targeted young men and women—exactly the group that we wanted to target. A bought a bunch of the books, and the next day, we began working on the same type of series.

The interviewer wants to know that—even when you're not working—you are able to synthesize information and apply what you see to your profession. You want to be sure that you are portraying yourself as an innovative and creative person. Don't talk about a great idea that you saw another business doing and chose to copy. Show that your work is something you are naturally inquisitive about rather than something you have to do. Are you able to "think outside of the box" to come up with fresh ideas? Be sure to give specific examples.

Q: How is your personality reflected in the kinds of activities you enjoy?

✔ **YES:** I love to cook and entertain. That's the salesman coming out in me. I love sharing experiences with people, and I'm very outgoing. I don't particularly enjoy being alone. I always feel as if I should be doing something.

✘ **NO:** I love to play sports. I think that this shows my fiercely competitive nature; I am not satisfied until I have pummeled the competition.

Talk about the way in which your natural skills, values, and ethics are reflected in things you do in your spare time. What do your hobbies and passions outside of work say about your personality? Remember, everything we do says something about us as a person. A detailed, precise hobby reflects something different from a risk-oriented, aggressive sport.

Q: What are some of the things you do to relax?

✔ **YES:** The main thing that helps me to relax is my family. For me, my weekends are like a vacation. I make the most of all the time I have to spend with my family. When I'm at work, I focus on what is going on in my professional life, but when I am at home, it's all about my family. When I began working at my current job, my wife and I decided to buy a home about 20 miles outside of the city. It was really one of the best things we ever did; now, even the drive home is relaxing.

✘ **NO:** The only way I know of to relax is to sleep!

The interviewer wants to be reassured that you do not spend all your time—physically or mentally—in the office. Describe at least one part of your life or activity that you engage in that you find to be relaxing. Talking about what you do in your free time is a great way to give the interviewer an insight into who you are as a person.

Insider Tips

Follow Up

Following the interview, it is important to keep your candidacy fresh in the interviewer's mind. Send samples of work that intrigued the interviewer. Or if you discovered that you share common interests with the interviewer, such as sailing or rock climbing, consider sending the person a great article you just found on the topic.

Q: Have you ever found yourself really burned out from a job, and if so, what did you do about it?

✔ **YES:** Because I know how dangerous it can be to begin experiencing those sorts of feelings, I don't allow myself to get locked into an unchanging routine. I am the type of person who will continually ask for new assignments and tasks so that I can keep motivated and challenged.

✘ **NO:** Burned out is exactly what I am feeling right now in my current job. That is why I'm sending out resumes and interviewing for new positions.

The interviewer is trying to figure out a few different things here: Are you smart and disciplined enough to avoid burnout? When you are not being productive, do you recognize it? What do you do to cope with stress? The interviewer wants to be sure that in a few months, you will not be running from this job and company.

Q: Our company believes that employees should give time back to the community. How do you feel about that?

✔ **YES:** I completely agree. In my last job as a manager, I allowed employees to spend one day a month, as long as the entire staff wasn't gone on one day, giving back to the community as a volunteer. I myself spend one Friday per month working with an adult literacy program.

✘ **NO:** As long as it is not a requirement of the job, I don't see a problem with it.

If you have spent time giving back to your community in some way, this is a great time to talk about it. Even if you have not, this is a good opportunity for you to discuss the issues, charities, and world problems that concern you. If you were given the time to do something for the community, what would you do? Showing a lack of excitement at the prospect of helping others is probably not the type of spirit a company is looking

for. Do you use your skills productively? Are you unselfish—a real team player? Demonstrate how your personal interests make you productive even when you aren't being paid. What incentives other than a paycheck inspire you?

Q: Are there any community projects that have benefited from your professional experience?

✔ **YES:** As a marketing professional, I have been able to help out at our local high school in drumming up publicity and awareness for its fund-raisers.

✗ **NO:** I don't know that any local organizations would have a real need for a professional writer.

This question gives the interviewer a sense of your values and lets him or her know whether you will be a good corporate citizen. Showing that you like to apply your professional expertise to situations in which the only reward is good will impress an interviewer. Be sure not to get sidetracked describing a cause that doesn't demonstrate job-related skills. Above all, avoid discussing any charity or organization that may be considered controversial; the last thing you want to do is offend the interviewer.

Q: Describe how a sport or hobby taught you a lesson in team work or discipline.

✔ **YES:** I used to play football, and my coach always taught us that the most important part of the game was watching out for the other guy, that if you do that job well, you'll always have someone watching out for you as well. It is exactly this strategy that I have tried to apply to my professional life. Help out when and where you can, and you'll always have others to rely on as well.

✗ **NO:** My football coach's philosophy was sort of a "take no prisoners" type attitude. Keeping this in mind, I have been able to quickly push my way up the corporate ladder.

Remember that the key to this question is teamwork! Rather than focus on how you have applied a certain strategy to work to your advantage, talk about a way in which you have used lessons learned to help your entire department or work group. Talk about a time when you had to use teamwork to get a desired result. Tell a specific story, then explain how the same skill or lesson has been used in your work.

Q: When you aren't at work, do you prefer to stick to a schedule, or do you prefer to be spontaneous? Why?

✔ **YES:** My workday is very structured because I'm generally in four or five meetings a day. On the weekends, I like to have a plan, but not necessarily a set schedule. That in itself is a relaxing change of pace for me, but I feel I'd be wasting time with no plan at all.

✘ **NO:** Since I don't set much of a schedule at work, I certainly don't when I'm at home.

Be careful that whichever answer you choose, it's consistent with the job you're interviewing for. For example, since accounting is a profession that requires discipline and precision, your answer should reflect your natural inclination toward agendas, schedules, and precision. However, for a sales job, you'd probably want to show that you are prepared to wing it. Though this question is essentially about your personality, it is also about your compatibility with the job.

Q: Tell me about an interest that you outgrew.

✔ **YES:** Early on, I wanted to be a research physician. Then I spent time in a chemistry lab and realized that I wasn't looking forward to the next two years of lab work. That's why I've chosen marketing for medical equipment instead. It combines my respect for the medical profession with a job that's more suited to my personality.

✗ NO: As a child, I always thought I would grow up to be a chemist. I loved playing around with my chemistry set and thought that I would be well suited to the profession. When I got to high school and college, I realized that there was a lot more to the job than just mixing chemicals and seeing what happens. It was then that I decided a job in insurance is where I would fit in best.

Describe a former interest or hobby that you no longer pursue, making sure that the interest isn't related in some way to the job you're interviewing for. Talk about why you outgrew the interest and how it's not compatible with your current interests. Be sure to discuss how your current interests are related to your career.

Q: Describe a movie you've seen that really inspired you.

✔ YES: I loved one part of an otherwise depressing movie, *One Flew over the Cuckoo's Nest*. In one scene, the nurse refuses to turn on the TV for the World Series, so Jack Nicholson looks at the blank screen and starts narrating as though the game were actually on. The other patients gather around him and follow the game. I thought that scene was an example of the power of visualization in making things happen.

✗ NO: After seeing the film *Mommy Dearest*, I knew that I wanted to be an actress.

Demonstrate that you can assimilate knowledge from a wide variety of sources, including books and film. Tell the interviewer about a specific book or movie that taught you something. Discuss how and where you've applied that knowledge. Make sure that the lesson you are relating is a positive one and that it somehow relates to the job at hand.

CHAPTER FOURTEEN

Special Situations

Students and Recent Graduates

Whether you are currently enrolled in or just graduating from high school or college, younger job seekers face a similar problem: a lack of professional experience. Though internships and part-time jobs in the industry you are interested in certainly count for something, recruiters may press you a little bit harder to figure out whether or not you have the personality to make it in a particular field or career.

The best piece of advice students and recent graduates can take to the interview with them is to remember that even though they have not had much experience in the workplace, they have had the experience of gaining an education and therefore have certainly been able to determine where their strengths and weaknesses lie.

Q: Why weren't your grades better in school?

✔ **YES:** School was a wonderful experience for me. I really enjoyed learning new ideas, I studied consistently, and I was attentive in class. But I never believed in cramming the night before an exam just to get a higher grade or staying up all night to finish a term paper. I really believe I learned just as much as many students who went for the grades.

✘ **NO:** As president of my university's most popular fraternity, I had a lot of social and philanthropic issues to attend to. I took this position very seriously and chose to devote more time to my brothers than my studies.

If you've made it to the interview stage, it is likely that your qualifications meet what the employer is looking for. In this case, the interviewer is just interested in how you react to his or her inquiry. The most important thing in responding to this question is not to get defensive or to place blame on someone else. Instead, try to put a positive spin on the question. For example, you could focus your answer on what you learned and the extra effort you put in to learn, rather than on the actual grades you received. Be aware that your grades could be just

fine; don't take this question personally and don't think it is an insult in any way.

Q: Why did you decide to major in history?

✔ **YES:** Deciding to major in history was a fairly difficult decision for me, as I was also very attracted to an education in government, international relations, and economics. But the study of history allowed me to combine all three of these subjects, especially considering that my major focus was on economic history. What's more, I found several of the professors in the department to be exceptionally knowledgeable and stimulating, which made my college experience that much more enriching and valuable.

✘ **NO:** The one history class that I had taken my freshman year in college was fairly easy and interesting, so I thought that majoring in it would be a great idea.

Show that you have solid, logical reasons for choosing your major. If you can't defend your choice of major, the interviewer will wonder how much thought you've put into choosing a career. You should also be sure that your reasons for choosing your major are compatible with your career choice. For instance, if you're applying for a position as a banker, don't say you were an English major because you love literature and writing.

Q: Was there any course in particular that you found to be especially challenging?

✔ **YES:** Initially I was completely overwhelmed by the introductory chemistry course that I took last year. No matter how hard I studied, I seemed to be getting nowhere. I even failed the first three quizzes. So I decided to try a new approach. Instead of just studying by myself, I asked a friend who's a chemistry major to help me with my studies. I also began seeking help from the professor after class. I found that more time spent in the lab was critical. I ended up with a B-plus in the course and thought I achieved a solid understanding of the material. More

Come Overprepared!

As hiring managers and recruiters are often under a lot of pressure to review candidates and get a position filled quickly, it shouldn't surprise you if you are left in the waiting room for a few minutes.

That said, it may be a good idea to bring along some reading material. That way when you're told that it's going to be another few minutes, you can show them how understanding you are by sitting quietly and reading.

Insider Tips

than that, I learned that tackling a new field of study sometimes requires a new approach, not just hard work, and that the help of others can be crucial!

✗ NO: Not really.

We all have difficulties mastering certain ideas and concepts, so don't be afraid to admit your own. Be careful that the "subject" you mention, however, does not directly correspond with the subject matter of the position you are looking to fill. The interviewer will want to see how well you respond to difficult situations. Demonstrate that you will not fold in the face of difficulty and that you're willing to put in the extra effort to meet a challenge. Show the recruiter that when the going gets tough, you get *thinking*!

Q: Why didn't you participate more in extracurricular activities?

✔ YES: I wanted to give as much effort as possible to my studies. Though I had done very well in high school, I lived in a very small town, and the school didn't prepare me very well for college. In order to keep getting the A's I had become accustomed to, I was forced to study very hard. Luckily, I was able to grasp material quickly enough that I found time to explore the city and make new friends. Still, between studying, working a part-time job, and socializing with friends, I never had much time for organized, extracurricular activities.

✗ NO: I never found one that interested me enough to participate in.

The interviewer is a bit concerned that you don't have many outside interests and, therefore, that you may eventually suffer from burnout. Employers like candidates who are well rounded and have interests outside of work. If you didn't participate in formal extracurricular activities in college, you still may want to talk about some of your interests, such as reading or exercising, that you participated in on a more informal level. For instance, you may have a passion for running, even if you weren't on the college track team.

Career Changers

Throughout the course of your life, it is likely that you will be involved in as many as five separate careers, maybe even more. Still, the fact that everyone is likely to change his or her career at one point still does not make the task of changing careers an easy one. The main concern you should have going into an interview is whether you can convince the interviewer that your interest in this new industry and career is sincere. Though you probably won't have much experience in exactly that field, be sure to point out all the skills that you have acquired in past jobs that could easily translate to this type of career. You should also feel free to think about the events that led to your decision to enter this profession and use that desire and dedication in answering the interviewer's questions.

Q: Why do you want to leave your current position?

✔ **YES:** My current position has allowed me to learn a great deal about the plastics industry, and I am very glad to have had that opportunity. However, I've also found that my interests really lie in research and development, which my company has recently decided to phase out over the next two years. That is why I am so interested in your organization. As I understand, your company places a great deal of importance on research and development and is also a highly respected leader in the industry.

✗ **NO:** I like change.

The interviewer's foremost concern with career changers will always be why they want to switch careers. But people do it every day, so don't think you will not get the job just because you don't have any hands-on experience in the field. Show the interviewer that your decision to switch careers has been based on careful consideration. Explain why you decided on this particular position and how the position will allow you to further your skills and interests.

Insider Tips

It's Good to Know...

An understanding and knowledge of computers is the most sought-after skill in new employees. Using electronic resources to find a job demonstrates your computer savvy to an employer.

Electronic business directories, either online or on CD-ROM, allow you to identify companies that hire employees in your field and with your background. These databases also contain enough company information to give you an indication of whether a company is right for you.

The Internet and commercial online services are available 24 hours a day, and their national and international scopes are ideal for job seekers.

Q: Why would you want to leave an established career at an employment agency for what is essentially an entry-level marketing job?

✔ **YES:** During my many years at the agency, I have acquired many valuable skills. At the same time, I feel as if I've stopped growing. There's only so far you can go in such a career, and I am nearing the end of the career path. I am no longer challenged by my work, and being challenged is what keeps me motivated. I've thought about this for a long time, as switching careers is not an easy decision to make. Still, I am confident that I am doing the right thing by looking for a job within another industry, even if it means starting over. My interest in marketing arose last year when a local family lost their home to a fire. A group of people from my community decided to pitch in and help this family raise enough money to rebuild their home. I helped by designing and distributing posters, placing advertisements in local newspapers, and selling T-shirts outside grocery stores and shopping malls. When I began to see the result of what my work was doing, I became very excited about this task. I learned that you can have a great product and a great cause but that if nobody knows about it, you are dead in the water. I felt as if the work I was doing was making a difference—and I was good at it, too. Since then, I have taken two introductory marketing courses and am planning to enroll in a part-time degree program this fall. Also, I'll be able to use many of the skills I've acquired working at an employment agency to benefit me in a marketing career as well. After all, working in an employment agency is marketing—that is, marketing the agency to corporate clients and job seekers, and marketing the job seekers to corporate clients.

✗ **NO:** I am feeling rather bored and unchallenged and want to learn something new—anything really.

The interviewer wants to determine two things: the candidate's motivation for choosing a new career and the likelihood that the candidate will be comfortable in a position in which he or she

will probably have less power and responsibility than in previous jobs. To dispel the interviewer's fears, discuss your reasons for switching careers and be sure to show that you have a solid understanding of the position and the industry in general. Many candidates expect to start their new career in a job comparable to the one they held previously. The truth is that most career changers must start in a lower, if not entry-level, position in their new company to gain basic experience and knowledge in the field.

Re-entering the Job Market

There's no doubt about it: If you've been out of the work force for an extended period of time, you will face some troubling issues upon your re-entry. You may feel anxious, wondering whether you've still got what it takes to make it out there, and it's not uncommon for employers to feel the same way.

The first thing you should do before trying to re-enter the work force is to make sure all your skills, technical and otherwise, are up to date. Read some articles about the industry and make sure the techniques, computer programs, and so forth, being described are all familiar to you. If you think your own skills could use a little tweaking, consider retraining by either taking courses or learning a new program. The main things you will want to focus on during your interview are the jobs you've had previously and the skills they called for, the ways in which you've kept up your learning during your absence (e.g., reading trade journals, doing freelance work, attending seminars, networking with industry professionals), and the skills you've learned at home that can be transferred to the workplace.

Q: Your resume indicates that you have not worked for several years. Would you mind explaining this absence?

✔ **YES:** I have spent the last five years raising my son, Liam, who's now in kindergarten. Leaving the workplace was a very difficult decision for me, but as this was our first child, I didn't

think I would be able to commit to my career 100 percent, knowing what responsibilities I had at home. Since I didn't think it would be fair to my employer to give any less than 100 percent, I believe it was the right decision for me at the time. Now that my son is old enough to be in school, I feel refreshed and am completely ready to devote myself to a full-time career.

✗ NO: Yes, I *would* mind explaining this, as it really is none of your business.

Whatever the reason for your hiatus, be honest. The interviewer has the right to know why you have not worked in so long, as it could definitely relate to the job you are being considered for. Discuss the decisions behind your absence, whether they were to stay at home and raise a family or recuperate from a debilitating injury. Be sure to emphasize the reasons why you want to return to work and why you think you are ready. Most importantly, stress your eagerness to resume your career.

The Abominable Zinger

One fear that is embedded in the mind of every interviewee—and rightfully so—is the thought of being asked a question you don't know the answer to. Even worse is stumbling over a question because you don't know the answer or because the question itself caught you by surprise. These unpopular questions—known as zingers—are questions that you can't really prepare for. They are questions that require more than a simple yes or no retort, and they are questions that by nature are meant to catch you off guard. The key to rising above such attempts to rile you is to remain calm, cool, and confident in your answer. Try your hardest to be diplomatic and—above all—positive, no matter what you are asked.

Again, while you can't exactly prepare for these questions, as it is their nature to be surprising, you can be made aware of some of the most popular zingers that exist and prepare an answer for them ahead of time. But more importantly, you can learn to expect the unexpected.

Q: Tell me about yourself.

A: I am a production assistant for a local morning talk show with a BA in communications and three years of solid broadcasting and public relations experience. I have extensive experience developing and researching topics, preinterviewing guests, and producing on-location television segments. I have a tremendous amount of energy and love to be challenged. I'm constantly taking on additional responsibilities so that I may learn new things. I have watched your station for quite some time now and have always been impressed with your innovative approach to broadcasting and programming. I'd definitely like to be part of that winning team.

> This is the perfect opportunity to sell yourself to an employer in just a few seconds. You need to "package" yourself into one small paragraph in which you mention your experience, skills, accomplishments, goals, and personal qualities. Declare your interest in the company and how you could make a difference if you were hired. If you are a recent college graduate with not too much real world experience, be sure to mention your educational qualifications and emphasize the classes you took that pertain to the job.

Q: Tell me about a project in which you were a bit disappointed in your own performance.

A: In my last job with a manufacturing company, I had to analyze all the supplier bids and present recommendations to the vice president of logistics. Because the supplier bids weren't in an organized format, my analysis often consisted of comparing dissimilar items. This caused some confusion in my final report, and by the time I'd reworked it and presented it to the vice president, we'd lost the critical time we'd needed to improve our approval process for these bids. In hindsight, I should have taken a similar approach to the problem and not tried to make it so complex or all inclusive. Ever

Insider Tips

Money Isn't Everything

The point of your job search isn't salary negotiation; it's finding a job that you'll be happy with, that you'll grow with, and that will allow you to be yourself. If your starting salary isn't the one you dreamed about, but the job presents the right opportunity, think about the possibility of commanding a higher salary once you've had a chance to make yourself invaluable to the organization.

Insider Tips

Stress Questions

If you encounter a question about stress, your best bet is to stay calm, be diplomatic, and remain positive in your response. Don't get defensive or allow your confidence to be shaken, and try to answer the question to the best of your ability.

since, I've paid much more attention to making recommendations in a timely manner.

Describe the barriers you've come across in past experiences and how you've worked around them. How have your skills come into play? In hindsight, what could you have done differently? Most importantly, turn this roadblock into a lesson and tell the interviewer what you learned from having gone through the experience.

Q: Tell me about the most difficult work or personal experience you've ever had to face.

A: A coworker, with whom I was very close, was going through a very difficult time and had begun to abuse drugs and alcohol. After a long talk, he decided that the best thing for him was to attend a rehabilitation center. For the next six months, I had to take on much of this person's work in addition to my own. While the long hours and added pressure were not the ideal situation for me to be in at the time, I know that he would have done the same for me, so I never once regretted my decision. It's very important to me to have that kind of trust among the members of my work group, and I am glad that I was able to help someone out in their time of need. It is certainly something I will always be proud of.

The ultimate goal of this question is to find out how well you handle pressure. Ideally, you want to describe a situation—personal or professional—that involved a great deal of conflict and challenge and, as a result, placed you under an unusual amount of stress. Explain, specifically, what the problems were, and what you did to resolve them. What was the end result? Is it something you would do again?

Q: How have you handled criticism of your work in the past?

A: The first time I ever had a client complain to me, I was devastated. The client was upset about the downtime in ATM machines.

Though her complaint had nothing to do with my professional service of the account, I couldn't help but take her complaints personally. However, rather than dwell on my own disappointment, I began to work very closely with this client to see whether there wasn't something I could do about her suggestion. Though in the end there was nothing I could do personally, I was able to learn a lot from the experience. I learned that showing empathy usually calms an unpleasant situation. I also learned that no client is going to be happy with everything, even if that client's overall experience is positive. I know that I should not take things personally and, instead, should put myself in that person's shoes to see if I can't do something to help them feel better.

> The interviewer is trying to learn something about your accountability and professional character. Talk about a time when you were engaged in a specific project or work habit that caused you a problem. Then discuss how you finally faced up to the problem and overcame it. Alternatively, you might describe a time you responded objectively and professionally to particularly harsh or unreasonable criticism of your work. In either case, finish the comment by talking about what you learned from this experience. Remember to always keep things on a positive note and to refrain from complaining or slandering any past work associates.

Q: Which aspects of your work are most often criticized?

A: In my first job as marketing assistant, I spent endless hours analyzing a particular problem that I knew there was a better solution to. I came up with a revised marketing plan that was extremely well received by my coworkers. Unfortunately, when it came time to present the plan to the top-level management, I hadn't prepared the fine points of the presentation—overheads and slides—and the proposal was turned down. I'd failed to make clear the real benefits of my plan, such as the savings that would result from implementing it. I spent the next two weeks working on my

presentation, and on my second try, management approved it; my recommendations were carried out to everyone's satisfaction. I was very grateful to have been given that second chance. Since then, I certainly make sure that all the details have been taken care of when I am proposing something new to a group so that there are no questions left unanswered.

> Though the answer given here seems to skirt the issue a bit, that's okay. The best way to answer this question is to give an example of something you overlooked—or a mistake that you made—earlier in your career. Discuss the ways in which you worked to overcome the situation and to improve your work. Talk about how the failure has changed the way you work now, or how it has caused you to pay more careful attention to detail in all your work.

Q: If your current boss could change anything about your work habits, what do you think he or she would do?

A: She would definitely try and turn me into more of a night owl. My current boss and I make a fantastic team. The only problem is that I like to arrive to work a bit early and get the day started by 7 A.M., and she prefers to start at 9 A.M. and end at 7 P.M. As a result, we tend to put in our extra time at opposite ends of the day. If there were one thing she could change about me, she'd probably make it so that we worked the same hours every day.

> The interviewer wants to know how well you fit in with your current boss. He or she also wants to feel confident that he or she has uncovered any surprises about your corporate style. One good way to answer this question is to point out a minor difference or preference between you and your supervisor. Another way to answer this question would be to talk about a weakness of yours that you and your boss have worked on together to improve. The key to answering this question is to make sure that the answer you give is not something that would be a major concern

to the company. You also want to make sure that the answer continues on a positive note. If you plan to describe a weakness, make sure it's a weakness that you recognized early on and have worked hard to fix.

Q: Tell me about a situation that frustrated you at work.

A: I was frustrated once when a client who had insisted on purchasing a high-growth stock called in a panic because the stock had dropped more than 20 points in one day. I had a hard time convincing him to ride it out rather than cut his losses. I think what frustrated me most was that this happened despite my attempts from the beginning to explain the short-term volatility of that stock.

This is another question designed to probe the candidate's professional personality. The interviewer will want reassurance that you are able to withstand pressure on the job. Describe how you've remained diplomatic, objective, or professional in a difficult situation. Pick a situation in which, again, you will not raise any major doubts or concerns in the mind of the interviewer. Also be sure that you depict yourself as someone who is able to work through the problems that arise in any job with tact and no hard feelings.

Q: Tell me about one of your projects that failed.

A: I've always been somewhat of a workaholic and have the attitude that I can tackle anything and achieve good results. After a rather destructive hurricane, my insurance company was inundated with claims. I really believed that I was completely capable of handling all the claims in my area and dove right into a series of 18-hour workdays. Even when others in the office would offer to help, I reassured them that I had it all under control. After about a week and a half, I realized that there was no way I could complete all of the claims on time and on my own. I had to begin delegating some of the responsibility to my investigators. What I learned was

that no matter how efficient and competent you are, there are always situations in which you need to ask for help from others.

Make sure that you demonstrate the ability to be humble when answering this type of question. One of the worst answers you can come up with in a situation such as this one is "I can't think of anything I've ever failed at" or "I've never had a project that failed." Everyone has failed at one time or another, and it's okay to admit it. Show the employer how much you can learn from your mistakes. In hindsight, what do you think you could have and should have done differently? How have you altered your leadership or professional style as a result of this experience?

> **Q: Tell me about a time when your employer wasn't happy with your work performance.**

A: When I first began working as a paralegal, I handed in two letters with typos in them during my first week on the job. I am not sure why my work was sloppy; perhaps it was my nervousness at beginning a new career and actually working instead of going to school. After that first week, however, my boss did tell me regularly how happy she was with my work.

Talking about your role in causing a company to go completely under certainly will not win you any points here. Instead, try to think of a relatively minor incident in which you made a mistake but were able to learn from it. Also, show your willingness to accept responsibility for the problem—don't blame others or make excuses. Simply describe what happened and what you did to successfully resolve the situation. In the time since that incident, how have you redeemed yourself or improved upon your past mistakes?

Q: Give me an example of a time when you were asked to complete a task but weren't given enough information to get it done.

A: At my first job as a publicity assistant, I was given the task of assembling five hundred press kits for immediate mailing. The work had already been done, but I was unsure of whether or not there was a specific order in which each of the pages needed to be arranged. My supervisor had already left for a meeting, but I was able to track her down in her car. She explained to me the order in which the kits needed to be assembled, and the work was completed in a fairly speedy amount of time. In the end, I managed to prevent a problem that would have cost several hours of time to rectify, not to mention a bunch of headaches.

> In answering this question, you want to reassure the interviewer that you are mature and responsible enough to handle problems that are likely to occur. Think of a situation in which you were able to think quickly enough to prevent a problem. Talk about your own resourcefulness and initiative in getting the job done in a timely and professional manner.

Q: Tell me about a time when you failed to resolve a conflict that had arisen.

A: I wasn't able to keep a good employee who had been working in one of my company's manufacturing facilities for more than 20 years. As part of the company's modernization policy, all job descriptions were rewritten to require some sort of computer skills. Though I offered to pay the cost of classes so that he could gain these skills, he refused. Unfortunately, I had no other option than to replace him, as the new equipment we were using required the said skills. When I look back on the experience, I really wish I had been more vocal to him and the other employees about acquiring new training periodically. That way,

when new techniques were introduced, he may not have been so overwhelmed. Now I am vigilant about encouraging those in my work group to attend seminars and training classes to enhance their job skills. I have even had various professionals come into work and teach some classes on-site.

The best way to answer this question is to discuss a difficult situation, but one that was not really yours to solve in the first place. Briefly introduce the problem, but focus more on the steps that you took to solve the problem. What was the result of your work? What did you learn from the experience? How has that experience changed your professional behavior today?

Q: When was the last time you really put your foot in your mouth?

A: As part of my college yearbook staff, I tended to have creative differences with the yearbook editor. Though I respected his opinion on many topics, his desktop publishing skills were not the greatest. When I told the committee that I was considering leaving, they all wanted to know why. Being a fairly close group, I told them that it was because I thought the editor was a bit talentless. Little did I know that one of the people on my committee was the editor's sister. Once I found out, I immediately called to apologize for making such a foolish comment. Luckily, she and I are still good friends today.

Everyone makes mistakes; you and the interviewer are no exceptions. If and when the interviewer asks you about a time when you have made a fool of yourself, don't be afraid to talk about it. Don't go into a full-length story here; set up the situation and let the interviewer know what the foolish comment was that you made. The interviewer is interested in whether you have a sense of right and wrong, and how far you will go to fix those mistakes that you have made. Show the interviewer that you are well aware of the way in which a bad impression of *you*

can extend to your company and that you would never do anything to intentionally damage the company's reputation.

Q: How do you feel when things go wrong on a project? How do you handle it?

A: Though I would obviously prefer that all of the projects I work on run smoothly, I am realistic enough to know that this cannot happen. This is especially true in the case of the biotechnology industry, in which changes can and will happen to any plan at any time. I try to realize from the outset of any project that the plan we come up with is only the best case scenario plan and that it may need to be changed at any given moment. When plans begin to unravel, my approach is just to cross each bridge when I come to it and not to think too much about it beforehand. One of the ways in which I try to prepare for complications is to come up with some alternative plans. Though this does work in some cases, it doesn't help in all; sometimes you can't prepare for a problem until it's right there in front of you. My basic attitude is to just take it all in stride.

This is a very tricky question, and as the interviewee, it's important that you understand that from the outset. What the interviewer is really trying to get at here is whether or not you have the ability to work under pressure. Without going into too much detail about all the projects that have somehow gone wrong in your professional history, reassure the interviewer that you can and do handle pressure with ease and professionalism.

Q: Have you ever been passed up for a promotion you thought you deserved?

A: A couple times in my early career, I thought I was unfairly passed up for a promotion. However, in retrospect, I now realize that I probably wasn't ready to perform those jobs. In fact, the additional training I received remaining where I was proved invaluable in the last few years, as I've made significant progress moving

Insider Tips

Body Language

As you answer the questions, watch for signals from the employer as to whether your responses are too short or too long. For example, if the employer is nodding or looking away, wrap up your answer as quickly as possible.

up the corporate ladder. I've also learned to appreciate that being ready for a promotion doesn't necessarily mean it will happen. There are many external factors, aside from a person's performance and capabilities, that need to be taken into consideration.

> The interviewer wants to gauge the candidate's self-confidence as well as his or her objectivity about personal or professional limitations. Be sure to give evidence here that you have enough patience to learn what is important before you get bored in one position or frustrated because you have not been promoted. After you've mastered your own job, would you stay motivated long enough to be productive? If you've never been passed up for a promotion— or if you've never been up for a promotion at all—it's okay to say so. Perhaps you've only been in the work force for a short period of time and don't think you've acquired strong enough skills to be promoted. Whatever the case, be honest.

Q: If this meeting were your first annual review with this company, what do you think I would be saying to you right now?

A: You would be thanking me for a job well done over the past 12 months, and I would be explaining how much I am looking forward to the next 12 months. I would tell you that you could certainly look forward to watching my performance get even better in the forthcoming year. Furthermore, I would anticipate your thanking me for putting in so much extra time to ensure that key projects were completed on time and your letting me know how much my innovation and creation had helped the company to solve some of their existing problems.

> Though you may be tempted to give some sort of witty retort such as "You'd be telling me that I got an enormous raise!" DON'T! Now is not the time or place for humor. Instead, talk about the way in which you think you could most impact this company in the coming months.

Mention the characteristics you plan to showcase and the ways in which you hope to make a difference if hired. Focus on one or two strengths based on the personal themes that you have developed.

Q: Have you ever been fired?

A: When I was in college, I was fired from a summer internship. I was working for a software consulting company, and midway through the summer, a new president was appointed because of some financial difficulties. As one of his first orders of business, he requested the resignation of my entire work group. I was swept out with everyone else, though my work performance had never been criticized.

If you've never been fired, this should be an easy question to answer. If you have been fired, you'll need to be prepared to discuss the situation in detail and possibly answer a series of specific follow-up questions. If the termination was the result of a situation beyond your control, like corporate downsizing, most interviewers will be understanding. If you were fired due to poor performance or some other personal problem, you'll need to admit your fault and convince the interviewer that you've corrected the problem. Although this may be a difficult question to answer (and one that makes you—ultimately—nervous about the overall impression you will leave behind), you should be completely honest. If you aren't honest and the recruiter finds out as much from your references, you will definitely not be offered the job; if you have been made an offer or have already accepted one, it may be revoked or you may be subject to an immediate dismissal.

Q: Why have you changed jobs so frequently?

A: My frequent job changes over the last five years have been due to the rapid changes in my profession. My jobs

have been based on government contracts, and over the last several years, congressional appropriations have been up and down, causing some companies' contracts to be canceled while other companies land huge, unexpected contracts. The unpredictability creates some good opportunities but also causes a lot of uncertainty. Because your business is based mostly on consumer products and not on government products, I welcome the opportunity to work in an environment where the business cycle is more stable and predictable.

> If you've been with the same company for an extended period of time, it is not likely that this question will be asked—even just to trip you up. If you have had a fairly high number of job changes though, be prepared to talk about them. Be candid when answering this question. Personal growth, a larger budget, or other career-enhancing experiences are all valid reasons for moving on. The last thing a recruiter wants to do is hire a fickle employee, only to have him or her quit just a few months after being hired. Convince the interviewer that you are interested in his or her company for the long haul.

Q: Why did you stay in your last job for such a long period of time?

A: I was in my last job for over seven years. During that time, I completed an advanced technical degree at an evening university and also had two six-month assignments in which I was loaned out to different departments. As a result, I acquired some additional skills that normally aren't associated with that job. Therefore, I think I've made good progress and am ready to accept the next challenge.

> On the opposite end of the spectrum, an interviewer may also be curious as to why you would stay in one particular position for too long. If you've been with the same company for an extended period of time, the interviewer may be curious about your interest in personal improvement, tackling new assignments, and so on. He or she

may also be concerned about whether you have a tendency to get too comfortable with the status quo. Demonstrate how you've developed job responsibilities in meaningful new ways in your many years on the job and that you are expecting to do the same with this company.

Q: Tell me about your least favorite manager or professor.

A: Well, I've been pretty fortunate as far as managers go, and I didn't have any problems with my professors. In my first job out of college, I worked with a manager who was pretty inaccessible. If you walked into his office to ask a question, you got the sense that you were bothering him, so we just learned to get help from each other instead. I wouldn't say he was my least favorite manager, because he was good in a lot of ways, but I would have preferred that he'd been more available to us and given us more direction.

Answering this question will be a little bit like walking across a minefield, so be careful! Keep in mind that the interviewer doesn't really want to learn about your former supervisors but about the way you speak of them. Though the interviewer may bait you to make a negative statement about your former employer, doing so can create a host of problems. Even if your claim is completely true and entirely justified, the recruiter may conclude either that you don't get along well with people in general (or specifically with those in authority positions) or that you often shift blame to others. The best way around this dilemma is to choose an example that's not too negative, touch upon it briefly, then focus the rest of your answer on what you learned from the experience.

Q: Who's the toughest employer you've ever had to work for and why?

A: The most difficult employer I've ever had would definitely have to be Mrs. Rogers at the Brady Project. She would push people to

Job Search
Odds and Ends

Bring a Good Book

The corporate controller at one large company makes everyone wait for at least an hour before he will interview them. He feels his time is more valuable than anyone else's. This is where you have to ask yourself, "How much do I really want this job—especially if I have to report to this person?"

Insider Tips

Thank-You Letter Required

While the thank-you letter is a relatively new part of the whole job search process, it is quickly becoming a step that is expected and almost required by certain employers. Sending a quick thank-you or follow-up letter reinforces your enthusiasm for a position and restates your desire to be hired, even after the interview. Don't take chances. Stay in the good graces of each employer you interview with, and always send a thank-you letter.

their limits when things got busy, and she was a stickler for detail. But she was always fair, and she always rewarded people when they worked hard and did a good job. I'd definitely call her a tough boss, but I'd also call her a good boss.

This question is another in which the interviewer is sort of daring you to make negative statements about a previous employer. Just remember that even the most difficult of bosses has taught you something new, so be sure to focus on that part of the experience. Turn the question around with a positive, upbeat response. Be sure to mention the positive aspects of this boss in addition to the qualities that made him or her so tough.

Q: Tell me about a time when you had a real problem getting along with one of your work associates.

A: I have always thought of myself as a pretty easygoing person; I tend to get along with most people. However, I do remember one time when we brought in a new associate who was very bossy—bossy to the point where his attitude really offended one of our interns. As this was not the type of management style that our employees were used to, I took it upon myself to pull the new associate aside and explain to him that I found it more productive to ask people for help than to give orders. Unfortunately, he seemed more offended by my concern for our employees and about the sour relationship he was beginning to form with them than pleased with or grateful for my attempt to help him. The advice didn't change anything with his attitude, but we were much more careful with our hiring process after that experience.

The best way to answer this question is to discuss a difference in work ethic between you and an associate, not an all-out hatred for each other. Avoid discussing a personality clash between you and a coworker. Instead, speak about a situation in which the interviewer is likely to empathize. For example, you might describe someone

whose standards of excellence were perhaps less stringent than yours. Be sure to talk about the steps you took to mend this problem and what the result was.

Q: Have you ever had to work with a manager who you thought was unfair to you, or who was just plain difficult to get along with?

 A: Fortunately, I've never really run into that problem. Of course, my current boss has to work under time constraints—just like everyone else—and she sometimes has a tendency to phrase things rather bluntly to push our department to meet its goals. But I've never considered that unfair or hard to handle; it's just part of the job. My supervisors and I have always gotten along quite well.

Again, no matter how many times an interviewer gives you the opportunity to do so, never criticize a current or former employer! The interviewer is not really interested in finding out whether or not you have worked for difficult people in the past—we all have. What he or she is trying to discover is whether or not (and how easily) you are willing to badmouth these people.

Q: What are some of the things your supervisor has done that you disliked?

 A: The only thing I really don't like is to get feedback in front of others. I want to hear good or bad feedback in private so that I have time to think and react to the issue without other distractions. I believe that's the fair way to improve learning or to change future behavior.

Again, avoid being overly negative about your ex-boss or manager. Discuss a relatively minor example of one with which the interviewer is likely to empathize. Put a positive spin on your answer by describing what you learned from this difficult situation.

Q: How do you handle tension with your boss?

A: The only tension I've ever felt occurred only once, when we both got too busy to keep each other informed. My boss overcommitted me with a short deadline, not knowing I was bogged down with another client problem. I believe firmly in the importance of staff meetings to keep coworkers aware and respectful of the demands on each other's time, and I worked closely with my boss to develop a formalized meeting schedule.

> Though the question itself is set in the present tense, your best bet in answering it is to use the past tense. The safest ground here is to describe an example of a miscommunication in your early relationship with a boss and how you resolved it. Talk about the problem itself, but focus more on how the two of you handled the problem. Describe the steps you have you taken since that incident to ensure that a similar problem does not reoccur.

Q: Tell about two or three aspects of your last job that you never want to repeat.

A: One of the skills that I am most proud of is my fairly extensive background in credit collections; it has enabled me to make better risk assessments in my everyday job. Though I really enjoyed the experience I received from having worked in collections, it was not a job that I particularly enjoyed, and it isn't something that I would want to do again.

> In a completely constructive way, describe one or two things you've done that you didn't especially enjoy or that didn't play upon your greatest strengths. Though this question specifically targets a negative topic, it's easy to turn this around: After talking about why you didn't like a particular job or task, describe your strengths and their relevance to the job you're applying for.

Q: Would you be able to work extended hours as the job needed you to?

A: I'm accustomed to working long hours during the week. I usually work until at least 6:30, because I get a lot done after the office closes at 5. I can make arrangements to be available on weekends, if necessary, though I do prefer to have at least 24 hours' notice.

> Your response should match closely the position you are applying for and should reflect a realistic understanding of the work and time required. Ask about seasonality of your work if you're unsure, and show a willingness to work occasional extended hours. If you are completely unwilling to work any overtime, it's not likely that many companies will consider you a very valuable asset. Recent studies have shown that a large majority of Americans are working, on average, closer to 50 hours per week, rather than 40.

Q: What are your salary requirements?

A: If hired, I would expect to earn a salary that is comparable to the going rate for someone in my field, with my same skills, amount of experience, and expertise. However, the salary of the job is not my only consideration. The opportunity, as you have presented it, is much more important to me. I really believe that this job is exactly in line with what I hope to accomplish, and that is the most important thing to me. What kind of figure do you have in mind?

> Recruiters weed out people whose financial goals are unrealistic or not in line with what the position at hand is offering. This question is a direct hit, and both the interviewer and the candidate know that. It forces you to respond—directly—to a question relating to a very touchy subject. On the one hand, you may cite a salary that is too low. As a result, you will seem uninformed or (even

Job Search
Odds and Ends

Check, Please?

Here is one story of a company checking up on a candidate's pay history: "I had been interviewing with a company for several weeks, and everything looked great. I had passed the screening interview, met with various members of the department I would be working for, and even had lunch with James, the man who would be my boss. During lunch, James told me he would like to offer me the position but wanted to know my current pay rate so that he could pay me accordingly. I was truthful with him, which was very lucky for me, as the next thing he asked for was a copy of my latest pay stub."

Job Search Odds and Ends

Relocating

If you're looking for work and need to relocate to a different part of the country, check out *http://homes.wsj.com.* This Web site offers resources for moving to a new city and buying a new home. The one hundred largest cities in the United States are profiled. Another option of this site is the "Best Places to Live," which allows you to choose from different criteria and then tells you which metro areas are your best match.

worse) desperate. On the other hand, if you throw out a salary amount that is too high, you may immediately eliminate yourself from any further consideration. The best way to handle "the salary question" is to turn the question back on the recruiter. Mention that the salary isn't your primary consideration, and ask what the salary range for the position is. Next, ask the recruiter to consider how your qualifications compare to the average requirements for the position and go from there.

Q: What is your current salary?

A: I currently earn an annual salary of $45,000 per year with full benefits.

If you're asked a question this direct, consider yourself lucky. Telling the recruiter how much money you make now is a heck of a lot easier than trying to negotiate a salary with absolutely no information to go on (as in the previous question). Be sure not to embellish your salary, as this information can be very easy for an employer to find out. More and more companies are starting to verify applicants' pay history, some even demanding to see W-2 forms from job seekers. If you get the job, a falsehood discovered even years later may be grounds for immediate dismissal. Don't leave yourself open to this kind of trouble.

Q: Would you be willing to relocate to another city?

A: Though I would prefer to be based here, it's certainly a possibility I'd be willing to consider.

Just because you're asked this question does not mean that the interviewer wants to fly you off to the other side of the country for a job. You may, even in some first interviews, be asked questions that seem to elicit a tremendous

commitment on your behalf, such as this one. Although such questions may be unfair during an initial job interview, you may well conclude that you have nothing to gain and everything to lose with a negative response. If you are asked such a question unexpectedly during an initial job interview, simply say something like "That's certainly a possibility" or "I'm willing to consider that." If and when the interviewer says something along the lines of "Well, we have nothing for you in our Boston office, but our outfit in Wichita would certainly benefit from someone with your experience!" then you can begin to panic.

If you do receive an offer, you can find out the specific work conditions as far as relocation goes and then decide whether you wish to accept the position. Remember, at the job-offer stage, you have the most negotiating power, and the employer may be willing to accommodate your needs. If that isn't the case, you explain that upon reflection, you've decided you can't (for instance) relocate, but you'd like to be considered for other positions that might open up in the future.

Q: Does the frequent travel that is required for this job fit in with your lifestyle?

A: The frequent travel in this consulting position is no problem for me or my family. I was recently married, but my wife is an airline flight attendant, so neither of us follows the typical routine.

If you feel comfortable enough to divulge information about your family situation, now is the time to do so. The interviewer's main concern here is that the candidate may not be able to travel as much as the job requires. In order to alleviate this concern, emphasize your flexibility or explain why travel wouldn't be a problem. Remember to be honest. If you were unaware that the job required any sort of travel—and if it would most likely be a problem—say so.

> **Q:** Time management has become a necessary part of strong productivity. Give me an example of a time management skill that you have learned and applied to your work.

A: I always use some form of scheduling software, which allows me to effectively plan for the day, week, month, or year ahead. It also has a to-do list feature as well as an alarm option, which is helpful in meeting timely deadlines. In general though, I consider myself to be a very goal-oriented and self-disciplined individual. I like to focus clearly on one project at a time for a set number of hours. In the past, I've found that this has helped me to save time, which in turn has given me the opportunity to implement new procedures that have ultimately saved the department time and money.

> The interviewer wants to hear about a technique that you have implemented that allows you to save time both at work and in your personal life. In most jobs, time is a very precious resource. You want to convince the interviewer how much you respect this fact and how you have worked to make your work environment— and the one around you—a more productive one. Try to think of a time when you have been able to increase productivity because of your time management skills, and talk about it.

> **Q:** What would you say are the broad responsibilities of an editorial assistant?

A: Though the job description differs from company to company, and medium to medium, I see the role of the editorial assistant as being a pivotal one in getting an entire publication brought together. If I were hired, I would expect to be doing a lot of typing, filing, and general administrative work. In addition, I imagine that I would also be asked to read and evaluate various book proposals, write and send manuscript rejection letters, speak with some of the authors about various subjects, and generally assist the editor in whatever it was that needed to be done.

> Though the job title itself will change from job interview to job interview, the question is one that is likely to be asked. The interviewer wants to get an idea of how *you* see your future with this

company. He or she is also checking to make sure that you have a clear understanding of the duties this job entails and that you are willing and able to do these things. If you are applying for an entry-level position, you might get this question more often. If you are applying for an entry-level position within an industry that is often glamorized, you can almost count on this question as being one of the interviewer's favorites. Many new recruits are often surprised by the lack of fun that an entry-level position offers them. They are unhappily surprised to find themselves engaged in a lot of clerical work and don't last too long in the industry as a whole. In asking this question, the employer wants to make sure that you know exactly what you are being hired to do and that it's a position you are likely to be happy in for years to come.

Q: What would you do or say if I told you that I thought you were giving a very poor interview today?

A: Well, the first thing I would do is ask you whether there had been any specific parts of the interview that you thought I mishandled. After that, I'd think back and try to remember if there had been any faulty communication on my part. Then I'd try to review possible problems I had understanding your questions, and I'd ask for clarification if I needed it. Finally, if we had time, I'd try to respond more fully and appropriately to the problem areas you identified for me.

Interviewers like to ask stress questions like these to see how well you hold up under pressure. Your best bet is to stay calm and relaxed; don't allow your confidence to be shaken.

Q: Sell me this stapler.

A: This professional quality stapler is designed to be functional as well as attractive. It will help you reduce clutter on your desk by enabling you to fasten pages together. And since papers relating to the same subject will now be attached, you'll be more efficient and will take less time searching for papers. Finally, its sleek shape and black color are coordinated to match the rest of your office furniture.

Job Search Odds and Ends

The Impossible Question

What is the best way to answer those questions that just seem to have no answer? Take this interview question for instance: How would you respond to a defaulted form Z-65 counterderivative renewal request if your manager ordered you to do so, and if the policy under which the executive board resolves such issues were currently under review?

Being asked an impossible question is actually a good sign. The recruiter is not really looking for an answer but rather trying to discover how you will hold up under the pressure. If you're asked a tough question that you can't answer, think about it for a few seconds. Then, with a confident smile, simply say something like "I don't know, but if you hire me, I'll be happy to find out for you."

The Mother of All Zingers

Let's say you are faced with this statement: You have seven minutes to convince me that you're the best candidate for the job. Go. How would you react?

This question is essentially *the* question that can determine whether or not you've been paying attention to the material in this book. This is the question that only the most prepared of job interviewees will survive, and that's exactly what the recruiter is looking for. In answering this question, you should refer back to everything this book has taught you. Review your personal themes and make sure to touch upon each and every one of them. Assure the interviewer that you know all there is to know about the job, the company, and the industry. Essentially, try to be every recruiter's dream candidate.

The interviewer is curious as to how quickly you can react to a situation. Do you have the ability to think on your feet? Do you know how to communicate effectively and succinctly? This is one question that you're likely to be asked if you're applying for a sales or marketing position in particular. If you want to get into either of those industries, be prepared to give a 30-second sales pitch on the benefits and advantages of any common office staple, from a paper clip to a fax machine.

Q: Prove to me that your interest in this job and company is sincere.

A: I know that there are a lot of people out there who would like to work in television because of large income potential or the opportunity to be on camera, but my reasons go far beyond that. To me, communication is an art form, and the television industry is the ultimate test of how well one communicates. Working in television isn't like working for a newspaper, where, if a reader misses a fact, he or she can just go back and reread it. A television news story can go by in a flash, and the challenge is to make sure the audience understands it, learns from it, and, in a broader sense, can use the information to better their lives or their situations. It's the way television can evoke action that's always made me want to be a part of the industry. I'm particularly interested in this station because I like your focus on the community. Though the on-air products have a great look, the station seems to remain focused on the tradition of local news and what matters to its audience. The special reports that emphasize town politics, go on location each week to a different town for a live shot, and explain the big issues facing a community make the viewer feel that the station is a part of the community. In my opinion, this is a great way to maintain a loyal audience.

Being unprepared to answer this question can eliminate you from further consideration. On the other hand, if you are able to demonstrate a strong interest in the company and the position, you'll have an advantage over the competition. Be sure to talk about the specific position and give the details of the company that make you want to become an employee.

APPENDIX

Sample Job
Interview Questions

Accounting and Marketing

Q: Explain how you would handle the following situation: Unusual bills are received and, though a purchase order is referenced, the money due exceeds the amount authorized.

Q: How long would it take you to post an average daily batch?

Q: Have you ever worked with any of the major spreadsheet programs? If so, describe how and why it was used.

Q: Have you ever performed the order-entry function, billing function, or customer-service function?

Q: How would you handle the following situation: An important, regular customer overpays an open invoice.

Q: Describe your knowledge of, or expertise with, the valuation process and, specifically, the role you play in such projects.

Q: What other kinds of actuarial projects do you participate in?

Q: Do you participate in other specialized projects? If so, describe them.

Q: Describe your exam progress to date and your intentions regarding enrollment and fellowship designations.

Q: Generally, how do you acquire your professional knowledge, beyond the academic experience of exam sitting?

Q: Have you participated in any marketing-related activities? In general, how do you feel about marketing and business development responsibilities?

Q: Describe to me what client service means to you and how you promote this activity on the job.

Q: Tell me about your early career development in banking.

Q: If the consumer price index is off this month, how does that impact our bank?

Q: Suppose your portfolio under management consisted of automotive corporate bonds, retail department store corporate bonds, and options on a major retailer's stock. How would you balance the risk in that?

Q: If you were looking at how a company financed a large equipment purchase, where would you find that information?

Q: If you are an account officer and are presented with a problem loan, what would you want to do?

Q: So many deals in the corporate finance group take a long time to develop. Describe a time when persistence over the long run got you the desired result.

Q: What are appropriate actions to take after you've made a proposal to a potential banking customer? How would you follow up?

Q: As banks move toward relationship management, what does that mean to you?

Q: What do you see as the role of the credit department in a lending operation?

Q: How big are the loans you have typically dealt with?

Q: What types of borrowers have you analyzed?

Q: What types of loans were involved in your analyses?

Q: What would you consider when analyzing a business loan request?

Q: How would a term loan analysis differ from that of a line of credit?

Q: Can you provide a sample presentation?

Q: Have you done industry surveys? Describe why and how.

Q: What class have you taken that has helped you the most in the business place?

Q: If you were a finance or accounting person new to the job at a manufacturing plant and you wanted to know how your costs compared, whether good or bad, what would you do? Where would you start?

Q: How important do you think qualitative concerns are to financial analysis?

Q: What publications do you read on a regular basis?

Q: Do you have experience preparing budgets?

Q: What is the yearly sales volume of your current company?

Q: How do insurance companies make profits?

Q: In what order would you prioritize the following tasks: completing a new-business proposal, resolving a service problem for an existing client, and renewing an in-force account?

Q: In general terms, what three or four demographic characteristics might distinguish a good risk from a bad risk for group life insurance?

Q: What are the five Cs of credit? Which is the most important, and why?

Q: How would you go about increasing the size of your loan portfolio?

Q: When you take collateral for a loan, what factors do you consider?

Q: Tell me about the new business you've developed.

Q: Is there any new business success story that stands out in your mind?

Q: If you could work with anyone in finance, whom would you want to work with?

Q: What are the differences between financial management in private and in public firms?

Q: Would you prefer to work for a full-service or a specialty firm?

Q: Do you have any experience with intangible sales?

Administration

Q: What is your typing speed?

Q: What word processing, spreadsheet, and database management programs are you familiar with?

Q: On a scale of 1 to 10, rate your proficiency with these applications.

Q: Do you have any experience taking dictation?

Q: Can you take shorthand?

Q: Have you ever screened telephone calls?

Q: Do you plan to further your education?

Q: How do you typically organize your work and plan your day?

Q: What's your theory on customer service?

Q: How do you deal with difficult people?

Q: In your opinion, what kinds of aptitudes, skills, and traits are necessary to be successful in this position?

Q: Which of these required aptitudes, skills, and traits do you consider to be your strengths?

Q: Which of these required aptitudes, skills, and traits give you the most difficulty or offer you the greatest opportunity for improvement?

Q: What five traits do you value most in your close working relationships?

Q: How do you handle conflict?

Q: Do you think it's important to maintain optimum working relationships?
Why or why not?

Q: How would you rate your grammatical skills?

Q: How do you approach the challenges of maintaining confidentiality?

Q: Give an example of a situation in which you faced conflicting priorities, and tell me what you did to resolve the conflict.

Q: What's your experience with employee relations?

Q: Do you have any experience managing budgets?

Q: How do you handle staff development?

Q: Do you have proofreading experience?

Q: Are you comfortable on the telephone? Tell me about your customer service skills.

Art and Design

Q: How do you see yourself functioning as art director?

Q: How would you rate yourself in terms of organizational, managerial, and interpersonal skills?

Q: How do you respond to criticism from management, editorial, and sales?

Q: How do you go about giving your staff critical feedback on their design submissions?

Q: How do you feel about using the latest trends when it comes to cover design?

Q: Have you ever implemented new procedures in or introduced new concepts to your department?

Q: Do you have any traditional production experience?

Q: Do you have a background in graphic design?

Q: Have you, in any previous jobs, had any graphic design responsibilities?

Q: What software applications are you familiar with?

Q: Have you ever worked with style sheets in Quark?

Q: Have you ever had to create from scratch a set of style sheets and templates for use on a project?

Q: Have you worked with Photoshop? Which version are you most familiar with?

Q: Have you done any basic Photoshop work with masques and silhouettes?

Q: Have you ever done any color correcting?

Q: Have you done any scanning?

Q: Have you done any streamlining of existing scans in Illustrator or Freehand?

Q: Have you ever created Illustrator files from sketches or image templates?

Q: What makes you an "expert" in QuarkXPress?

Q: What is the difference between RGB and CMYK colors?

Q: Suppose I gave you a piece of artwork and told you to scan it and that it was going to be used in a printed brochure and as part of a disk-based presentation. What would you do?

Q: Which are your favorite serif and sans-serif fonts?

Q: Suppose you were setting type at 12/14 and had a 3¾ inch column to fill. How would you figure the number of lines that would fit?

Q: Describe a trap and why it's important.

Q: Suppose I gave you two sets of specifications, one on Monday and another on Wednesday, for the same piece—let's say a poster—and they were different. What would you do?

Q: How fast can you produce a 32-page catalog?

Q: Have you ever missed a deadline?

Q: How do you feel when someone finds an error in a finished piece?

Q: How many times will you redo a piece? What is the greatest amount of times you have redone a piece?

Q: How often do you back up your work?

Q: How would you deal with freelancers?

Q: May I see your portfolio?

Q: How would you react if you were assigned to photograph the dog of the week?

Q: What positions did you hold on your college newspaper?

Q: When did your interest in this subject change from a hobby to a career?

Q: Tell me what you know about reproduction photography.

Q: Tell me what you know about digital imaging. Have you ever done any digital imaging yourself?

Q: How would you rate your writing skills?

Communications

Q: Give me an example of a great idea you've had.

Q: Describe three examples of leadership that I would find on your resume.

Q: What do you think about purple hair? When would you advise someone to have it?

Q: What is the story behind your pin?

Q: What publications do you read regularly?

Q: Give me your ideas for selling a pencil.

Q: What writing classes did you take in college?

Q: How do you think that new information technology will affect this industry?

Q: Do you have any experience with identity management consulting?

Q: Do you approach your projects from a task- or a project-oriented position?

Q: Do you have any experience with budgeting?

Q: Do you belong to any professional associations?

Q: What would you do if a client asked you to stretch the truth in a press release or press conference?

Q: Do you have experience with a diverse client base and diverse mediums?

Q: How much client interaction have you had?

Q: How did you come up with the idea for this particular piece?

Q: Can you write lengthy copy? Do you have any corporate capability brochures or annual reports under your belt? If so, do you have them with you?

Q: What environments have you worked in? How well have you worked with account executives?

Q: What's your favorite advertising campaign, and why?

Q: Name three books you've read recently.

Q: Who is your favorite author and why?

Q: How fast can you type?

Q: How necessary is it for you to be creative on the job?

Q: What is your impression about the industry in general?

Q: What in your background has prepared you for hard work and long hours?

Q: Organization and the scheduling of people and tasks are necessary functions in any account role. Give me an example that illustrates your organization and scheduling ability.

Q: Give an example of a time when you've used facts and reason to persuade another person to take action.

Q: Give an example of a time when you used your authority to influence another individual.

Q: Tell me about a time when you were able to learn a difficult concept without the direction of another person.

Q: Tell me about the last time you decided to withhold information from someone.

Q: Tell me about a time when you felt inappropriately reprimanded by a supervisor. How did you handle the situation?

Q: Tell me what you know about market research.

Q: Tell me about a project in which your input made a difference.

Q: How persuasive are you?

Q: What kind of contacts have you been able to establish in your previous positions?

Q: How do you handle deadline pressure?

Q: What sorts of things are you interested in?

Q: What books do you keep on your desk?

Q: If you had extra time to devote to some project, what would that project be?

Computers

Q: What type of programming experience do you have?

Q: Do you have any analysis-and-design experience?

Q: Have you ever programmed in a Windows-based environment?

Q: Do you have experience with client/server technology?

Q: Explain the concept "referential integrity" as it applies to relational databases.

Q: How much experience do you have using SQL (Standard Query Language)?

Q: Have you ever worked on mission critical applications before?

Q: How did you become interested in interactive multimedia?

Q: What platform do you feel most comfortable with?

Q: What kind of computer do you have at home?

Q: What kind of training have you done?

Q: Tell me about the local-area network at your current company.

Q: Consider this situation: My PC's sound card isn't working. It's configured at IRQ 7 and I/O 220. What could be causing the problem?

Q: Describe your philosophy of what would be important if you were the senior systems analyst and had to staff your organization with programmers and systems analysts.

Q: Are there certain personal qualities you believe are compatible with the information-systems profession?

Q: Is it sometimes difficult to get clients to reveal what they're thinking in terms of information output?

Q: How do you get people to embrace a new software product?

Q: Describe a new system that was a great success in terms of ease of implementation.

Q: What new technology do you think will be most significant over the next few years?

Q: What role do you play in the design and development of the system conversion to C++?

Q: When you start a project, do you prefer to create a flowchart or to immediately start coding?

Q: Do you feel comfortable sharing information with other specialists?

Q: What do you think is the most challenging product to support?

Educational Services

Q: Tell me about any previous experience you've had with children.

Q: What has your involvement been with other teachers or counselors?

Q: Describe the reading program you'd use with your grade.

Q: How do you incorporate writing into your curriculum?

Q: What do you think should be included in the math programs for this grade level?

Q: How would you teach multiculturalism in your classroom?

Q: In the past several years, classrooms have become much more diverse, with the inclusion of special-needs children, children from different socioeconomic backgrounds, and children from different cultures in the same classroom. How do you expect to meet the needs of all the students in your class?

Q: If I walked into your classroom, what would it look like?

Q: What computer experience have you had, and how will you integrate computers into your classroom?

Q: Have you had experience leading parent conferences?

Q: How would you tell a parent about a negative situation involving his or her child?

Q: With all the materials being covered in today's classroom, how do you plan to gather information for assessments?

Q: How do you handle discipline in your class?

Q: How do you go about planning and developing units or lessons for your students?

Q: In what areas of teaching would you like to improve?

Q: A student comes into your office. The teacher's note states that the student was being disruptive in class. The student says the teacher is prejudiced and hates him. How would you deal with the situation?

Q: What do you consider to be the role of parents in the school, and how would you involve them? Also, how would you promote their involvement at school?

Q: How do the needs of the high-school student differ from those of the elementary- or middle-school student?

Q: What do you perceive as your strengths in regard to working with racially, culturally, and ethnically diverse urban youngsters?

Q: Do you feel that community and other external agencies should have a role in complementing what our school system has to offer? If so, how would you go about tapping into these community and other external resources?

Q: What are the advantages and disadvantages of electronic media?

Q: What do you think are the most important aspects of supervision?

Q: What positive personal attributes would you bring to this position?

Q: Describe the ways in which you believe a teacher could establish a positive classroom environment.

Q: How do you measure student progress? How do you use that information?

Q: What do you believe contributes to the problem of identifying certain groups of students as handicapped, and what suggestions do you have for addressing the problem?

Q: What's your understanding of due process as it pertains to parents and children with respect to Chapter 766 and the IDEA?

Q: How would you advocate for a child and balance the needs of the child with the system's ability to deliver services?

Q: How would you deal with angry or upset parents?

Q: How do you integrate educational goals with a child's social or emotional needs?

Q: How do you react when you have a conflict between the reality of a situation and your professional beliefs?

Q: Say you are providing direct service to a special-needs student within the classroom. Give an example of how you would adapt the curriculum and instructional strategies for that student.

Q: What's been your most rewarding experience?

Engineering

Q: Tell me about significant team projects you've worked on.

Q: How proficient are you with using process-simulation software?

Q: Tell me about your last project. What were you trying to accomplish? How did you optimize the process?

Q: Do you have knowledge of and experience with GMP, TQM, and/or ISO-9000? If so, where? What was your role?

Q: What products have you designed?

Q: What kind of design experience do you have with high-power components?

Q: What type of lab tools are you comfortable using?

Q: What microprocessors, microcontrollers, or Digital Signal Processors (DSPs) do you have experience with?

Q: Describe any experience you've had with metastability.

Q: Tell me about any application notes you've written.

Q: Do you have experience in water treatment and distribution systems?

Q: Are you familiar with federal EPA sludge regulations?

Q: Are you a member of any professional associations?

Q: Tell me about the most interesting manufacturing job or project you've successfully completed.

Q: Tell me how you'd respond to the following scenario: You've just been hired to work in my factory, and your job as an industrial engineer is to get more output from the work force. The work force is made up of 20-year employees and is unionized. How would you go about implementing your ideas?

Q: Tell me about some specific technical subjects you would like to learn more about.

Q: Tell me about your experience with product optimization.

Q: Have you facilitated any systems training?

Q: Are you certified as a professional engineer?

Q: Do you have experience purchasing materials and/or equipment?

Q: Have you been involved with patenting a product or process?

Executive and Management

Q: How many people reported to you in your last position?

Q: Compare managerial styles of people you've reported to.

Q: How do you establish yourself when you're assuming a new management position?

Q: How closely do you tend to monitor your employees' work?

Q: How do you get people who report to you to give you their best performance?

Q: What techniques have you used to bring an underperforming employee up to speed?

Q: When do you think meetings are an appropriate use of time?

Q: Have you ever had to let an employee go?

Q: Tell me about the biggest challenge you've experienced as a manager.

Q: What do you find to be the most rewarding, and the most frustrating, aspects of managing people?

Q: What would you do if you were dealing with an angry customer?

Q: How would you rate your communication skills?

Q: What type of companies do you have experience with? What were their sizes in terms of sales revenue?

Q: How many years have you had responsibility for month- and year-end closings? Was there ever a year when the year-end audit adjustments were unfavorable or exceeded acceptable levels or standards?

Q: Do you have experience with acquisitions, leveraged buyouts (LBOs), or initial public offerings (IPOs)? Do you have experience with 10K filings?

Q: Have you had direct involvement establishing company benefit programs, including insurance, 401(k) plans, or SERPS?

Q: Briefly describe why accurate financial reporting is important to any organization.

Q: What experience do you have with annual budgeting and monthly forecasts?

Q: Do you have experience preparing tax returns or managing tax audits?

Q: Why is it important for most companies to exercise strict inventory controls? What experience do you have with inventory management?

Q: Describe in detail improvements you've made in manufacturing, both in operating efficiency and in cost reduction.

Q: There are a number of different management styles, from authoritarian to team oriented. In your own experience, which management style do you find to be the most effective, and why?

Q: What's your opinion of the value of training at all levels of the organization? Describe any training programs that you either initiated or participated in.

Q: Consider this hypothetical situation: One of the senior managers who reports to you has reached the top of her salary grade, and you are not able to give her a salary increase. How would you explain to that person that she's important to the company and keep her motivated in the face of the fact that she's not getting a raise this year?

Q: Tell me about the last course of educational study or seminar that you attended on a particular business issue. What value did you get from it?

Q: In your experience, what type of organization is most effective in driving improvements and allowing you to manage effectively? For example, what managers ought to report to you, how would you relate to people in other departments, and so on?

Q: We ask more of people, at all levels, than we used to, so it's becoming more important every day to understand how they're feeling. What method do you use to make sure that you're aware of the feelings or concerns of those in your work force?

Q: How do you feel your company treats its employees?

Q: This position is all about interacting with people. What are your best skills in this area?

Q: How important is recognition to you? What do you feel are the most and least effective ways to recognize people for a job well done, and why?

Q: Tell me some of the ways you might motivate the employees where you work.

Q: How would you describe your negotiating style?

Q: What are your feelings toward labor unions? What's the best way to handle unions?

Q: How do you stay current with changing labor laws?

Q: Consider this hypothetical situation: An important shipment for a key customer is ready and loaded on the truck. Just before the trailer is to be taken away, one of your supervisors reports to you that he or she believes there is possibly a defect on some of the merchandise in the trailer. This defect may not be immediately noticeable but has been mentioned by the customer in a previous complaint. What would you do?

Q: Consider this hypothetical situation: You arrive at work one morning to find that all of your manufacturing people are standing in a group outside their department, refusing to go to their workstations. They're protesting the firing of a coworker on the previous day. What would you do?

Q: What comments do you have regarding ISO-9000?

Q: What interests you about business analysis and strategic planning?

Q: Do you have any experience in an operations area such as insurance claims or customer service?

Q: Describe a business process that you determined wasn't value added.

Q: What's your approach to managing costs per hire?

Q: When you have an opening, do you tend to search for a candidate within the industry or outside it?

Q: Suppose you had a new PC delivered to your office. How would you learn to use it?

Q: How would you plan and organize a campus recruiting program?

Health Care

Q: Which of your clinical affiliations did you enjoy the most?

Q: Upon what do you base your clinical decisions?

Q: What would you do with a patient whose expectations for treatment outcome were unrealistic?

Q: Tell me about a difficult experience in your life. How did you overcome it?

Q: What kind of patient situation do you feel most comfortable with?

Q: What type of situation would make you most nervous?

Q: Why are you interested in our facility?

Q: Are your licenses and certifications current?

Q: Have you ever worked with children?

Q: Do you have any academic honors or awards?

Q: Have you taken any continuing education courses?

Q: Do you volunteer your professional skills?

Q: Will you be willing to pick up several clients and maintain them on an ongoing basis?

Q: Have you had experience using Hoya lifts?

Q: Tell me about your experience working with quadriplegics or paraplegics. Do you have a particular specialty?

Q: Are your CEUs (certified education units) up to date?

Q: Would you be willing to take on more than one case per day?

Q: Have you ever worked with terminally ill cases?

Q: How do you rate your ability to work with equipment and to troubleshoot problems?

Q: Consider this scenario: You've just finished training, and this is the first week you are "on your own." The supervisor is on break and you receive a call from OB asking for a STAT magnesium. Your control is out low. What would you do?

Q: Describe a positive work experience you've had with a physician.

Q: Describe a negative work experience you've had with a physician. How were you able to cope with the situation?

Q: What's your position on the use of vitamin and mineral supplements?

Q: Do you have experience developing patient-education materials?

Q: Are you familiar with nutritional therapy for wound healing?

Q: Would working long shifts cause you to lose concentration?

Q: How do you feel about working with the elderly?

Q: Do you feel you're good at making quick decisions?

Q: How would you handle a situation in which you thought a client was handing you a phony prescription?

Q: If you didn't know the proper dosage of a drug, where would you turn?

Q: What do you think about managed care?

Q: Do you think high technology will play an important role in the medical industry?

Q: What would you do if you found a friend and coworker stealing medical supplies?

Q: What do you think is the greatest problem with the way hospitals are run today?

Q: What do you do when you encounter procedures that you are unfamiliar with?

Q: What is an HMO?

Q: What type of disorder do you feel most comfortable treating?

Q: What type of disorder do you feel least comfortable treating?

Q: When assessing children younger than three, do you believe it's better to separate them from their parents or have the parents present during the evaluation?

Q: If a parent expressed dissatisfaction with your discipline procedures or with your therapy expectations, what would you do?

Q: Have you found your age to be a problem when working with elderly patients?

Q: If you were seeing a lot of the same type of disorder, would you lose interest and become bored with your caseload?

Q: Paperwork is a constant demand, and timeliness is important. How well have you managed to fulfill your administrative obligations?

Legal and Protective Services

Q: Do you have any experience preparing budgets?

Q: Tell me about a time when you saved the company money through security measures.

Q: What kind of interview and interrogation skills do you possess?

Q: What kind of employee-awareness training have you done?

Q: What are your skills in safety or fire prevention?

Q: Do you have any experience with executive protection? What would you do if your CEO received a death threat?

Q: What would you do if an employee threatened the safety of another employee and no witnesses were present?

Q: Have you ever dealt with protection of proprietary information?

Q: What experience do you have with liability prevention?

Q: How can you develop a new plan that you know will work when put into action?

Q: Tell me about some of the emergency management activities you have actually participated in.

Q: What important contacts and resources could you bring to the job?

Q: Do you have any licenses or memberships that are helpful to you in your career?

Q: If you could represent anyone as a lobbyist, who would that be?

Q: What opportunities do you see in the future of government relations?

Q: What issues have you been involved in, specifically?

Q: What coalitions have you been involved in?

Q: Could you lobby for something you didn't believe in?

Q: What are your expectations of working in a law office?

Q: What was your favorite class, and why?

Q: Tell me about a long-term project you've worked on.

Q: Do you have any experience or training in legal research?

Q: How would you rate your writing skills?

Q: Describe your familiarity with computers. What software programs do you know?

Sales and Marketing

Q: Tell me about the product you are currently selling.

Q: Do you prefer marketing products or services?

Q: How much of your time is spent cold calling new accounts versus servicing existing ones?

Q: How many new accounts did you acquire last year?

Q: What is your biggest difficulty in selling?

Q: In an ideal job, would you like to spend more or less of your time cold calling?

Q: What lead sources have you found most productive?

Q: Tell me about some of the most extreme lengths you have gone to in order to close a sale.

Q: How have you performed relative to your goals or quotas?

Q: Did you meet your goals during the previous year?

Q: What sales angle might you use in selling our product line?

Q: How do you feel about overnight travel?

Q: What do you imagine is different about working on a new product as opposed to working on an established brand?

Q: What have you learned in your various marketing positions that will help you in new product development?

Q: If you had to describe brand management as more creative or more financial, which would you choose?

Q: Here are some packaging changes we implemented. Take a look and give me your opinion on what we wanted to accomplish.

Q: In the context of brand management, what do you think are the differences between a leader and a manager?

Q: Tell me how you've mentored your marketing assistants.

Q: How do you use in-store promotions?

Q: Describe how you can use off-seasons to expand the use of a seasonal product.

Q: If you had to recall a product, what might you do?

Q: This is your 30-second commercial. What else do you want to tell me?

Q: Do you consider yourself to be left- or right-brained?

Q: Discuss the main difference between secondary and primary research. When is the best time to use each?

Q: What's the difference between qualitative and quantitative research?

Q: Here's some data from a research study. Take a few minutes to review the cross-tab table. What do the numbers say to you?

Q: Consider the following scenario: A client has sunk a lot of money into a product. Your research indicates that the product wasn't well received by consumers. In fact, it's a total failure. How do you present your findings and still please the client?

Q: After being a marketing representative for a period of time, where would you want to go next?

Q: It can be challenging to work with field-sales reps who manage their own time and have home offices. How might you manage a group of reps?

Q: What experiences helped you to be prepared and qualified to manage national accounts?

Q: People in this business tend to have creative natures. How would you manage such people?

Q: How do you motivate your sales associates?

Q: If a customer had a complaint, would you prefer to handle it directly or refer the call to customer service?

Q: If your corporate office advertised an item in error, would you explain to the customer that it wasn't your fault?

Q: What were the last five sales-related learning tools that you utilized?

Q: As you may be aware, this company has a Web site. Sell it to me.

Q: Do you prefer tangible sales or intangible sales?

Q: What do you think may slow you down, potentially impeding your sales, during the sales cycle?

Q: Who inspired you the most to do what you are doing now?

Q: What do you think is the best way to approach a potential customer?

Q: How do you respond to the word *no*?

Scientific

Q: What is your level of experience with HPLC?

Q: Are you familiar with gas chromatography?

Q: Tell me about your experience with spectroscopy abilities. What are some common problems associated with spectral analysis?

Q: Using spectroscopy, describe a simple experiment to validate the accuracy of a delivery system, such as a pump or pipette.

Q: What do you perceive as the similarities between microbiology and chemistry? What about the differences?

Q: Tell me about your experience with statistics.

Q: You notice a drift in pH readings over a three-day period. What might you attribute this to?

Q: Have you had to make defined molarity concentration solutions? Tell me how to do it.

Q: Explain how you would handle the following situation: Customers are reporting that a particular lot of test panels are not performing to specifications. They believe stated concentrations are not in tolerance when they follow the package insert exactly.

Q: Are you affiliated with any professional societies?

Q: Have you taken any significant engineering courses that are relevant to your career in biotechnology?

Q: Did you participate in a cooperative work-study program?

Q: Have you ever taken a technical writing course?

Q: Do you consider yourself to be a good communicator?

Q: What types of projects have you worked on in your current job?

Q: Do you have any professional registrations or certifications that are relevant to this position?

Q: How proficient are you with a computer?

Q: Can you complete projects on time and within a budget?

Q: Describe the most difficult crisis in a work situation that you've experienced. How did you resolve it?

Q: How do you see biotechnology changing the way consumers perceive fresh produce?

Q: Consumers are becoming increasingly educated about the use of pesticides. Do you think this will affect the biotechnology industry?

Q: What kind of validation experience have you had?

Q: What kind of training experience do you have, either as a trainee or a trainer?

Q: What kind of auditing experience do you have?

Q: Tell me about your documentation background.

Q: Describe the batch-record review and product-release systems you use at your current facility.

Q: What experience do you have with on-site investigations?

Q: Describe the product-complaint system at your current company.

Q: Do you have a stability program at your current company? Tell me about it.

Q: Describe the change-control system at your current company.

Q: Have you ever had experience writing research or grant proposals?

Q: This position requires experimentation with animals. Do you mind working with laboratory animals?

Q: Have you had any experience lecturing or presenting research material before?

Q: Have you ever supervised and trained anyone before? If so, tell me a bit about that experience.

Q: What is the research environment in your present position like? Do you prefer a flexible or a regular schedule?

Q: Tell me about your research experience characterizing DNA.

Q: Have you published any articles in a scientific journal?

Q: How much experience have you had with microscopy techniques?

Q: How familiar are you with electrophoresis?

Q: Have you ever had any unexpected or unpredictable results with your research? If

so, what happened, and what did you do to defend your position?

Q: Tell me about any future plans you might have for schooling or furthering your scientific career.

Q: I see that previously you were working in the physics arena. Tell me why you are thinking of switching fields to molecular biology. Isn't this a rather large leap for you?

Service

Q: Do you believe that the customer is always right?

Q: How do you handle unruly or demanding customers?

Q: What level of decision-making authority have you had in your last two positions?

Q: How did you handle a situation when the customer was totally wrong?

Q: Why did you go into the customer service department of your company, as opposed to sales?

Q: After a difficult day, how do you handle the stress associated with your job?

Q: What was the most difficult situation you had to face at your last company?

Q: What type of industry do you prefer to work in?

Q: When you start work with a new company or industry, how do you go about gaining an understanding of that company and its products?

Q: What was the pace of the company at your most recent position?

Q: How are you able to interact effectively with others in your most recent company?

Q: What do you feel are the personal qualities necessary to make a success of this job?

Q: What types of decisions are difficult for you?

Q: At your most recent position, what were some of the things that you spent most of your time working on?

Q: If you were head of the customer service department with authority to effect changes, what three things would you change?

Q: How many days were you absent from work last year? Why?

Q: Everyone talks about managing the people that work for you, but nobody ever bothers to talk about managing the people who manage you. Do you have the ability to "manage up" within an organization?

Q: What specific personal skills have you developed over your last several jobs, and what experiences helped you build these skills?

Q: Working with a large group of semiskilled, entry-level employees is difficult. How will you handle it?

Q: Business has been good, but your clientele isn't what you'd like it to be. What would you do to change your customer base?

Q: A new employee is great in some aspects of the job, but not in all. How would you get this person to excel in all aspects of the job?

Q: Give me an example of a time when your actions helped change a customer's attitude.

Q: Name the top three states you'd like to live in.

Q: Have you worked with profit-and-loss statements?

Q: Tell me about the toughest termination you've ever had to make.

Q: How would somebody best manage you?

Q: What are your recommendations for lowering employee turnover?

Q: How do you feel about rote paperwork?

Social and Human Services

Q: Do you have experience working with children or adolescents who are technologically dependent?

Q: What skills do you believe are important for dealing effectively with young children?

Q: Do you have any additional skills to deal specifically with children who are medically fragile or technologically dependent?

Q: What skills do you believe are important in dealing with the families of patients?

Q: Tell me about a time you needed someone's cooperation to complete a task and that person was uncooperative.

Q: How do you evaluate conflicting information or intervention approaches?

Q: Discuss your knowledge of handling confidential information while advocating for a client's needs.

Q: Discuss your methods for documenting your case-management work in individual case files, as well as for reimbursement purposes.

Q: Discuss your experience with, and knowledge of, medical terminology, developmental stages, and disability groupings.

Q: How do you manage multiple concurrent deadlines and demands on your time?

Q: What's your familiarity with computers and electronic client-record-keeping systems?

Q: What do you consider to be your most beneficial assets in your professional work?

Q: What are your future goals, if any, in advanced educational training?

Q: What's your experience in dealing with individuals who exhibit inappropriate behavior?

Q: Are you able to perform a mental-status assessment?

Q: What do you believe is your true mission statement?

Q: Do you know what to do and what to ask of a patient or client who announces that he feels suicidal, or who's making suicidal ideations or gestures?

Q: How do you determine when a client needs to be referred to a psychiatrist for medication?

Q: How do you best distinguish organic from emotional disturbances?

Q: What psychological theories do you believe have weathered the decades?

Q: What do you think are the best safeguards in a clinical agency to ensure that safe clinical interventions are being used?

Q: Identify and describe relevant issues when you were growing up that have been significant in understanding your life.

Q: What kind of messages did you receive from significant adults when you were growing up?

Q: Are there any issues from your personal life that might potentially have an impact on your professional career?

Q: What does leadership mean to you?

Q: Tell me about your experience relating to treatment planning, discharge planning, and case management.

Q: What knowledge do you have of eating, personality, attention-deficit, and disruptive-behavior disorders?

Q: How do you think the services we provide can best be delivered?

Q: The human services field works with divergent populations, and each of these has different needs. What is it about this particular area that interests you?

Q: What has been your experience with crisis intervention?

Technical

Q: What were your responsibilities in a professional project that you've worked on?

Q: What construction responsibilities have you handled?

Q: How much client contact have you had?

Q: Which of your strengths are particularly important to architecture?

Q: What things hold you back as an architect?

Q: Are you computer literate?

Q: How competent are you at drawing and drafting?

Q: Do you like dealing with clients?

Q: How do you think dealing with contractors differs from client interactions?

Q: Show me three of your best drawings.

Q: Were you able to earn your requirements for the AIA's IDP?

Q: What do you think the job of project manager would entail?

Q: What did you get out of your architecture-school training?

Q: What do you think one lacks after graduating from architecture school?

Q: Why did you want to become an architect?

Q: What publications do you read?

Q: What licenses do you have?

Q: If you could work on a special project for this firm, what would it be?

Q: Give an example of a project you've worked on.

Q: Do you have any experience with computer-aided drafting systems?

Q: How would you shoot line copy that's gray or light blue?

Q: Have you ever used FrameMaker? How do you feel about learning or using desktop publishing software?

Q: What kind of a typography background do you have?

Q: Can you explain "kerning" to me?

Q: Have you ever worked with standards before? Do you understand why they're important?

Q: Have you ever written online help? If so, what tools did you use?

Q: Have you ever attended industry seminars? Which ones?

Q: If you could join an SIG (special interest group) tomorrow, which would you pick?

Q: Have you published with HTML? Adobe Acrobat?

Q: How organized are you? Do you use any project planning strategies?

Q: What programming skills do you have?

Index

We Have EVERYTHING!

Everything® **After College Book**
$12.95, 1-55850-847-3

Everything® **American History Book**
$12.95, 1-58062-531-2

Everything® **Angels Book**
$12.95, 1-58062-398-0

Everything® **Anti-Aging Book**
$12.95, 1-58062-565-7

Everything® **Astrology Book**
$12.95, 1-58062-062-0

Everything® **Baby Names Book**
$12.95, 1-55850-655-1

Everything® **Baby Shower Book**
$12.95, 1-58062-305-0

Everything® **Baby's First Food Book**
$12.95, 1-58062-512-6

Everything® **Baby's First Year Book**
$12.95, 1-58062-581-9

Everything® **Barbeque Cookbook**
$12.95, 1-58062-316-6

Everything® **Bartender's Book**
$9.95, 1-55850-536-9

Everything® **Bedtime Story Book**
$12.95, 1-58062-147-3

Everything® **Bicycle Book**
$12.00, 1-55850-706-X

Everything® **Breastfeeding Book**
$12.95, 1-58062-582-7

Everything® **Build Your Own Home Page**
$12.95, 1-58062-339-5

Everything® **Business Planning Book**
$12.95, 1-58062-491-X

Everything® **Candlemaking Book**
$12.95, 1-58062-623-8

Everything® **Casino Gambling Book**
$12.95, 1-55850-762-0

Everything® **Cat Book**
$12.95, 1-55850-710-8

Everything® **Chocolate Cookbook**
$12.95, 1-58062-405-7

Everything® **Christmas Book**
$15.00, 1-55850-697-7

Everything® **Civil War Book**
$12.95, 1-58062-366-2

Everything® **Classical Mythology Book**
$12.95, 1-58062-653-X

Everything® **Collectibles Book**
$12.95, 1-58062-645-9

Everything® **College Survival Book**
$12.95, 1-55850-720-5

Everything® **Computer Book**
$12.95, 1-58062-401-4

Everything® **Cookbook**
$14.95, 1-58062-400-6

Everything® **Cover Letter Book**
$12.95, 1-58062-312-3

Everything® **Creative Writing Book**
$12.95, 1-58062-647-5

Everything® **Crossword and Puzzle Book**
$12.95, 1-55850-764-7

Everything® **Dating Book**
$12.95, 1-58062-185-6

Everything® **Dessert Book**
$12.95, 1-55850-717-5

Everything® **Digital Photography Book**
$12.95, 1-58062-574-6

Everything® **Dog Book**
$12.95, 1-58062-144-9

Everything® **Dreams Book**
$12.95, 1-55850-806-6

Everything® **Etiquette Book**
$12.95, 1-55850-807-4

Everything® **Fairy Tales Book**
$12.95, 1-58062-546-0

Everything® **Family Tree Book**
$12.95, 1-55850-763-9

Everything® **Feng Shui Book**
$12.95, 1-58062-587-8

Everything® **Fly-Fishing Book**
$12.95, 1-58062-148-1

Everything® **Games Book**
$12.95, 1-55850-643-8

Everything® **Get-A-Job Book**
$12.95, 1-58062-223-2

Everything® **Get Out of Debt Book**
$12.95, 1-58062-588-6

Everything® **Get Published Book**
$12.95, 1-58062-315-8

Everything® **Get Ready for Baby Book**
$12.95, 1-55850-844-9

Everything® **Get Rich Book**
$12.95, 1-58062-670-X

Everything® **Ghost Book**
$12.95, 1-58062-533-9

Everything® **Golf Book**
$12.95, 1-55850-814-7

Everything® **Grammar and Style Book**
$12.95, 1-58062-573-8

Everything® **Guide to Las Vegas**
$12.95, 1-58062-438-3

Everything® **Guide to New England**
$12.95, 1-58062-589-4

Everything® **Guide to New York City**
$12.95, 1-58062-314-X

Everything® **Guide to Walt Disney World®, Universal Studios®, and Greater Orlando, 2nd Edition**
$12.95, 1-58062-404-9

Everything® **Guide to Washington D.C.**
$12.95, 1-58062-313-1

Everything® **Guitar Book**
$12.95, 1-58062-555-X

Everything® **Herbal Remedies Book**
$12.95, 1-58062-331-X

Available wherever books are sold!
To order, call **800-872-5627**, or visit everything.com
Adams Media Corporation, 57 Littlefield Street, Avon, MA 02322. U.S.A.

Visit us at everything.com

Everything® is a registered trademark of Adams Media Corporation.

We Have

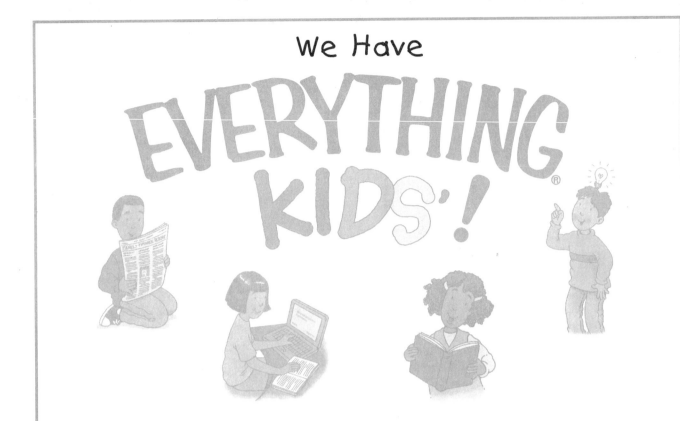

EVERYTHING KIDS'®!

Everything® Kids' Baseball Book, 2nd Edition
$6.95, 1-58062-688-2

Everything® Kids' Joke Book
$6.95, 1-58062-686-6

Everything® Kids' Mazes Book
$6.95, 1-58062-558-4

Everything® Kids' Money Book
$6.95, 1-58062-685-8

Everything® Kids' Nature Book
$6.95, 1-58062-684-X

Everything® Kids' Puzzle Book
$6.95, 1-58062-687-4

Everything® Kids' Science Experiments Book
$6.95, 1-58062-557-6

Everything® Kids' Soccer Book
$6.95, 1-58062-642-4

Everything® Kids' Travel Activity Book
$6.95, 1-58062-641-6

Available wherever books are sold!

For more information, or to order,
call 800-872-5627 or visit everything.com

Adams Media Corporation, 57 Littlefield Street, Avon, MA 02322. U.S.A.

Everything® is a registered trademark of Adams Media Corporation.